OXFORD MEDIEVAL TEXTS

General Editors

D. E. GREENWAY B. F. HARVEY

M. LAPIDGE

WILLIAM OF MALMESBURY
HISTORIA NOVELLA
THE CONTEMPORARY HISTORY

William of Malmesbury

HISTORIA NOVELLA

The Contemporary History

EDITED BY
EDMUND KING

TRANSLATED BY
K. R. POTTER

CLARENDON PRESS · OXFORD
1998

Oxford University Press, Great Clarendon Street, Oxford OX2 6DP

Oxford New York

Athens Auckland Bangkok Bogota Buenos Aires Calcutta
Cape Town Chennai Dar es Salaam Delhi Florence Hong Kong Istanbul
Karachi Kuala Lumpur Madrid Melbourne Mexico City Mumbai
Nairobi Paris São Paolo Singapore Taipei Tokyo Toronto Warsaw
and associated companies in
Berlin Ibadan

Oxford is a registered trade mark of Oxford University Press

Published in the United States
by Oxford University Press Inc., New York

British Library Cataloguing in Publication Data
Data available

Library of Congress Cataloging in Publication Data
William, of Malmesbury, ca. 1090–1143.
Historia novella: the contemporary history / edited by Edmund
King; translated by K.R. Potter.
p. cm. – (Oxford medieval texts)
English text and translation with the original Latin manuscript.
Includes bibliographical references and index.
1. Great Britain–History–Stephen, 1135–1154. 2. Stephen, King
of England, 1097?–1154. I. King, Edmund. II. Potter, K. R.
(Kenneth Reginald) III. Title. IV. Series.
DA198.5.W52 1998
942.02'4–dc21   98-27485
ISBN 0-19-820192-3 (hb)

1 3 5 7 9 10 8 6 4 2

Typeset by Joshua Associates Ltd., Oxford
Printed in Great Britain
on acid-free paper by
Biddles Ltd., Guildford & King's Lynn

PREFACE

The special subject which I teach at the University of Sheffield on the reign of King Stephen was first offered in 1970 and—now rechristened 'The Age of Brother Cadfael'—continues to attract a good number of students, from whom over the years I have learnt a good deal. I turned to the period initially, having worked on the medieval peasantry for my Ph.D., because R. H. C. Davis and H. A. Cronne had just produced their fine edition of the royal charters of the reign, and had additionally each produced a monograph, while the main chronicles were also available in translation. The special subject has always given pride of place amongst the chronicles to the NMT editions of the *Gesta Stephani* and of William of Malmesbury's *Historia nouella*; these two volumes were both edited by K. R. Potter, and both published in 1955 (and so were amongst the earliest volumes in the series). The *Gesta Stephani* was revised by R. H. C. Davis for OMT in 1976. The *Historia nouella* now joins it in the same series.

All that is left of the NMT edition here is K. R. Potter's translation. This stands for the most part, though it has been revised, and for help in this revision my first specific thanks—rather than, as tradition dictates, my last—go to my wife Jenny. All the introduction, and the annotation, are new. So also, at times, is the Latin text. William of Malmesbury's *Historia nouella*, so at least I have come to believe in working on the manuscripts, differs in some respects from the text which was printed in NMT and in earlier editions. The arguments for this are fully set out in the introduction, and I hope will provoke some discussion.

This has been a most enjoyable and intellectually rewarding commission, and it is a pleasure to thank the many friends, colleagues, and institutions who have helped in the work. I was able to make the first serious progress during a term's study leave from the University of Sheffield, which I spent as a Visiting Fellow at All Souls College, Oxford. I must thank the College for its most

generous support, its librarians (particularly Norma Aubertin-Potter), and Andrew Watson (who was then cataloguing the College's manuscripts, which include a copy of the *Historia nouella*). The work was largely completed in the academic year 1995–6. The University was by now blessed with semesters, and to a semester's study leave I was able to add a further semester from the HRB/British Academy's new study leave scheme. The Academy also awarded a generous 'small grant' for research expenses.

I owe a considerable debt to the three general editors of OMT, Diana Greenway, Barbara Harvey, and Michael Lapidge. All have read the text, much of it more than once, and have been characteristically generous of their time and expertise. I owe an equal debt of gratitude to Michael Winterbottom whose knowledge of William of Malmesbury's Latin has been put at my disposal unstintingly. If I have any measure of confidence in presenting this new edition for scholarly appraisal and I hope some enjoyment it is because of the generous help I have received. I would like to thank also Nigel Hope for skilfully copy-editing my typescript, which has benefited greatly from his care, and also Anne Gelling and all the staff of the Press for making the actual production of the volume so pleasant an experience. Any faults—the standard disclaimer is certainly necessary here—are entirely my responsibility.

William of Malmesbury and his contemporaries are currently well represented in new and forthcoming volumes in OMT. Diana Greenway's edition of Henry of Huntingdon's *Historia Anglorum* was published in 1996; the text volume of William of Malmesbury's *Gesta regum*, edited by Roger Mynors, Rodney Thomson, and Michael Winterbottom, is in press; and R. R. Darlington and Patrick McGurk's edition of *The Chronicle of John of Worcester* is in active progress, with vol. ii (the annals up to 1066) published in 1995, and vol. iii (the annals from 1067 to 1140) in press. Proofs of the *Gesta regum* and John of Worcester have kindly been made available to me by the series and the volume editors, and so readers will find cross-references to the new editions in my text. I would not wish to claim, however, that I have fully assimilated all the findings and the learning of these magisterial new editions.

I am grateful for assistance in my work to the staffs of Cambridge University Library, the Bodleian Library, Oxford, the Manuscripts Room of the British Library, and Sheffield University Library; also for access to manuscripts at Corpus Christi College, Cambridge, Corpus Christi College, Oxford, and Trinity College, Cambridge. Papers based on my work have been given to the medieval groups at Liverpool and Sheffield Universities, and to the conference on the Medieval Chronicle held in 1996 at Utrecht: I am grateful to the audiences on these occasions for their comments. Martin Brett kindly provided me with concordances to the main writings of William of Malmesbury, which have been most useful. The following have also offered a variety of much-appreciated support: Marjorie Chibnall, David Crouch, Paul Dalton, Judith Green, Christopher Harper-Bill, Thomas K. Keefe, Simon Keynes, Daniel Power, Sandra Raban, Timothy Reuter, Kathleen Thompson, Rodney Thomson, and Kenji Yoshitake. Two scholars who have supported the enterprise I sadly cannot now thank. Ralph Davis, over dinner in Merton College in 1990, encouraged me to recollate the manuscripts. And twenty years ago now, driving me towards the crenellated campus of the University of California at Santa Barbara, Warren Hollister asked my views about the events of December 1135. I have left it too late, but here they are.

Edmund King
January 1998

CONTENTS

LIST OF PLATES
(following p. cix)

1. London, BL, Royal MS 13. D. v (Cd) fo. 132^v: reproduced by kind permission of the British Library.
2. Oxford, Bodleian Library, MS Laud Misc. 548 (Ag) fo. 200^v: reproduced by kind permission of the Bodleian Library.
3. Oxford, Bodleian Library, MS Bodley 712 (Bk) fo. 198^r: reproduced by kind permission of the Bodleian Library.
4. London, BL, Royal MS 13. D. ii (Ce^1) fo. 123^v: reproduced by kind permission of the British Library.

ABBREVIATED REFERENCES

Actes de Louis VI	*Receuil des actes de Louis VI, roi de France (1108–1137)*, dir. R.-H. Bautier, ed. J. Dufour, 4 vols. (Paris, 1992–4)
Ann. Mon.	*Annales Monastici*, ed. H. R. Luard, 5 vols. (RS xxxvi, 1864–9)
ANS	*Anglo-Norman Studies*, being the Proceedings of the Battle Conference on Anglo-Norman Studies
ASC	*Anglo-Saxon Chronicle: Two of the Saxon Chronicles parallel*, ed. C. Plummer and J. Earle, 2 vols. (Oxford, 1892–9)
Bale, *Index*	J. Bale, *Index Britanniae Scriptorum*, ed. R. L. Poole and M. Bateson, int. C. Brett and J. P. Carley (Woodbridge, 1990)
Brett, 'John of Worcester'	M. Brett, 'John of Worcester and his contemporaries', *The Writing of History in the Middle Ages: Essays presented to Richard William Southern*, ed. R. H. C. Davis and J. M. Wallace-Hadrill (Oxford, 1981), pp. 101–26
Castellarium Anglicanum	D. J. Cathcart King, *Castellarium Anglicanum: An Index and Bibliography of the Castles in England, Wales and the Islands*, 2 vols. (New York, 1983)
Chartrou, *Anjou*	J. Chartrou, *L'Anjou de 1109 à 1151: Foulque de Jérusalem et Geoffroi Plantagenet* (Paris, 1928)
Chibnall, *Matilda*	M. Chibnall, *The Empress Matilda* (London, 1991)
Chronica majora	Matthew Paris, *Chronica Majora*, ed. H. R. Luard, 7 vols. (RS lvii, 1872–84)
Chronicles	*Chronicles of the Reigns of Stephen, Henry II and Richard I*, ed. R. Howlett, 4 vols. (RS lxxxii, 1884–9)
Councils and Synods	*Councils and Synods with other Documents relating to the English Church*, i: *A.D. 871–1204*, ed. D. Whitelock, M. Brett, and C. N. L. Brooke, 2 vols. (Oxford, 1981)
CP	*The Complete Peerage of England, Scotland, Ireland,*

	Great Britain and the United Kingdom, by G. E. C., rev. edn. 13 vols. in 14 (London, 1910–59)
Crouch, *Beaumont Twins*	D. Crouch, *The Beaumont Twins: The Roots and Branches of Power in the Twelfth Century* (Cambridge Studies in Medieval Life and Thought, 4th ser. 1: Cambridge, 1986)
Davis, *Stephen*	R. H. C. Davis, *King Stephen 1135–1154*, 3rd edn. (London, 1990)
Diceto	Ralph de Diceto, *Opera Historica*, ed. W. Stubbs, 2 vols. (RS lxviii, 1876)
EEA	*English Episcopal Acta* series, in progress
EHR	*English Historical Review*
EHS	English Historical Society
Eulogium	*Eulogium Historiarum sive Temporis: Chronicon ab Orbe Condito usque ad Annum Domini 1366, a Monacho quodam Malmesburiensi exaratum*, ed. F. S. Haydon, 3 vols. (RS ix, 1858–63)
Farmer, 'Lamentations'	[D.] H. Farmer, 'William of Malmesbury's commentary on Lamentations', *Studia Monastica*, iv (1962), 283–311
Farmer, 'Life and works'	[D.] H. Farmer, 'William of Malmesbury's life and works', *Journal of Ecclesiastical History*, xiii (1962), 39–54
Fasti, ed. Greenway	John le Neve, *Fasti Ecclesiae Anglicanae 1066–1300*, compiled by D.E. Greenway, vols. i–v (London, 1968–96)
GF, *Letters*	*The Letters and Charters of Gilbert Foliot*, ed. A. Morey and C. N. L. Brooke (Cambridge, 1967)
Gloucester Charters	*Earldom of Gloucester Charters: The Charters and Scribes of the Earls and Countesses of Gloucester to A.D. 1217*, ed. R. B. Patterson (Oxford, 1973)
GND	*The Gesta Normannorum Ducum of William of Jumièges, Orderic Vitalis, and Robert of Torigni*, ed. E. M. C. van Houts, 2 vols. (OMT, 1992–5)
GP	William of Malmesbury, *De Gestis Pontificum Anglorum*, ed. N. E. S. A. Hamilton (RS lii, 1870)
GR	William of Malmesbury, *De Gestis Regum Anglorum*, ed. W. Stubbs, 2 vols. (RS xc, 1887–9); ed. R. A. B. Mynors, R. M. Thomson, and M. Winterbottom, i (OMT, 1998): cited by paragraph

Gransden, *Historical Writing*, i   A. Gransden, *Historical Writing in England, [i,]* c. *550 to* c.*1307* (London, 1974)

Gransden, *Historical Writing*, ii   A. Gransden, *Historical Writing in England, ii,* c. *1307 to the Early Sixteenth Century* (London, 1982)

Green, 'Financing'   J. Green, 'Financing Stephen's war', *ANS*, xiv (1992), 91–114

Green, *Henry I*   J. A. Green, *The Government of England under Henry I* (Cambridge Studies in Medieval Life and Thought, 4th ser. 3: Cambridge, 1986)

GS   *Gesta Stephani*, ed. K. R. Potter and R. H. C. Davis (OMT, 1976)

Handbook of Chronology   *Handbook of British Chronology*, ed. E. B. Fryde, D. E. Greenway, S. Porter, and I. Roy, 3rd edn. (London, 1986)

Hardy   William of Malmesbury, *Gesta Regum Anglorum, atque Historia Novella*, ed. T. D. Hardy, 2 vols. (EHS: London, 1840)

Haskins   C. H. Haskins, *Norman Institutions* (Cambridge, Mass., 1918)

Heads   *The Heads of Religious Houses. England and Wales 940–1216*, ed. D. Knowles, C. N. L. Brooke, and V. C. H. London (Cambridge, 1972)

HH   Henry, Archdeacon of Huntingdon, *Historia Anglorum*, ed. D. Greenway (OMT, 1996)

Hollister, *Anglo-Norman World*   C. W. Hollister, *Monarchy, Magnates and Institutions in the Anglo-Norman World* (London, 1986)

Hugh the Chanter   Hugh the Chanter, *The History of the Church of York 1066–1127*, ed. C. Johnson, rev. M. Brett, C. N. L. Brooke, and M. Winterbottom (OMT, 1990)

Hüls, *Kardinäle*   R. Hüls, *Kardinäle, Klerus und Kirchen Roms* (Bibliothek des Deutschen Historischen Instituts in Rom, xlviii: Tübingen, 1977)

JW   *The Chronicle of John of Worcester*, ii, ed. R. R. Darlington and P. McGurk (OMT 1995); iii, ed. P. McGurk (OMT, 1998)

Kealey, *Roger*   E. J. Kealey, *Roger of Salisbury: Viceroy of England* (Berkeley, CA, 1972)

King, *Anarchy*   *The Anarchy of King Stephen's Reign*, ed. E. King (Oxford, 1994)

King's Works	R. A. Brown, H. M. Colvin, and A. J. Taylor, *The History of the King's Works*, vols. i–ii (London, 1963)
Law and Government	*Law and Government in Medieval England and Normandy: Essays in Honour of Sir James Holt*, ed. G. Garnett and J. Hudson (Cambridge, 1994)
Knowles, *Monastic Order*	D. Knowles, *The Monastic Order in England*, 2nd edn. (Cambridge, 1963)
Leland, *Collectanea*	J. Leland, *Collectanea*, ed. T. Hearne, 2nd edn., 6 vols. (London, 1770)
MGH SS	*Monumenta Germaniae Historica, Scriptores*
Migne, *PL*	*Patrologiae Cursus Completus*, ed. J. P. Migne
Mynors	'The text', in William of Malmesbury, *Historia Novella*, ed. K. R. Potter (NMT, 1955), pp. xxxviii–xliii
NMT	Nelson's Medieval Texts
OMT	Oxford Medieval Texts
OV	Orderic Vitalis, *The Ecclesiastical History*, ed. M. Chibnall, 6 vols. (OMT, 1969–80)
Peter the Venerable	*The Letters of Peter the Venerable*, ed. G. Constable, 2 vols. (Harvard Historical Studies, lxxvii: Cambridge, Mass., 1967)
Regesta	*Regesta Regum Anglo-Normannorum 1066–1154*, ed. H. W. C. Davis *et al.*, 4 vols. (Oxford, 1913–69)
Robinson, *Papacy*	I. S. Robinson, *The Papacy 1073–1198: Continuity and Innovation* (Cambridge, 1990)
Round, *Geoffrey*	J. H. Round, *Geoffrey de Mandeville* (London, 1892)
RS	Rolls Series
RT	*Chronique de Robert de Torigni*, ed. L. Delisle, 2 vols. (Rouen and Paris, 1872–3)
Saltman, *Theobald*	A. Saltman, *Theobald Archbishop of Canterbury* (London, 1956)
Schmale, *Schisma*	F.-J. Schmale, *Studien zum Schisma des Jahres 1130* (Forschungen zur kirchlichen Rechtsgeschichte und zum Kirchenrecht, iii: Cologne and Graz, 1961)
Scott, *Glastonbury*	J. Scott, *The Early History of Glastonbury: An Edition, Translation and Study of William of*

	Malmesbury's De Antiquitate Glastonie Ecclesie (Woodbridge, 1981)
SD	*Symeonis Monachi Opera Omnia*, ed. T. Arnold, 2 vols. (RS lxxv, 1882–5)
Southern, *Anselm*	R. W. Southern, *Saint Anselm: A Portrait in a Landscape* (Cambridge, 1990)
Stubbs	Introductory material to RS edition of *GR*
Suger	Suger, *Vie de Louis VI le Gros*, ed. H. Waquet (Classiques de l'histoire de France au moyen-âge, xi: Paris, 1929)
Thomson	R. M. Thomson, *William of Malmesbury* (Woodbridge, 1987)
TRHS	*Transactions of the Royal Historical Society*
VCH	*Victoria History of the Counties of England*
Winchester Studies, i	*Winchester in the Early Middle Ages*, ed. M. Biddle (Winchester Studies, i: Oxford, 1976)

INTRODUCTION

I. THE AUTHOR AND HIS WORK

T H E *Historia nouella* (henceforth *HN*) is the last work of one of England's greatest historians. William of Malmesbury saw his place in history as being the first man since Bede to write a continuous history of the English people in Latin. He made the claim in the Prologue to the first book of the work that was intended to supply the lack, the *Gesta regum* ('The Deeds of the Kings', henceforth *GR*), which covered the period from the *adventus Saxonum* to the reign of Henry I.[1] He restated it in the Prologue to the third and final book of the *HN*.[2] 'As we men of the present day severely and rightly blame our predecessors, who since Bede have left no record of themselves and their doings, I, who have set myself to remove this disgrace from us, may fairly claim the kindly favour of my readers if they judge aright.' While his Prologues were directed to his contemporaries he looked beyond them, to a time, as he hoped, 'when love and envy are no more';[3] there would be an audience for his life of Wulfstan, a contemporary saint, he believed, 'as long as the pole turns the stars and literature survives'.[4] So indeed it has proved. The comparison with Bede has not been found fanciful by the authorities of the present day.[5] The audience for William's work currently grows apace, with several important studies of his career,[6] and new and

---

[1] *GR*, book i. prologue.   [2] *HN*, prologue.
[3] *GR*, book i. pro. 8.
[4] *The Vita Wulfstani of William of Malmesbury*, ed. R. R. Darlington (Camden Soc., 3rd ser., xl, 1928), p. 3; cf. ibid., p. v, and JW, ii, p. xvii.
[5] Knowles, *Monastic Order*, pp. 499–500; R. W. Southern, 'Aspects of the European tradition of historical writing: 4. The sense of the past', *TRHS*, 5th ser., xxiii (1973), 243–63, at pp. 253–6; R. Thomson, 'William of Malmesbury', in *The Blackwell Dictionary of Historians*, ed. J. Cannon *et al.* (Oxford, 1988), pp. 451–2.
[6] Thomson; Farmer, 'Life and works'; Gransden, *Historical Writing*, i. 166–85. Stubbs's prefaces to the two volumes of the Rolls Series edition of the *GR* remain fundamental: on William's life and work, Stubbs, i, pp. xvii–xliii; on the historical value of his work, ibid., ii, pp. xv–cxlii.

revised editions of some of his works.[7] The present study offers a
new edition of the *HN*, and a reassessment of the significance of
the work. William of Malmesbury's career, and his other works,
are brought into commission only so far as this is necessary for an
understanding of the *HN*. The 'judging aright' of this text is in
itself a difficult enough task.

William of Malmesbury's date of birth is usually given as
*c.*1095, following a literal reading of his reference to himself,
'quadrigenarius sum hodie', in the Prologue to his commentary on
the Lamentations of Jeremiah, a work which refers to Henry I as
recently dead.[8] Stubbs saw the difficulties in accommodating what
was then known of William of Malmesbury's career with so late a
date; and subsequent work has made it all but impossible to
sustain. Sir Richard Southern saw William as hard at work in the
Canterbury archives, collecting material for the *GR* and his other
main historical work the *Gesta pontificum* ('The Deeds of the
Prelates', henceforth *GP*), in the years from 1115 to 1120.[9] Letters
of dedication prefacing a copy of the *GR* surviving in Troyes show
that the work was first taken up at the invitation of Henry I's
queen, Matilda, who died in 1118.[10] That request came to a
religious house, and a library, and a scholar, with an established
reputation. If 'quadrigenarius' is taken as 'in my forties',[11] then a
date of birth of *c.*1090 seems to be preferable, and would still do no
damage to William of Malmesbury's reputation as a prodigy.

It is known that William of Malmesbury was of mixed
parentage—English and Norman—for when he paused to

[7] Among the new editions are: Scott, *Glastonbury*; P. N. Carter, 'An Edition of William of Malmesbury's Treatise on the Miracles of the Virgin', D.Phil. thesis (Oxford, 1959), and also J. M. Canal, 'El libro *de laudibus et miraculis Sanctae Mariae* de Guillermo de Malmesbury, O.S.B. (†*c.*1143)', *Claretianum*, viii (Rome, 1968), 71–242; R. W. Pfaff, 'The *Abbreviatio Amalarii* of William of Malmesbury', *Recherches de théologie ancienne et médiévale*, xlvii (1980), 77–113, xlviii (1981), 128–71; *William of Malmesbury, Polyhistor: A Critical Edition*, ed. H. Testroet Ouellette (Medieval and Renaissance Texts and Studies, x: Binghamton, NY, 1982).

[8] The relevant passages are fully discussed in Stubbs, i, pp. xiii–xvii.

[9] Southern, *Anselm*, pp. 390–1, 400–2, 470–3.

[10] E. Könsgen, 'Zwei unbekannte Briefe zu den *Gesta regum Anglorum* des Wilhelm von Malmesbury', *Deutsches Archiv*, xxxi (1975), 204–14.

[11] Stubbs had suggested this as a possibility (i, p. xvi), and it was seen as a probability by Farmer, 'Life and works', p. 50. The date *c.*1095 is retained by Thomson, pp. 1–2, and in *Dictionary of Historians*, pp. 451–2.

comment on the significance of the Battle of Hastings, he claimed an understanding of both sides of the argument, 'having the blood of both nations in my veins'.[12] It is presumed that, as is demonstrably the case with his older contemporary Orderic Vitalis, his father was of Norman stock and his mother was English.[13] It was from his father that he gained his love of books and of learning.[14] He entered the monastery of Malmesbury in Wiltshire as a boy,[15] and is presumed to have been born either in that county or in Somerset.[16] He is unlikely to have travelled far to find his vocation, for Malmesbury in the late eleventh century did not cast a long shadow.[17] In terms of endowment it was barely in the first division of the Benedictine monasteries as they are recorded in Domesday Book in 1086.[18]

If not wealthy in terms of endowment, Malmesbury was rich in the heritage of sanctity that William would come to see as the chief contribution of the Anglo-Saxon to the Anglo-Norman world. He would travel widely collecting material for his writings, most notably the *GP*,[19] and books for his library. 'You can scarcely pass any settlement of consequence but that you hear the name of some new saint'; but of the majority of these, 'all memory had perished'.[20] A saint without a c.v. was a sad specimen. Where he could, and using any material that came to hand, William sought to supply the lack. Southern has described his study of St

---

[12] *GR*, book iii, prologue; cf. §228.12.

[13] On Orderic's background, see OV i. 1–6.

[14] *GR*, book ii, prologue.

[15] This cannot have been much, if at all, later than 1100, for the memory of the community in his day (*nostro tempore*) stretched back to Abbot Wulfsige, who died *c*.1033/4: Stubbs, i, pp. xvii–xviii, citing *GP*, p. 411; *Heads*, p. 54.

[16] Matthew Parker's manuscript of the *GP* was identified as written 'per . . . Guilhelmum Malmesburiensis Benedictine sodalitatis monachum qui Somerset proprio cognomine dictus est': Cambridge U.L., MS Ff. 1. 25, part 1, fo. 3ʳ. William described Stephen Harding monk of Sherborne (Dorset) and later third abbot of Citeaux as 'one of us' ('noster ille': *GR* §334), but in the context this may mean no more than that he was English.

[17] On the history of the monastery, see A. Watkin, 'The abbey of Malmesbury', in *VCH Wiltshire*, iii. 210–31.

[18] It occurs in sixteenth place in the list given in Knowles, *Monastic Order*, pp. 702–3 in terms of wealth recorded in Domesday Book (£178).

[19] The book was edited from William's autograph by N. E. S. A. Hamilton in the Rolls Series.

[20] *GR* §245.2.

Aldhelm, the most notable of the early abbots of Malmesbury, which forms book v of the *GP*, as 'his masterpiece of historical method. . . . He had to rely on a mixture of charters, inscriptions, archaeological remains, pictures, legends and chronicles; and to these he added Aldhelm's own theological writings and letters.'[21] He offered his expertise also to the neighbouring, and very wealthy, monastery at Glastonbury in Somerset, writing biographies of four of its saints, Benignus, Dunstan, Indract, and Patrick.[22] These works were all seen by John Leland at Glastonbury early in the sixteenth century,[23] but they have suffered the more subtle iconoclasm of the destruction of the great monastic libraries, and only the *Life of Dunstan* now survives.[24] William's materials for this work were 'writings both in Latin and English', which the monks had found for him in a very old chest.[25] He showed his independence as a historian by rejecting some of the traditions of the community, finding no evidence, for instance, that they possessed the body of St Dunstan as they claimed;[26] while, without mentioning the possibility of forgery, he noted as remarkable a charter of Cædwalla attested by a cross while that king remained a pagan.[27] The saints still lived in the places where their bones lay. In writing their lives, William was writing contemporary history.

Archival research had its fascination and its challenges, in dealing both with texts and with their custodians; but the foundation of serious study was a good library. The building up of a library was an essential part of William of Malmesbury's work. He describes the library in his time as the joint achievement of

[21] Southern, 'The sense of the past', p. 255.

[22] *The Chronicle of Glastonbury Abbey: An Edition, Translation and Study of John of Glastonbury's 'Cronica siue Antiquitates Glastoniensis Ecclesie'*, ed. J. P. Carley (Woodbridge, 1985), pp. xxxvii–xlii.

[23] Leland, *Collectanea*, iv. 155.

[24] The *Life of Dunstan* is printed in *Memorials of St Dunstan*, ed. W. Stubbs (RS lxiii, 1874), pp. 250–324.

[25] Scott, *Glastonbury*, p. 7, quoting *Memorials of St Dunstan*, ed. W. Stubbs, p. 252.

[26] Scott, *Glastonbury*, pp. 4–5, 23. For a discussion and translation of Eadmer's letter on the subject, see R. Sharpe, 'Eadmer's letter to the monks of Glastonbury concerning St Dunstan's disputed remains', *The Archaeology and History of Glastonbury Abbey: Essays in Honour of the Ninetieth Birthday of C.A. Ralegh Radford*, ed. L. Abrams and J. P. Carley (Woodbridge, 1991), pp. 205–15.

[27] Scott, *Glastonbury*, pp. 92–3.

Abbot Godfrey of Jumièges (1091–1109) and himself. In the time of Abbot Godfrey[28]

the foundations of a library were laid; and if I draw attention to this activity of his, I believe this is within my rights, for in this respect I have not yielded to any of my predecessors; indeed, if it is not boastful to say so, I have outstripped them all . . . I have collected much for reading, emulating the vigour of one who, in this respect at least, deserves praise.

Modern study has confirmed this description. The range of William's interests can be gauged by considering a small sample of this collection, the books that survive in his own handwriting.[29] These include the autograph of the *GP*, a portable copy, in which the text was much revised over time;[30] a collection of authors 'designed to provide a reasonably connected account of Roman history, from the siege of Troy to the Greek and Roman emperors of William's own day';[31] treatises on the calendar, annotated and corrected by William;[32] the works of Julius Frontinus and Eutropius, and the *De re militari* of Vegetius;[33] John Scotus's *Periphyseon*;[34] and canons from the Church councils.[35] A study of these and other surviving manuscripts from the *scriptorium* at Malmesbury, which William directed with meticulous care, has shown how he galvanized the community.[36] When William

[28] *GP*, pp. 431–2; trans. Farmer, 'Life and works', p. 41.
[29] The manuscripts are listed in *Medieval Libraries of Great Britain: A List of Surviving Books*, ed. N. R. Ker, 2nd edn. (London, 1964), p. 128 and n. 9, and ibid., *Supplement to the Second Edition*, ed. A. G. Watson (London, 1987), p. 48. On William's handwriting see N. R. Ker, 'William of Malmesbury's handwriting', *EHR* lix (1944), 371–6; Thomson, pp. 76–7 and plates 1 and 2.
[30] Magdalen College, Oxford, MS 172; facsimiles are printed as frontispieces to the *GP*, and in Gransden, *Historical Writing*, i, plate v.
[31] Oxford, Bodleian Library, MS Arch. Selden B. 16; description from Thomson, p. 66, with facsimile plate 2.
[32] Oxford, Bodleian Library, MS Auct. 3. 14; discussed, without the attribution to William of Malmesbury, by W. H. Stevenson, 'A contemporary description of the Domesday survey', *EHR* xxii (1907), 72–84, and, with attribution, by Ker, 'William of Malmesbury's handwriting', pp. 374–5.
[33] Oxford, Lincoln College, MS Lat. 100.
[34] Trinity College, Cambridge, MS 1301; discussed by E. Jeauneau, 'Guillaume de Malmesbury, premier éditeur anglais du *Periphyseon*', *Sapientiae Doctrina: mélanges de théologie et de litterature médiévales offerts à Dom Hildebrand Bascour* (Recherches de théologie ancienne et médiévale, numéro spécial, 1: Louvain, 1980), pp. 148–79.
[35] Oxford, Oriel College, MS 42; discussed by Thomson, pp. 64–6.
[36] Thomson, pp. 76–97.

introduced himself in the Prologue to the *HN* it was as 'librarian of Malmesbury', a simple title that encapsulated his life's work.

William of Malmesbury's own studies, continuing alongside the building up of a library, formed clear preferences in his mind. In the Prologue to book ii of the *GR* is found perhaps the best known of the many fragments of autobiography in his writings:[37]

To Logic, the armourer of speech, I no more than lent an ear. Physic, which cures the sick body, I went deeper into. As for Ethics, I explored parts in depth, revering its high status as a subject inherently inaccessible to the student and able to form good character; in particular I studied History, which adds flavour to moral instruction by imparting a pleasurable knowledge of past events, spurring the reader by the accumulation of examples to follow the good and shun the bad.

This latter point is more fully developed in the Prologue to the *HN*.[38]

What is more to the advantage of virtue or more conducive to justice than recognizing the divine pleasure in the good and punishment of those who have gone astray? Further, what is more pleasant than consigning to historical record the deeds of brave men, that following their example the others may cast off cowardice and arm themselves to defend their country?

It was as a historian that William of Malmesbury became best known, particularly for the *GR* and the *GP*, which may originally have been intended as a single work. The *GR* was started, as has been seen, before 1118, and was completed by 1125, with two further editions appearing soon after 1134.[39] The *GP* was also completed in 1125, and revised over the next fifteen years.[40] There are about thirty surviving medieval manuscripts of the *GR* (fewer than half of which have additionally a text of the *HN*); and there are about twenty surviving manuscripts of the *GP*.[41] The *Liber*

---

[37] *GR*, book ii. pro. 1.
[38] *HN*, prologue. This is modelled very closely on the Prologue to Bede's *Ecclesiastical History*.
[39] Könsgen, 'Zwei unbekannte Briefe zu den *Gesta regum Anglorum*'; *GR* i, pp. xix–xxxi, xliii–xlv.
[40] The date 1125 is given in the text: *GP*, p. 442. On the revisions, *GP*, pp. xiv–xvii, and Farmer, 'Life and works', pp. 44–6.
[41] These figures are found in Farmer, 'Life and works', p. 43 n. 4; the locations are briefly described in Gransden, *Historical Writing*, i. 179–80.

pontificalis, identified as his by Rodney Thomson, was also a major work of historical scholarship, completed soon after 1119.[42]

The historian who wrote the *HN* was not just supremely well-read,[43] but also very well-travelled, and very well-connected. His travels took him the length and breadth of England, to the north (where he found the dialect of Yorkshiremen all but incomprehensible)[44] to the fenlands (where the monks of Thorney were misogynists),[45] and widely in southern England (where the fertility of the Vale of Gloucester was singled out for particular commendation).[46] Much of the civil war would be fought over what for William was home ground. The *HN* is not, however, a text in which the sense of place is well developed, for William of Malmesbury is less interested in the struggle for castles than in the struggles for men's minds. Here the quality and the range of his connections, his 'networking', become important. In the 1120s he wrote of himself as being 'of a retiring disposition and far from the secrets of the court';[47] but this may be tongue in cheek, as are many of his asides. It certainly was not true in the last decade of his life. After the death of Queen Matilda in 1118, the monks of Malmesbury looked to her stepson Robert earl of Gloucester, established at Bristol 24 miles away, for support. The later editions of the *GR* were dedicated to Robert;[48] and the *HN* was his commission. Roger of Salisbury was often at Malmesbury, and he can be heard in the *HN*, explaining why he felt himself no longer bound by his oath to the empress, and confiding his fears before setting off for the meeting of the court at Oxford in June 1139.[49] The *HN* also confirms that William of Malmesbury remained closely tied to Henry of Blois, abbot of Glastonbury (1126–71), bishop of Winchester (1129–71), and papal legate (1139–43). It was Henry of Winchester above all who brought

---

[42] Thomson, pp. 119–38.

[43] Ibid., pp. 39–75; N. Wright, 'William of Malmesbury and Latin poetry: further evidence for a Benedictine's reading', *Revue Bénédictine*, ci (1991), 122–53; idem, '*Industriae testimonium*: William of Malmesbury and Latin poetry revisited', ibid., ciii (1993), 482–531.

[44] *GP*, p. 209.   [45] *GP*, p. 327.   [46] *GP*, pp. 291–2.

[47] *GR*, book v, prologue.

[48] *GR*, ep. iii; also *GR* §446–9 (epilogue).

[49] *HN* §3, 'sepe audiui dicentem'; *HN* §23, 'audiui eum dicentem'.

William close to the secrets of the court, into the cloisters of power. William went to the legatine councils at Winchester in 1139 and 1141,[50] and there saw the behaviour of kings put under scrutiny, and the fate of nations decided. His brethren would not be allowed to forget it: 'my memory is very clear'.[51] William of Malmesbury gives us the clearest picture of a prelate in perpetual motion; and at times he seems almost to echo Henry's patterns of thought.[52]

William of Malmesbury was also well-connected in literary circles. Indeed it may be, following up Martin Brett's observations,[53] that his is the first generation of which we may speak of the existence of a historical profession within England, a group of scholars in regular contact, collecting material, distributing drafts of their writings to one another for comment, confident both of their methodology and of the market for their work. It is the fruit of the close textual work of the last two decades that this world starts to come to life. Three centres of contact have been shown to have been particularly important in determining the shape of William of Malmesbury's academic career. The first chronologically, and which may have retained its primacy for him throughout his life, was Canterbury.[54] At Canterbury William met Eadmer, whose work he admired,[55] and made extensive use of in the *GR*;[56] he heard of the deeds of—and

[50] *HN* §25–30 (1139); §46–51 (1141).

[51] 'Egregie quippe memini': *HN* §46.

[52] The following may be noted: (i) he 'was not slow to carry out what he had once taken in hand': *HN* §59 (and also §58); cf. references to lay brothers of Sempringham, 'men who had put their hand to the plough of divine service': *The Book of Saint Gilbert*, ed. R. Foreville and G. Keir (OMT, 1987), pp. 146–7; (ii) 'knowing that it was the special concern of his office that peace should be agreed upon': *HN* §40; cf. 'on him [England] depends for peace or war, agitation or rest': Henry of Blois enamel plaques, *English Romanesque Art 1066–1200*, ed. G. Zarnecki *et al.* (London, 1984), nos. 277 a and b, pp. 261–2 (which refer also to his eloquence, cf. *HN* §58); (iii) both William (of Roger of Salisbury) and Henry (of himself) use the—admittedly common—tag *uel prece uel pretio* ('by prayer or by price'): *HN* §33; *EEA*, viii: *Winchester 1070–1204*, ed. M. J. Franklin (Oxford, 1993), App. I, p. 209.

[53] Brett, 'John of Worcester', pp. 101–26.

[54] Thomson, pp. 46–7, 70, 73.

[55] 'He expounds everything so clearly that all seems to happen under our very eyes': *GP*, p. 74, trans. Southern, *Anselm*, p. 247.

[56] Much of book v of the *GR* was taken from Eadmer's *Historia novorum*: Stubbs, ii, p. cxxxiv. As to which version of Eadmer's work was used, see Brett, 'John of Worcester', p. 112 n. 1, and references there cited.

perhaps even saw—Anselm,[57] whom some already revered as a saint; and he could not fail to note the importance for contemporary history of the Canterbury archive, with its 'huge piles of material'.[58] Sir Richard Southern has recently identified William of Malmesbury as the 'unauthorised person' who had carried off parts of this archive,[59] but he sees him also as maintaining a collaboration with the house,[60] and his autograph collection preserves the texts of some of Anselm's letters not found elsewhere. At Canterbury, William drew on the libraries both of Christ Church and of St Augustine's, taking from the latter a copy of the 'E' text of the *Anglo-Saxon Chronicle*, and a distinctive version of an early *Life* of Dunstan.[61] The second of the major centres was Glastonbury. William must have visited Glastonbury at least once before 1125, whilst he was writing the *GP*, for he refers to its fine library, but in that work it was given comparatively short shrift.[62] About 1129, however, and thus shortly after the appointment of Henry of Blois as abbot, William made a longer visit to Glastonbury. Whilst there, as has already been noted, he wrote the lives of its local saints, but he also completed a substantial monograph, *On the Antiquity of Glastonbury*. This last work has a fulsome Prologue dedicated to Henry of Blois, in which he describes himself as 'a son of your church',[63] which it is suggested shows that he had been admitted to the abbey's fraternity.[64] Worcester is the third centre where William found important material and congenial colleagues, who included Prior Nicholas, a protégé of Wulfstan, and the monk John. As at Glastonbury, at least two visits must be posited, one to work on the *GP*, and the second to work on the monograph, the *Life of Wulfstan*.[65] William of Malmesbury and John of

---

[57] Anselm is described as 'uir qui omnes quos quidem uiderimus sapientia et religione praestaret', in *GP*, p. 121.

[58] *GP*, p. 113. The dispute between Canterbury and York he had condensed from many tedious volumes (*GP*, p. 44), and what have become known as 'the Canterbury forgeries' were coming to light as he wrote (*GR* §294; Southern, *Anselm*, pp. 359–62).

[59] Southern, *Anselm*, pp. 390–4. [60] Ibid., pp. 400–2, 473.

[61] Thomson, pp. 45–7, 70, 73–5. [62] *GP*, pp. 196–8.

[63] Scott, *Glastonbury*, pp. 40–3. [64] Stubbs, i, pp. xxvii–xxx.

[65] *GP*, pp. 278–89; *Vita Wulfstani*, ed. R. R. Darlington; and for comment see E. Mason, *St Wulfstan of Worcester c.1008–1095* (Oxford, 1990), pp. 289–94, 295–6, and D. H.

Worcester drew on each other's work, as Martin Brett has shown in detail in his fine study.[66] More speculative must be the suggestion that it was from his contacts at Worcester that William derived his interests in the calendar and in cosmology.[67] It is interesting also that it was at Worcester, twenty years after William's death, that a son of Robert of Gloucester (to whom the *HN* is dedicated) became the diocesan bishop.[68] Roger of Worcester owned a copy of William of Malmesbury's *Commentary on Lamentations*,[69] and probably one of the *HN* also.

The *Commentary on Lamentations* was written early in the reign of King Stephen. It is almost certainly the last surviving work written by William of Malmesbury before the *HN*, and it is important for this reason. It has not been edited, but the main themes are picked out in an admirable article by David Farmer, which in quotation and paraphrase reproduces substantial parts of the text.[70] The *Commentary* is pessimistic, not least in its references to the history of recent events:[71]

We have both heard from our elders and ourselves seen Christian kings, princes, and bishops destroying abbeys and putting monks to flight. We have seen the church's ornaments put up for sale or given to other churches. Our prince's religion consists in carrying away for his own followers spoils from ancient monasteries, whilst what has been filched from the poor countrymen is offered up to God.

The themes of this passage occur elsewhere in the *Commentary*, and they would recur no less insistently in the *HN*. Under Stephen:[72] 'the treasures of some churches were plundered and their landed property given to laymen; churches belonging to

Farmer, 'Two biographies of William of Malmesbury', *Latin Biography*, ed. T. A. Dorey (London, 1967), pp. 165–74.

[66] Brett, 'John of Worcester', pp. 113–17.

[67] Cf. R. W. Southern, *Medieval Humanism and Other Studies* (Oxford, 1970), pp. 158–80, at 168–9, and plates VII and VIII.

[68] M. Cheney, *Roger, Bishop of Worcester 1164–1179* (Oxford, 1980). See further below, pp. xci–xciv.

[69] Oxford, Bodleian Library, MS Bodley 868; Farmer, 'Lamentations', p. 286; Stubbs, i, pp. cxxi–cxxiii.

[70] Farmer, 'Lamentations'.   [71] Farmer, 'Lamentations', pp. 294–5.

[72] *HN* § 19; cf. the complaint of Henry of Winchester in 1139 that church property had been given to 'laymen and moreover men of little religion', *HN* § 24.

clerks were sold to strangers; bishops were made prisoners and compelled to alienate their property; abbacies were granted to unfit persons either to oblige friends or to pay off debts.' When he came to summarize the state of the nation, in the year 1140, he would conclude in the same vein: 'everything in England was up for sale, and now churches and abbeys were split up and sold not secretly but openly'.[73] And if in the *HN* the bishops were among the victims, in the *Commentary* they were chief among the culprits. They should preach the Word and live in holy simplicity, but instead they oppressed the poor, and served as 'yes-men' (*assentatores*) to the rich; their proper sobriety had been turned to worldly pomp; they ruled their subjects but profited them not at all.[74] Here, we may be sure, the 'ancient monastery' of Malmesbury, and its diocesan bishop Roger of Salisbury, were uppermost in William's mind.

Roger of Salisbury under Henry I, and briefly under Stephen, had all the authority which would later be associated with the formal title justiciar, and a good deal more besides.[75] His writ ran throughout England. The four great castles with which he is particularly associated—Salisbury (Old Sarum), Devizes, Sherborne, and Malmesbury—show the scale of his ambition within his comparatively small diocese. At Malmesbury he took over both the monastery and the borough. In 1118 the abbot Eadwulf was deposed;[76] and Roger appropriated the abbey to the bishopric, 'insofar as this was within his power'.[77] Stubbs saw the importance of this episode,[78] but later writers have perhaps discounted it a little. The monks felt themselves, and seem to have been, totally defenceless against the suspension of their liberties. Their feelings are best expressed in the letters to David of Scotland and to the empress found in the early Troyes manuscript of the *GR*, which

[73] *HN* §37; cf. the complaint of Henry of Winchester in 1141 that abbacies had been sold and churches despoiled of treasure, *HN* §47. On the lack of respect for graveyards, *HN* §17, 36, and discussion below, p. xcvi and n. 403.

[74] Farmer, 'Lamentations', pp. 293–4.   [75] Kealey, *Roger*; Green, *Henry I*.

[76] 'Edulfus abbatiam Malmesberiae sine causa amisit': 'Annals of Winchester', in *Ann. Mon.*, ii. 45; but other sources say that the abbot died: *VCH Wiltshire*, iii. 216. In either event, he was not replaced.   [77] *HN* §33.

[78] 'This eclipse of the monastic independence of the house must have been a very notable thing': Stubbs, i, p. xxiii.

have been dated to 1126–7.[79] The abbey was leaderless, they said, and for the lack of a shepherd the sheep were being dispersed.[80] The protests of the monks fell on deaf ears, and the bishop only tightened his grip. When the oaths to the empress were renewed at Northampton in September 1131, the king granted the monastery of Malmesbury to the church of Salisbury and its bishop, 'ut dominium suum et sedem propriam', thus reducing it to the status of a cathedral priory.[81] This was cast as a 'restoration', made with the approval of the bishops present, since the monastery had earlier been united with the see.[82] Then, after Stephen's accession, the bishop obtained additionally the grant of the borough of Malmesbury, with the hundreds attached, as Henry I had held them in demesne.[83] He built a castle at Malmesbury, within a stone's throw of the abbey church.[84]

This was the outlook, as William composed his *Commentary on Lamentations* at Malmesbury, and England descended into civil war. Advancing years and worsening circumstances ('fortuna deterior'), he said in his Prologue, had led him to put aside historical work.[85] The monastery's circumstances, if not those of the country as a whole, were about to look up. The disgrace of Roger of Salisbury in summer 1139 was followed shortly thereafter by his death. The monks of Malmesbury then sought out the king, and obtained from him 'the restoration of their ancient privileges and their abbots'.[86] The abbatial election of 1140, suggested

[79] *GR*, ep. i, ii; Könsgen, 'Zwei unbekannte Briefe zu den *Gesta regum Anglorum*', pp. 211–14.

[80] Under the protection of Queen Matilda the house had been greatly blessed: 'Hoc solum in habundantia totius bonitatis superfuit, quod absque pastore gregem aecclesiae nostrae liquerit. Qua de causa oues ipsas, quas domina nostra congregauit, iniuste dispersas noueritis': letter to David, king of Scots, *GR*, ep. i. 7.

[81] *Regesta*, ii, no. 1715; full text in *Sarum Charters and Documents*, ed. W. Rich Jones and W. D. Macray (RS xcvii, 1891), pp. 6–7.

[82] The history behind this claim is elucidated in a valuable article by N. Berry, 'St Aldhelm, William of Malmesbury, and the liberty of Malmesbury Abbey', *Reading Medieval Studies*, xvi (1990), 15–38.

[83] *Regesta*, iii, no. 784.   [84] *HN* § 22: 'uix iactu lapidis'.

[85] Farmer, 'Lamentations', p. 288 and n. 17.

[86] *HN* § 35. It was the later tradition at Malmesbury that Stephen had kept Roger imprisoned at Devizes until the time of his death (BL, Cotton MS Vitell. A. x, fo. 159ᵛ), from which it has been suggested that the election may have taken place as soon as Roger was imprisoned (*VCH Wiltshire*, iii. 216 n. 60), but *HN* and the other contemporary sources argue against this.

Stubbs, 'may possibly have been one of the critical events of our author's life'.[87] Whether or not he knew it, this was a propitious moment for Robert of Gloucester to ask William to turn his talents to the writing of contemporary history. 'Now your highness's mind desires the transmission to posterity of those things that, by a very wonderful dispensation of God, have happened in England in recent times (*moderno tempore*).'[88] Here was a great challenge; but also great dangers. William of Malmesbury was well aware of the dangers. But now he could relish the challenge. His whole career had been a preparation for it.

II. THE WRITING OF THE *HISTORIA NOVELLA*

In response to Robert of Gloucester's commission, William of Malmesbury explained in his Prologue that he needed to go back in time, so that 'the history may be related in a more orderly sequence'. He would start, he said, with 'the empress's return to England after her husband's death'. The emperor Henry V died in May 1125, and the empress returned to England in September 1126. The final event described in the *HN* was the empress's dramatic escape from the siege of Oxford in December 1142. The text of the work is divided into three books (*libri*). The first book goes from 1126 to the siege warfare which followed Robert of Gloucester's renunciation of his homage to Stephen in summer 1138.[89] The second book covers the years 1139 and 1140, the first of these being the year in which the empress, 'eadem uirago', 'came to England to vindicate her right against Stephen', and concludes with the peace discussions of 1140.[90] The third book covers the years 1141 and 1142, starting with the battle of Lincoln on 2 February 1141, and concluding with the siege of Oxford in December 1142.[91] This last event, William explained, he had not the information to put in context. 'I am disposed to go into this

[87] Stubbs, i, p. xxxviii.
[88] *HN*, prologue.
[89] *HN* § 1–21.
[90] *HN* § 22–40.
[91] *HN* § 41–79.

more thoroughly if ever by the gift of God I learn the truth from those who were present.'[92]

Even without William of Malmesbury's initial disclaimer, it would have been clear that the text of the early part of the *HN* was not strictly contemporary with the events described. The reference to Henry of Winchester's prominent part in securing Stephen's coronation in December 1135 noted that he was 'now legate' ('modo legatus'),[93] a title he first used at the Council of Winchester in August 1139. Other anticipated references are to the death of the antipope Anacletus II, which occurred in January 1138, during the discussion of the dual papal election of February 1130,[94] and to the accession and marriage of Louis VII in the summer of 1137, noted under the year 1131.[95] So far as the structure of the *HN* is concerned, the importance of these references is that they show that book i (which finished in 1138), and book ii (which dealt with the events of 1139 and 1140), must be taken together and be viewed as a single composition.

These references within the text would suggest that the *HN* was commenced not earlier than 1140. Other evidence confirms this date, and indicates a date of composition possibly starting late in 1140 and stretching into the early months of 1141 for books i and ii. In the year 1140 England 'was troubled by the brutalities of war',[96] but for the monks of Malmesbury it was a year of liberation, when after an interval of more than twenty years they were given licence to elect an abbot.[97] They elected one of their own number, the monk John. Abbot John was no sooner elected than he was *en route* for Rome, a journey made (it may be supposed) to appeal against Henry of Winchester's rejection of the appointment on the grounds of simony.[98] John died on 19 August 1140,[99] and his companion on the journey, Peter Moraunt, was elected abbot in his place.[100] William of Malmesbury wrote a

---

[92] *HN* §79.
[93] *HN* §14: *modo* in AC texts, omitted in B.
[94] *HN* §7.
[95] *HN* §8.
[96] *HN* §36.
[97] *HN* §35.
[98] *HN* §35, says simply that Henry 'disapproved of the person elected, for in no way could he be convinced that the king had agreed to the election without a bribe'.
[99] The date of death is given in the Gloucester chronicle: JW iii. 280–1.
[100] This information also comes from the Gloucester chronicle: JW iii. 292–3.

history of this journey, a work now lost but seen by John Leland in the sixteenth century.[101] In the Prologue to this work—the *Itinerarium* or *Odoeporicon* of Abbot John—William of Malmesbury stated that he was currently hard at work on the *HN*.[102] If, as is possible, Abbot John died in Rome,[103] Peter cannot have returned, have been elected as abbot, and have started to brief William of Malmesbury on the journey, before October 1140. The *HN* may only have been commenced after the *Itinerarium* was completed. When dealing with the eclipse of March 1140, William comments that 'it was thought and said by many, nor were they wrong, that the king would not survive the year in office',[104] clearly anticipating the Battle of Lincoln in early February 1141. Books i and ii may have been written in their entirety in the weeks immediately following this battle, when for the Angevins everything was possible. They were certainly completed at this period, but they could have been commenced in late 1140.

There was then a break in the writing. Book iii of the *HN* has a separate, short Prologue, which starts as follows:

In the year of the Lord's Incarnation 1142, I am undertaking to unravel the trackless maze of events and occurrences that befell in England, with the aim that posterity should not be ignorant of these matters through our lack of care, it being worthwhile to learn the changefulness of fortune and the mutability of the human lot, by God's permission or bidding.

It is obvious that William here is writing after the battle of Lincoln, and that the reference to the changefulness of fortune was suggested to him, as to other chroniclers, by the outcome of that battle and by events later in 1141. It is less obvious, but it may be suggested, that when William wrote of 'inextricabilem laberinthum rerum et negotiorum' he was looking forward to the events of 1141, which he was about to describe, and not back to the period 1126 to 1140, which had been treated in his earlier text in terms of the straight line of legitimate succession. In 1141 a

---

[101] Leland, *Collectanea*, iii. 272; the incipit was *Principium et processum Malmesburiensis cenobii*: Bale, *Index*, p. 136; Stubbs, i, pp. xxxviii–xl.

[102] 'Iam vero in Novella Historia diligentur ad hoc nostra vigilavit oratio': Leland, *Collectanea*, iii. 272.

[103] 'de laboriosa . . . profectione versus Romam': ibid.   [104] *HN* §38.

treatment in these terms could no longer be sustained. If William
had lost his narrative line, had lost track, it was because the
Angevin party had suffered the same fate:[105] the labyrinth was in
their minds. William said that he was writing this section of the
HN in 1142. The scribe of the Margam manuscript, conscious that
the events described dated from 1141, altered the reading here
from '1142' to '1141'. This emendation was followed by Hardy
and by Stubbs, because they saw this manuscript as William's
definitive text;[106] but the reading 1142 was restored by Mynors.[107]
This was undoubtedly correct.

A further break in the text is signalled a little over half way
through book iii, after a description of the legatine council held in
December 1141:

It has occurred to me to join up the early events of this year, which is the
year of the Lord's Incarnation 1143, with what is left over from the year
before; and at the same time to make into a parcel, as it were, the main
points scattered through my text bearing on the conduct of Robert, earl
of Gloucester, King Henry's son, and to present them in a recapitulation
for the reader to evaluate.[108]

There are some problems in interpreting this passage. 'What is left
over from the year before' was the detail of negotiations for the
exchange of the king and the earl of Gloucester in the later months
of 1141. It follows that 'the early events of this year' should refer
to early 1142 and not early 1143. There is more than one possible
explanation of this confusion. The sentence, which is a long one,
reads slightly awkwardly, and it may be that spelling out 'huius
anni' was an interpolation; but, if so, it certainly comes from
Malmesbury before the text was disseminated. The conclusion to
the *HN* was certainly written early in 1143. It would appear that
the text from this passage onwards was written at this time, and
that the tie-in to the earlier sections of book iii has been carelessly
drafted. The final book is less polished than the previous two.
Certainly the work lacks a final revision.

The following sequence of writing is suggested:

[105] See below, pp. lxiv–lxvii. [106] Hardy, ii. 737; Stubbs, ii. 567.
[107] Mynors, p. 46. [108] *HN* §60.

Books i and ii: October 1140–April 1141
Book iii up to para. 57: early 1142
Book iii para. 58 to the end: early 1143

The writing of the text took place between late 1140 and early 1143, a period of mutability of fortune for both parties in the civil war, and much soul-searching in the Angevin camp. For the ideas of the Angevin party in the decisive years of 1141 and 1142 it is the crucial text.

III. THE HISTORICAL VALUE OF THE *HISTORIA NOVELLA*

The *HN* is William of Malmesbury's contemporary history. He was a historian who thought deeply about his craft, and in the Prologues that he wrote in the full range of his works, and in asides to his readers, he shows an awareness of the problems of writing in each particular genre. Contemporary history was one such. There were conventions in the writing of prologues,[109] and the reader must be aware of what was conventional in them; but William of Malmesbury was seldom content simply to copy,[110] and throughout all his works he is particularly tenacious in claiming his readers' attention. In writing about current affairs, he believed, the historian had some advantages, but faced several difficulties. One great advantage was immediacy. He wrote in the Prologue of book i of the *GR*:[111] 'I guarantee the truth of nothing in past time except the sequence of events; the credit of my narrative must rest with my authorities. But whatsoever I have added out of recent

---

[109] G. Simon, 'Untersuchungen zur Topik der Widmungsbriefe mittelalterlicher Geschichtsschreiber bis zum Ende des 12. Jahrhunderts', *Archiv für Diplomatik*, iv (1958), 52–119, v–vi (1959–60), 73–153; A. Gransden, 'Prologues in the historiography of twelfth-century England', *England in the Twelfth Century: Proceedings of the 1988 Harlaxton Symposium*, ed. D. Williams (Woodbridge, 1990), pp. 55–81; D. W. T. C. Vessey, 'William of Tyre and the art of historiography', *Mediaeval Studies*, xxxv (1973), 433–55.

[110] B. Guenée, 'L'histoire entre l'éloquence et la science. Quelques remarques sur le prologue de Guillaume de Malmesbury à ses *Gesta regum Anglorum*', *Académie des Inscriptions et Belles-Lettres. Comptes Rendues des Séances de l'Année 1982* (Paris, 1982), pp. 357–70.

[111] *GR*, book i, pro. 7–8.

history, I have either seen myself or heard from men who can be trusted.' The *GR*, it is clear from this passage, was intended to stretch to the present day. In the present day, the historian had the advantage of direct access to the protagonists,[112] and could draw on his own experience. The confidence which that gave him, certainly the confidence that William of Malmesbury gained thereby, should not be underestimated. And yet there were problems:[113] 'Most people, I know, will think it unwise to have turned my pen to the history of the kings of my own time; they say that in works of this character truth is often disastrous and falsehood profitable, for in writing of contemporaries it is dangerous to criticize, while praise is sure of a welcome.' The kings of his own time were William Rufus and Henry I. These were his contemporaries: William of Malmesbury was perhaps born a year or so after Rufus's accession. The issues of their day, and many of the protagonists, were still alive. In writing for contemporaries, in high places, there was the temptation to write what they wanted to hear. This temptation William said that he would resist: 'I will so summarize doings, both good and bad, that as my ship speeds unhurt between Scylla and Charybdis, my information may perhaps be found wanting, but not my judgement.' These are the prefaces of books written as, to use modern terminology, they are about to be sent to press. The author assumes, and he writes in the expectation, that his work will straight away go into circulation. And just as individuals are thanked in modern prefaces, so here. The friends whom William of Malmesbury addresses are real, even if they are not always named, and his thanks to them are genuine, for they were providing him with material as well as advice on methodology. William of Malmesbury saw the writing of contemporary history as a form of dialogue.

In the *HN* William of Malmesbury was setting up a dialogue, which in the event would have to be continued after his death, and which continues to the present day. He was concerned to emphasize that he remained a historian, and that he would exercise

[112] On William of Malmesbury's attitude to oral testimony, see Scott, *Glastonbury*, pp. 21–4.
[113] *GR*, book iv, prologue; cf. *GR*, book v, prologue.

care in what he chose to believe. Some material might have to be suppressed, he admitted, but he would not allow his own judgement to be compromised. Of all the modern commentators it is Stubbs, the earliest and the greatest of them, who has most clearly seen what William of Malmesbury in this work was trying to achieve. Of 'our author' he says:[114]

His personal character was not that of an earnest partisan; nor was his judicial faculty that of a judge; he wrote for the ear of great men, not simply for the love of his subject, yet he is not a flatterer; he is not an impartial critic; he is not an unsympathising cosmopolitan. He has a distinct personality; he is not the able editor, though not a few of his more ambitious sections have a little of the look of leading articles.

These staccato comments, though they do not exclusively concern the *HN*, are particularly valuable for an understanding of it. 'He wrote for the ear of great men': the allusive style of so much of the text is best explained on the basis of shared knowledge and shared experience. He 'was not an earnest partisan', though some recent commentators have found him so: 'the work smacks of a conscious effort to deceive' is the most direct modern criticism in this vein.[115] Such criticism makes no reference to William of Malmesbury's other work, and it quite mistakes this text. There was, there can have been, no intention to deceive those who knew the story already. On the basis of shared experience, William of Malmesbury in the *HN* was concerned to select information and ideas that he felt to be important to the main story. The story was that of a disputed succession, the moral problems that this caused for individuals, the impact that this had on men's behaviour and— but this only indirectly—on government. Here is high politics; and here is high-quality political commentary. The leader-writer presumes that the reader has read the front page.

William of Malmesbury had first to choose where 'the history of recent events' was to start. It was not an easy decision, for while he was here telling a new story, it followed on chronologically from

[114] Stubbs, ii, pp. cxli–cxlii.
[115] R. B. Patterson, 'William of Malmesbury's Robert of Gloucester: A re-evaluation of the *Historia Novella*', *American Historical Review*, lxx (1965), 983–97, at p. 996.

his earlier work in the *GR*, and he seems to have been aware that in time the texts would come to be transmitted together. Book v of the *GR* thus becomes the starting-point for this discussion. The concluding letter to Robert of Gloucester, in its earliest version, said that the *GR* dealt with 'the history of the English from their first arrival in the country till the twentieth year of your father's most happy reign'.[116] That year concluded in August 1120. The key event of the following year was very far from happy. On 25 November 1120 the *White Ship* went down off Barfleur, and William, Henry's only legitimate son, was drowned. 'No ship was ever productive of so much misery for England, none was so widely celebrated throughout the world.'[117] There would follow a revolution in the politics of northern Europe: 'when the death of this youth became known, it produced a remarkable change in the course of events'. William in the *GR* went on to particularize, first that Henry was married again, to Adeliza of Louvain, and second that Fulk of Anjou, returning from Jerusalem, 'faithlessly espoused' the cause of William Clito, the son of Robert of Normandy.[118]

These themes were not developed. William of Malmesbury turned next to Henry's other child, Matilda, and her marriage to the German emperor Henry V. This led him to the struggle over lay investiture, up to the settlement of 1122, the whole of this excursus being brought back to the empress with a summary of her conspicuous virtues.[119] William was then well in to tidying up, and it might even seem that he saw himself as concluding the *GP* as well as the *GR*: 'now having ended the series of the kings, it seems incumbent on me to speak of that of the prelates of all England'.[120] He had selected for special notice three monks, Serlo abbot of Gloucester,[121] Lanzo prior of Lewes,[122] and Godfrey prior of Winchester.[123] As to those more skilled in secular matters than in spiritual, he went on, 'if there were any, they endeavoured to mitigate their failings by costly ornaments for their cathedrals';

---

[116] *GR* §446.
[117] *GR* §419.6. On this passage as a piece of fine writing, using classical models, see Wright, 'William of Malmesbury and Latin poetry', pp. 150–2.
[118] *GR* §419.8.   [119] *GR* §420–38.   [120] *GR* §445.4.
[121] *GR* §441.   [122] *GR* §442–3.   [123] *GR* §444.

and Ranulf Flambard was singled out.[124] The letter to Robert of Gloucester then stated that no further additions would be attempted, it being better to bring any new material into a further book ('librum').[125]

In the Prologue to the *HN*, William of Malmesbury refers to his earlier writings on Henry I's reign: 'Most of the achievements of your father of illustrious memory I have not failed to set down, both in the fifth book of the *Deeds of the Kings* and in the three little books to which I have given the name of *Chronicles*.' The present book would be clearly differentiated from these, because it had a precise objective, which was to explain 'those things which by the wonderful dispensation of God have happened in England in recent times'. To do this he would need to go back: 'the history may be related in more orderly sequence (*ordinatius . . . historiam transigi*) if I go a little further back and open my annals after the empress's return to England after her husband's death'. The three *libelli* entitled the *Chronicles* appear to be a separate work, and William here refers to them amongst his writings, but they have not survived.[126] It is tempting to suggest that the *HN* was all along intended (or very soon seen) to supersede them.[127] It is quite understandable that in later centuries the *HN* would appear to be the book vi of the *GR* that William had advertised, 'when my life and my history will terminate together'.[128]

The death of the German emperor Henry V provides the starting-point of the *HN*. It was important because it reanimated the empress as a political force in the Anglo-Norman world. The first important set piece is the council held first at Windsor and then at London in December 1126–January 1127. Here the matter of the succession was to take pride of place.[129] In William's

---

[124] *GR* §445. William had earlier written in very severe terms of Ranulf Flambard, but he revised his judgement of him, as of other contemporary clerics: *GP*, pp. xiv–xvii; Farmer, 'Life and works', pp. 45–6.

[125] 'consultius uidetur alium de talibus librum procudere': *GR* §449 (epilogue).

[126] The evidence was discussed by Stubbs, i, pp. cxv–cxvi.

[127] This was the view of Stubbs, i, pp. xxxii–xxxiii.

[128] 'in altero erit idem uitae qui scripturae terminus': *GR* §449 (epilogue). On the *HN* viewed as Book VI of the *GR* see below, p. lxxxvi.

[129] *HN* §2–3. A valuable modern study, which also makes the council the focus of a discussion of the succession dispute, is found in Hollister, *Anglo-Norman World*, pp. 145–69.

judgement the history of recent events in England, up to the early 1140s when he was writing, was determined by what was said and done at this council. What was done was what Henry I wanted. What Henry is reported to have said is worth some attention. He referred back to the loss of his son William in the *White Ship* in 1120. William had been he 'cui iure regnum competeret', to whom the kingdom belonged by right. This echoes what William of Malmesbury had said in the *GR* about Henry I himself, that he alone of the sons of William the Conqueror was born in royalty, 'et ei regnum uideretur competere'.[130] Henry, as reported, did not use the same language of Matilda's title, but referred to her rather as the person 'cui soli legitima debeatur successio', 'in whom alone lay the lawful succession'. William of Malmesbury went on to emphasize the empress's royal descent, from both parents. He placed particular emphasis on her descent, through her mother, from the Anglo-Saxon royal house: 'the line of that same royal blood never failed or suffered impediment in succession to the monarchy'. This title lay behind the oaths sworn at the council, by all the great men of England, that if Henry I died without a male heir, they would immediately and without going back raise up Matilda as lady, 'dominam susciperent'. The empress would enjoy lordship over the Anglo-Norman political community.

The precise form of that lordship remained to be worked out. William of Malmesbury did not particularize on the details of the oath, but concentrated rather on those who swore it, and the personal commitment they thus made to support the empress's claims. He tells the story of Robert of Gloucester and Stephen of Blois competing to be the first of those of comital rank to swear the oath, 'the one claiming the prerogative of a son, the other the dignity of a nephew'.[131] John of Worcester also records the discussion,[132] and agrees that Stephen swore first,[133] but according

---

[130] *GR* §390.   [131] *HN* §3.

[132] JW iii. 176–8. The date and place are given as 29 Apr. 1128 at Westminster, which is impossible, as the king was then in Normandy. This comes at the beginning of a passage identified as a reworking in JW ii, pp. lxviii–lxix. The same episode is discussed earlier, JW iii. 166–7.

[133] When he came to his 'recapitulation', however, William of Malmesbury said that it was Robert who swore first: *HN* §61.

to him there was no competition. Roger of Salisbury acted as master of ceremonies, and he called first for Robert of Gloucester. 'Get up,' he said, 'get up, and take the oath as the king wishes.' Robert, however, deferred to Stephen, as the elder of the two;[134] 'and so it was done'. John of Worcester says that the oath followed the taking of counsel from the magnates; but there was no discussion of Matilda's marriage to Geoffrey of Anjou, which took place in 1128. William of Malmesbury introduced at this point the breaking of the oath, quoting Roger of Salisbury as having said to him many times that he was released from the oath because of this lack of consultation.[135] The remaining years of Henry I's reign, William now said, would be reviewed very briefly, 'so that posterity may not be deprived of the knowledge of events, and yet I may not appear to dwell too long on matters irrelevant to this history (*quae minus ad hanc historiam pertinent*)'.[136] Granted the regard in which Henry I was held, it could not have been made more plain that this *historia* was not the history of England but the history of the succession.[137]

There is little enough in the *HN* on the matter of the succession between Matilda's marriage in 1128 and Henry I's death in December 1135, even though—or it might be argued because—the events of this period provide the key to the civil war which followed.[138] John of Worcester says that when the oaths were sworn to the empress in 1127, associated with her were the rights of her husband should she have one.[139] There was scope for discussion as to what those rights should be,[140] but all the indications are that Henry refused to discuss them at all; and

---

[134] This passage challenges the dates commonly given for the birth of these two men, i.e. for Robert of Gloucester *c*.1090 (*CP*, xi, App. D, p. 106), and for Stephen *c*.1096 (Davis, *Stephen*, p. 1 n. 1). The two men must have been close contemporaries, and, if John of Worcester is correct, a date of birth for each of them of *c*.1092 would appear to be indicated.

[135] *HN* §3.   [136] *HN* §4.

[137] As was noted by Stubbs, *GR*, ii, p. cxxxix.

[138] The crucial modern discussion of this period will be found in Chibnall, *Matilda*, pp. 56–63.

[139] 'cum legitimo suo si habuerit sponso': JW iii. 176–9.

[140] The Durham chronicler, writing close to the event, thought that Geoffrey would succeed as king (SD ii. 281–2), and this view was widely held in Anjou (Chibnall, *Matilda*, pp. 56–7).

that this contributed to the couple's separation in 1129 after they had been married for just a year.[141] Henry's policy on the succession hung in the balance at this time; and a council was convened to meet at Northampton in September 1131 to decide what to do. This council, no less important than that of December 1126–January 1127, was less well reported, but by two different chroniclers we are given the two key elements of a single settlement. Henry of Huntingdon stated that it was agreed that Matilda should be restored to her husband: William of Malmesbury noted that the oaths were again sworn.[142] Matilda returned to Geoffrey, and at Le Mans in March 1133 their first son, Henry, was born. It is possible (though by no means certain) that in the same year, precipitated by this event, a further set of oaths were sworn at Westminster.[143]

Henry I crossed to Normandy for the last time in August 1133. 'It is not to be doubted that he did many things in Normandy with a just claim to be written down': but they are not found in the *HN*, for William of Malmesbury explains that he intends to pass over matters of which he is not fully informed. We are taken immediately to Henry's death-bed. 'When he was asked . . . about his successor, he assigned all his lands on both sides of the sea to his daughter in lawful and lasting succession.' He was at this time 'somewhat angry' with her husband because of his behaviour.[144] In this way William of Malmesbury introduces the quarrel between the old king and Matilda and Geoffrey of Anjou, which Warren Hollister has argued was the reason why the arrangements so carefully made for the succession were not put into effect. 'Maud's opponents in 1126 would probably have had no choice but to accept her in December 1135, had it not been for her violent break with her father several months before.'[145] In this analysis, Geoffrey and Matilda, almost in spite of themselves, became caught up in border warfare between the Normans and the Angevins, which had been going on for generations; and this cost

---

[141] Chibnall, *Matilda*, pp. 57–9.

[142] HH, pp. 486–9; *HN* §8.

[143] The relevant sources, Ralph de Diceto's *Abbreviationes chronicorum* and Roger of Howden's *Chronica*, are discussed below, pp. xcvii–xcviii.

[144] *HN* §11.   [145] Hollister, *Anglo-Norman World*, pp. 162–3.

them support at the crucial time.[146] It was just bad luck. The chroniclers, William of Malmesbury included, allow if they do not insist that the matter be put another way. The quarrel between Henry and his nominated successor (and her husband) was intimately linked to the succession. Orderic Vitalis said that Geoffrey of Anjou 'demanded castles in Normandy, asserting that the king had covenanted with him to hand them over when he married his daughter'.[147] The other Norman authority is Robert of Torigni, who was writing later, during the 1150s. He mentioned the border warfare, as it involved Henry's refusal to hand over the fortresses of William Talvas. And yet: 'There was another and more significant cause of dispute between them. The king had refused to do fealty to his daughter and her husband when they required it, for all the fortresses of Normandy and England; and this they did on behalf of their sons, who were King Henry's lawful heirs.'[148] The security was asked for—in respect of some castles, according to Orderic, or of all castles, according to Robert of Torigni—in the names of Henry's grandchildren, his 'lawful heirs'. This form of security, for the succession as thus defined, was seen as essential if Henry's plans were to be implemented after his death. Orderic saw Geoffrey as hotheaded, refusing good counsel, but all the indications are that it was Henry who was refusing to take counsel,[149] and that his senior advisers favoured the arrangements that Matilda and Geoffrey had proposed. Robert of Gloucester, advised to claim the throne himself after Henry's death, said that it should more properly go to his sister's son, Henry;[150] David of Scotland's views seem to have run exactly on the same lines.[151] These passages support a

---

[146] Ibid., pp. 162–4. [147] OV vi. 444–5. [148] RT i. 200.

[149] Writing of the five years which followed the loss of the *White Ship*, Karl Leyser commented that 'Henry's views on this anxious question [as to who was the next heir] differed profoundly from those of most of his vassals and barons and the outside world': 'The Anglo-Norman succession 1120–1125', *ANS*, xiii (1991), 225–41, at p. 226. This comment holds good for the whole of the period 1120–35.

[150] 'dicens aequius esse filio sororis suae, cui iustius competebat': *GS*, pp. 12–15.

[151] When he came south after the death of Henry I, he took oaths and hostages from the northern magnates 'ad conseruandam fidem imperatrici nepti suae'. This comes after a passage in which Geoffrey is introduced as having married the empress, 'cuius filio Anglia ac Normannia iurata fuit'. The two passages need to be read together: Richard of Hexham, in *Chronicles*, iii. 145.

literal reading of Robert of Torigni's text; and on such a reading that text has one further implication. The claims that Matilda and Geoffrey made, on behalf of boys the elder of whom was barely two years old, can only have involved a regency. When we read of Henry's refusing to hand over castles, we must see him as rejecting the most visible part of a more complex settlement; and in rejecting one part of the settlement he rejected the whole. Matilda was left to fight on her own, and for herself. She did not succeed.

After describing Henry I's death, William of Malmesbury tells the story of Stephen's succession. It is the story of a coup, which was made possible by an element of antipathy to Anjou, by a lack of clarity as to Matilda's title, and by Stephen's control of the key minds and bases of power within England. It was the royal title that was the prize. Stephen would do what was necessary to secure and defend it. William of Malmesbury explains, with no element of censure, what Stephen did.[152] He obtained the support of the citizens of London and Winchester, of Bishop Roger of Salisbury, who controlled the English administration, and of William Pont de l'Arche, who controlled the treasury. Most crucial of all, he had the support of Bishop Henry of Winchester, his brother; without this, 'all his efforts would have been in vain'. That support was granted in the hope that Stephen would continue the good customs of his grandfather William the Conqueror, 'in the governance of the kingdom, especially as regards strict uprightness in Church affairs'. In this way William alluded to the fact that Stephen also was a grandchild of the Conqueror; and he introduced the solemn undertakings made to the Church before Stephen was crowned, by the archbishop of Canterbury, on 22 December 1135. 'The terms of this oath were afterwards put in writing'; which is to say that Stephen's charter of liberties to the Church, issued early in April 1136, spelt out undertakings given before the coronation, which reported to Pope Innocent were the key to securing his confirmation of Stephen's title.

After Henry I's burial at Reading, King Stephen was recorded in the *HN* as heading north, where he met David, king of Scots,

---

[152] *HN* §14.

'who was said to entertain different views, and had no difficulty in obtaining from him what he wanted'.[153] This refers to a peace treaty made in Durham and confirmed at York, 'either a genuine or a pretended peace'. William of Malmesbury had in the *GR* written very warmly of David;[154] his dismissive tone here is at first sight rather surprising. To understand the reason for this we need more detail than is given in the *HN* of King David's behaviour and of the precise terms of the peace treaty. The detail is to be found in Richard of Hexham.[155] This account makes it clear that well before Stephen was crowned, the Scots had captured Carlisle and had made substantial incursions into Northumbria. On his progress, King David was described as taking oaths of fealty and hostages from the great men that they would maintain their faith to the empress.[156] The peace terms that were subsequently agreed, after negotiation, follow the standard pattern of such an agreement, with balanced concessions being made by both sides.[157] The first concession was made by the Scots: 'Henry son of King David did homage to Stephen at York.' David gained valuable concessions in return: most notably he retained Carlisle, which he claimed as part of his kingdom;[158] but Stephen 'got what he wanted', for David had dealt with him, and his son and heir had done him homage, as king of England. It was for this reason that, more in sorrow than in anger, William of Malmesbury wrote of the king of Scots as a spent force. He was writing after the battle of the Standard in August 1138, and after the conclusion of a further and equally significant peace treaty,[159] neither of which he mentioned. Significant they may have been, but they had no bearing on the succession.

---

[153] *HN* § 16.   [154] *GR* § 400.

[155] Richard of Hexham, in *Chronicles*, iii. 145–6; trans. A. O. Anderson, *Scottish Annals from English Chroniclers. A.D. 500 to 1286* (London, 1908), pp. 172–3.

[156] Other chroniclers also mention the oath: G. W. S. Barrow, 'The Scots and the North of England', in King, *Anarchy*, pp. 231–53, at p. 244 n. 62.

[157] It is discussed in these terms by E. King, 'Dispute settlement in Anglo-Norman England', *ANS*, xiv (1992), 115–30, at pp. 119–20.

[158] On these claims, see Barrow, in King, *Anarchy*, pp. 244–53.

[159] On the battle, see Richard of Hexham, in *Chronicles*, iii. 159–65, and HH, pp. 712–19 (for extracts in trans. from these and other sources see Anderson, *Scottish Annals*, pp. 190–207); on the peace, see Richard of Hexham, in *Chronicles*, iii. 177–8 (trans. Anderson, *Scottish Annals*, pp. 214–15).

After describing how the second layman to swear allegiance to the empress in January 1127 had seized the crown in December 1135, and how the first layman who had done so had tacitly recognized the legitimacy of that seizure in February 1136, William turned to consider the position of the third layman, Robert of Gloucester. The political situation in the early months of 1136 is well realized.[160] Stephen was the man in possession. He was a popular figure. He controlled the resources of the kingdom. His authority grew apace: 'already all the chief men of England had willingly gone over to his side'. The *Gesta Stephani* tells the same story: 'almost all the chief men of the kingdom accepted him gladly and respectfully, and having received very many gifts from him and likewise enlargement of their lands they devoted themselves wholly to his service by a voluntary oath, after paying homage'.[161] Stephen's authority was made visible at the Easter court, according to Henry of Huntingdon the most splendid ever held;[162] and charters issued on this occasion confirm the wide support which the king by then enjoyed.[163] William of Malmesbury depicted Robert of Gloucester as isolated. He had to undertake to recognize Stephen before he was allowed to cross to England; and when he came he did homage. But, William went on to say, he did so conditionally ('sub conditione quadam'), 'namely for as long as the king maintained his rank unimpaired and kept the agreement'.

This is an important passage, and by later historians it has been much commented upon, at times to William of Malmesbury's disadvantage. It is carefully phrased. 'Homagium regi fecit': Robert did homage. The form of that homage was routine. The forms of submission have been well treated by Jacques Le Goff, glossing the text of Galbert of Bruges, in which he described the reception of William Clito as count of Flanders in 1127.[164] Three

[160] *HN* § 17. [161] *GS*, pp. 12–13.
[162] HH, pp. 706–7; cf. *GS*, pp. 24–9, John of Hexham, in SD ii. 287.
[163] *Regesta*, iii, nos. 46, 944; cf. Round, *Geoffrey*, pp. 18–20, 262–6.
[164] J. Le Goff, *Time, Work, & Culture in the Middle Ages* (Chicago, 1980), pp. 237–87 (text), 354–67 (notes); Galbert of Bruges, *Histoire du meurtre de Charles le Bon, comte de Flandre (1127–1128)*, ed. H. Pirenne (Paris, 1891), p. 89, trans. J. B. Ross, *The Murder of Charles the Good, Count of Flanders, by Galbert of Bruges*, rev. edn. (New York, 1967), pp. 206–7; and for comment, S. Reynolds, *Fiefs and Vassals* (Oxford, 1994), pp. 268–9.

distinct stages are identified in these ceremonies. First the homage, a verbal undertaking to become the man of the lord, accompanied by the *immixtio manuum*, the lord taking between his hands the joined hands of his man. Second the fealty: the man who has done homage promises on his faith loyalty to the lord, swearing in the most solemn form, at which the two 'become allies with a kiss'. Thirdly there was the investiture: 'with the rod which he held in his hand the count gave investiture to all'. There is no equivalent description of what happened in England, but Henry of Blois, the king's brother and his stage-manager, wrote as follows concerning one of the tenants of Glastonbury Abbey: 'King Henry my uncle having gone the way of all flesh, and my brother Stephen having succeeded in the kingdom, the aforesaid Robert did homage and swore an oath of fealty as was the custom, together with the other magnates of the land.'[165] Here are noted the first two stages of the ritual which Galbert of Bruges described. What is at issue is the third stage, the form of investiture. Stephen, in what has become known as his first coronation charter, promised 'all my barons and men of England all the liberties and good laws which Henry the king of the English my uncle gave and conceded to them'.[166] But, as William of Malmesbury was concerned to stress,[167] few of the new king's barons and men were at the coronation to pay him homage and have their individual liberties confirmed. We must envisage a series of inevitably more private ceremonies, preceded in many cases by individual negotiation. In the case of Miles of Gloucester, the grant of his lands in return for homage was accompanied by an agreement (*conuentio*) granting him hereditary tenure of his offices.[168] In the case of Baldwin de Redvers a refusal to conclude a similar agreement caused his rebellion.[169] The ceremonial of the

---

[165] *Adami de Domerham de rebus gestis Glastoniensibus*, ed. T. Hearne, 2 vols. (Oxford 1727), ii. 310.

[166] *Regesta*, iii, no. 270.

[167] 'nullis abbatibus paucissimis optimatibus': *HN* § 15.

[168] *Regesta*, iii, nos. 386–7; for comment see Round, *Geoffrey*, pp. 10–17; King, 'Dispute settlement in Anglo-Norman England', pp. 120–1; D. Crouch, 'A Norman *conuentio* and bonds of lordship in the middle ages', *Law and Government*, pp. 299–324, at 313.

[169] Richard of Hexham, in *Chronicles*, iii. 146; *GS*, pp. 30–3; Davis, *Stephen*, pp. 22–4 (but the sources do not support the statement there that Stephen refused to confirm

Easter court might well have included a public renewal of fealty,[170] and a confirmation of investiture.[171] Robert of Gloucester took care to arrive a little later; there were discussions, and he 'obtained all that he demanded in accordance with his wish'; and then he did homage.[172] 'Sub conditione quadam': the homage created a contract, and all contracts were conditional. William here emphasized an element of the ceremony of submission that no contemporary would have found remarkable, and which the circumstances of Stephen's accession had served to highlight.

William of Malmesbury moved immediately from the earl of Gloucester doing homage to the king, *quamdiu* he kept to the agreement made with him, to the churchmen doing fealty to the king, *quamdiu* 'he should maintain the freedom of the Church'.[173] He then gave a full text, though lacking the reservation of the rights of the crown and the names of the witnesses (among whom was Robert of Gloucester), of Stephen's second charter of liberties.[174] This meant that when, as William would shortly describe, Robert renounced his homage on the advice of the clergy, both parties were able to claim that Stephen was in breach of an agreement with them: 'It is not right that I should hide the truth, with all respect for a very kindly man; if he had acquired the kingdom in a lawful way, and in administering it had not lent trusting ears to the whispers of those who wished him ill, then undoubtedly he would have lacked little that adorns the royal character.'[175] In William's analysis, political error was no less important than weakness of title in undermining Stephen's position.

The remainder of book i, having thus summarized the reasons

Baldwin 'in his lands'); R. Bearman, 'Baldwin de Redvers: Some aspects of a baronial career in the reign of King Stephen', *ANS*, xviii (1996), 19–46.

[170] 'fidelitates exegit': Diceto, i. 248.

[171] At the conclusion of Arthur's crown-wearing at Caerleon 'uocantur cuncti qui ei propter honores obsequium prestabant et singuli singulis possessionibus, ciuitatibus uidelicet atque castellis, archiepiscopatibus, episcopatibus, abbaciis, ceterisque honoribus donantur': *The Historia Regum Britannie of Geoffrey of Monmouth*, i, ed. N. Wright (Cambridge, 1985), § 157. This work was written early in Stephen's reign: C. Brooke, 'Geoffrey of Monmouth as a historian', *Church and Government in the Middle Ages: Essays Presented to C. R. Cheney on his 70th Birthday*, ed. C. N. L. Brooke *et al.* (Cambridge, 1976), pp. 77–91, at 87.

[172] *GS*, pp. 14–15.

[173] *HN* § 18.

[174] *Regesta*, iii, no. 271.

[175] *HN* § 19.

for Stephen's failure, leads the reader to Robert of Gloucester's *diffidatio*. No more is said of the events of 1136, but when Stephen crossed to Normandy early in 1137, Robert, after settling affairs in England, followed him there, 'putting to sea actually on Easter day', which fell on 11 April. Robert witnessed charters of Stephen at his own base of Bayeux;[176] at Évreux,[177] where Stephen concluded an agreement with his brother Theobald;[178] and at the Beaumont town of Pont Audemer,[179] to which the king had pursued a group of deserters after wide divisions had appeared in his army.[180] These charters are important in establishing Stephen's itinerary in Normandy, and if Robert of Gloucester did not cross the Channel until after Easter, the dates need to be looked at again.[181] Robert of Gloucester clearly wished to keep close to the action, but he was never fully trusted by elements in Stephen's court, and in particular by the Flemings. William of Malmesbury recorded an attempted ambush of Robert of Gloucester, instigated by William of Ypres, soon after the earl's arrival in Normandy. He stated that Stephen accepted responsibility for this, and that the two men were reconciled, the archbishop of Rouen standing as security to the earl that the king would not act in this way again. This is patently Robert of Gloucester's version of what had happened. The king and the earl thereafter treated one another with formal politeness. The earl is shown as distancing himself from the court, waiting to see how things would turn out.

---

[176] *Regesta*, iii, no. 594.   [177] Ibid., no. 69.   [178] RT i. 206–7.

[179] *Regesta*, iii, no. 749; cf. Crouch, *Beaumont Twins*, map on pp. 72–3.

[180] OV vi. 486–7.

[181] The sources are OV vi. 480–7, and RT i. 206–7. The problems of reconciling them to reconstruct an itinerary are noted by Davis, *Stephen*, p. 25, and Chibnall, OV vi. 484 n. 2; and a revision is offered by R. Helmerichs, 'King Stephen's Norman itinerary, 1137', *Haskins Society Journal*, v (1993), 89–97. All are constrained by the style of one of the chancery scribes, who has dated three charters (*Regesta*, iii, nos. 69, 594, 843) by calendar and by regnal year, in the form 'anno incarnationis dominice mcxxxvi, regni vero mei secundo'. The editors of the *Regesta* date these three charters variously to before Lady Day (25 Mar.) or before Easter (11 Apr.). Nos. 69 and 594, witnessed by Robert of Gloucester, must be later; and if they are released from the strait-jacket so also may be no. 843, a charter of Stephen's queen issued at Évreux. There is then no need for any of the state business of the year to take place before Easter, which one would expect the king to have kept at Rouen. Amaury I of Évreux died 18/19 Apr. 1137, a week after Easter (Crouch, *Beaumont Twins*, p. 34); Stephen's visit to Évreux may have been shortly thereafter.

When in the final chapter of book i Robert of Gloucester renounces his allegiance, the reader is invited to see this as both a political judgement and a question of conscience. The year 1138 saw much castle-building, and according to the *Annals of Winchester*, it was every man for himself: 'There was no man of any dignity or substance in England who was not building or strengthening fortifications in England.'[182] The king was torn this way and that, 'and always settled the business with more loss to himself than to his opponents'.[183] From now on in England there would be only the appearance of peace, 'simulatam ad tempus pacem'. An important element in this instability was uncertainty. It was being reported that Robert of Gloucester would move to support his sister, just as soon as he had defied the king. So indeed it turned out. According to Orderic it was not an easy decision for Robert to take even then, for 'he feared the factions on both sides'.[184] William's treatment had been structured from the beginning towards what Round called 'the famous *diffidatio*'.[185] He says that Robert of Gloucester, 'in the traditional way' (*more maiorum*), withdrew his homage to the king and broke with him (*rege . . . diffidato*)'.[186] A little later the same phrase introduces his criticism of Stephen for coming to besiege Lincoln early in 1141, since he had not formally withdrawn his friendship from Ranulf of Chester and his brother, 'which they call defiance' ('nec modo more maiorum amicitiam suam eis interdixerat, quod diffidiare dicunt').[187] Here, as elsewhere when he is dealing with the language of chivalric custom,[188] William is at some pains to keep his distance, whether from fastidiousness or from some other cause is not clear.[189] In consequence of his withdrawal of homage,

---

[182] *Annals of Winchester*, in *Ann. Mon.*, ii. 51.　　　　[183] *HN* §21.
[184] OV vi. 516–17.　　　　[185] Round, *Geoffrey*, p. 28.
[186] *HN* §21.　　　　[187] *HN* §41.
[188] Thus with the customs regarding escort, to deny which to an enemy 'laudabilium militum mos non est' (*HN* §31), and the rendering of castles, 'sicut moris est illorum hominum' (*HN* §77); and, in discussing the Battle of Lincoln, the phraseology used about jousting and imprisonment: 'proludium pugnae facere quod iustam uocant' (*HN* §43), 'iuxta morem illius generis hominum quos captiuos nominant' (*HN* §44).
[189] Differing interpretations of the *diffidatio* will be found in J. Gillingham, '1066 and the introduction of chivalry into England', *Law and Government*, pp. 31–55, at 48–9, and M. Strickland, *War and Chivalry: The Conduct and Perception of War in England and Normandy, 1066–1217* (Cambridge, 1996), pp. 40–1.

Robert of Gloucester lost many of his possessions in England, though he retained Bristol.[190] At this point, rather abruptly, book i ends.

Book ii deals with events of the years 1139 and 1140. The year 1139 is seen as overshadowed first by reports that the empress was about to arrive, and then in the autumn by her landing. Under 1140 William describes, almost in apocalyptic terms, the effect of the civil war on England, and the implications for his own monastery and for Robert of Gloucester. And yet neither Robert nor the empress, nor the rights and wrongs of their quarrel with King Stephen, lie in this book at centre stage. In their place are two great churchmen, Roger of Salisbury and Henry of Winchester. It is with the dilemmas of the churchmen, not of the laity, that book ii is concerned. It contains some of William's finest writing. As contemporary reportage of a high-level diplomatic conference it would be difficult to improve upon the description of the council of Winchester in 1139.[191] As an obituary of a great man, who had done the writer some harm, it would be difficult to improve upon the obituary given here for Roger of Salisbury.[192] As a summary of the effects of civil war it would be difficult to improve on William's lament for the state of England, which seems to echo many of the themes in the more famous description in the *Anglo-Saxon Chronicle.*[193]

William of Malmesbury had followed the treatment of the *pactum* which Robert of Gloucester had made with Stephen, with a similar *pactum* made with him by the Church. The rupture of the one, in Robert of Gloucester's *diffidatio*, was followed by a threat of rupture in the other, consequent on the 'arrest of the bishops' at Oxford in June 1139. The arrest is placed in the context of a political situation that had been briefly outlined in book i: reports that the empress would shortly land, and divisions within Stephen's court. Roger of Salisbury and his nephews were among a number of individuals, whom 'he arrested at his own court, in a manner unbefitting a king, in addition requiring the surrender of

---

[190] *HN* § 21.   [191] *HN* § 25–30.   [192] *HN* § 33–4.
[193] *HN* § 36–7; for a discussion of the relationship of the *HN* with the *ASC*, see below, pp. xcv–xcvi.

their castles and making other such terms as he pleased'.[194] William specified Newark castle, built by Alexander of Lincoln 'for the protection, as he said, and glorification of his bishopric', and four fortifications c˙ Roger of Salisbury—Sherborne, Devizes, Malmesbury, and Salisbury itself. The bishops' ostentation offended some powerful laymen, 'vexed that they would be surpassed by clerks in the amassing of wealth and the size of their castles'. This group of castles has suffered severely from the ravages of time, and there is little more than the shell of Sherborne to indicate now the awe inspired in William of Malmesbury by Roger of Salisbury's building works.[195] There is no reason, however, to doubt that they were the wonders of their day. William had a good eye for buildings.[196]

The 'arrest of the bishops', involving the fall of a man who was justiciar in all but name, was a sensational story, and it featured prominently in all the chronicles. Only William of Malmesbury, however, has a proper discussion of the issues which the arrests raised—the rights of the bishops to control castles, particularly in time of war, and the rights of the monarchy to subject ecclesiastics to the judgment of secular tribunals. These issues were discussed at length at the council which convened at Winchester on 29 August 1139.[197] The contestants were well matched. This was a legatine council, and so the legate could set the agenda. First he was able to choose the language of discourse: his complaints against the king were made in Latin, 'since he was addressing educated men'.[198] It was wrong for the king to arrest his men, and especially bishops, in the peace of his court; and wrong for him to make the charges levelled against the bishops the pretext for the spoliation of church property. The king had accepted a summons to the council, and so it was for the clergy, 'the archbishop and the

[194] *HN* § 22.

[195] See R. A. Stalley, 'A twelfth-century patron of architecture: A study of the buildings erected by Roger, bishop of Salisbury 1102–1139', *Journal of the British Arch. Assoc.*, 3rd ser., xxxiv (1971), 62–83.

[196] William of Malmesbury is one of the main authors discussed in A. Gransden, 'Realistic observation in twelfth-century England', *Speculum*, xlvii (1972), 29–51; and see also R. A. Brown, *Castles, Conquest and Charters: Collected Papers* (Woodbridge, 1989), pp. 227–34.

[197] *HN* § 25–30; *Councils and Synods*, i (2), no. 141, pp. 781–7.

[198] *HN* § 25.

others', to decide what should be done. After this, the king 'sent earls to the council to enquire why he had been summoned'.[199] The legate repeated the points he had made previously, more briefly and presumably in French. The king's case was made first and in terms of secular law by Aubrey de Vere, and then in terms of the canon law by Hugh, archbishop of Rouen. In arguing that Roger of Salisbury had been arrested 'not as a bishop but as a servant of the king',[200] those who advised Stephen were on familiar ground.[201] It is a part of the interest of the proceedings at Winchester that the king was more than ready for a fight on the clergy's own terms. William informs us, almost as an aside, that 'the king did not lack confidence in his own case'.[202] He represents the council, waiting for Hugh of Rouen, as all agog as to what he would say.[203] In fact, the king and his advisers knew very well. The archbishop of Rouen was a good canonist, and the canons offered little support for bishops as holders of castles.[204] He was familiar also with the custom of 'rendability' of castles, as it was applied in Normandy and elsewhere,[205] during what is termed here 'a time of uncertainty'. In William's description, which comes to us first-hand, the clergy's case was reduced to disarray.

The king's confidence in September 1139 was not just because he had a case to argue in canon law. Six months earlier, at the Lateran Council, the pope, Innocent II, had found for him in the

---

[199] *HN* § 26.   [200] *HN* § 27.

[201] William of Malmesbury reported Lanfranc as saying in 1082 that Odo of Bayeux was being held as earl of Kent not as bishop of Bayeux: *GR* § 306.3 (cf. the discussion of Chibnall in OV iv, pp. xxvii–xxx); and this was cited as a precedent at the trial of William of St Calais, bishop of Durham, in 1088: SD i. 184; trans. in *English Lawsuits from William I to Richard I*, ed. R. C. Van Caenegem, 2 vols. (Selden Soc., cvi–cvii, 1990–1), i. 99.

[202] *HN* § 26.

[203] *HN* § 29. In setting the scene for the council in *HN* § 24, William had anticipated the arrival of Hugh of Rouen and outlined his views.

[204] T. G. Waldman, 'Hugh of Amiens, archbishop of Rouen (1130–64), the Norman abbots, and the papacy: the foundation of a "textual community"', *Haskins Society Journal*, ii (1990), 139–53, at p. 147.

[205] On custom and practice concerning the 'rendability' of castles, see J. Yver, 'Les châteaux forts en Normandie jusqu'au milieu du xiie siècle. Contribution à l'étude du pouvoir ducal', *Bull. de la Soc. des Antiquaires de Normandie*, liii (1955–6), 28–115, esp. pp. 60–3, 80–1, 94–5; Haskins, pp. 277–84; C. L. H. Coulson, 'Rendability and castellation in medieval France', *Château Gaillard*, vi (1972), 59–67; idem, 'The French matrix of the castle-provisions of the Chester–Leicester *conventio*', *ANS*, xvii (1995), 65–86, citing *HN* § 29 at p. 82.

matter of the succession.[206] Ulger bishop of Angers had presented the empress's case against Stephen, 'charging the king with perjury and unjust seizure of the kingdom'.[207] Arnulf archdeacon of Lisieux had been one of those putting the case for the king: 'he did not deny the oath, but maintained that it had been extorted by force and was conditional only', for the king might designate another heir; and this he had done. Nor should the empress have been allowed to succeed, 'because she was the daughter of an incestuous union', her mother having taken the veil whilst at Romsey.[208] This last point was not totally frivolous, but it will not have taken the council long to deal with it.[209] That the king had changed his mind had been widely disseminated,[210] and this could not be disproved. Innocent cut the arguments short, 'and sent [Stephen] friendly letters confirming him in the kingdom of England and duchy of Normandy'.[211] Innocent will have been reminded of the reasons for his original decision. We know that this was so. Roger of Salisbury and his two nephews were among the churchmen who acquired privileges for their sees, issued at this council, and they drew attention to the king's defence of ecclesiastical liberty.[212]

[206] The sources are John of Salisbury, *Historia Pontificalis*, ed. M. Chibnall (NMT, 1956; OMT, 1986), pp. 83–5, and GF, *Letters*, no. 26; for comment, Chibnall, *Matilda*, pp. 75–6; C. Holdsworth, 'The Church', in King, *Anarchy*, pp. 207–29, at 210–11; and G. Constable, in *Peter the Venerable*, ii. 252–6 (discussing the possibility of an earlier hearing at Rome in 1136).

[207] John of Salisbury, *Historia Pontificalis*, ed. Chibnall, p. 84.

[208] Ibid., pp. 83–4.

[209] The marriage had been publicly celebrated by Anselm, and no impediment had been found; but the archbishop had had his reservations (Southern, *Anselm*, pp. 260–2, and the references there cited), and Gilbert Foliot felt it necessary to spell out the matter at some length (GF, *Letters*, pp. 65–6).

[210] The description of Stephen's accession in the *Liber Eliensis* reads as though copied from an official newsletter: *Liber Eliensis*, iii. 46, ed. E. O. Blake, Camden Soc. 3rd ser., xcii (1962), pp. 285–6.

[211] John of Salisbury, *Historia Pontificalis*, ed. Chibnall, p. 85.

[212] A bull for Alexander confirmed 'the liberty granted to the Church by that illustrious man Stephen the king of the English': *The Registrum Antiquissimum of the Cathedral Church of Lincoln*, ed. C. W. Foster, i (Lincoln Rec. Soc., xxvii, 1931), no. 249; and the same phrases were used in a bull for Roger de Clinton, bishop of Chester: W. Holtzmann, *Papsturkunden in England*, 3 vols. in 4 (Berlin and Göttingen, 1930–52), ii (2), no. 19. The bull for Nigel of Ely is ibid. ii (2), no. 21; and for Roger of Salisbury, ibid., ii (2), no. 20. The bull for the Lincoln diocese may have been procured by Henry of Huntingdon, who attended the council: HH, p. lv.

Hugh of Rouen's intervention at the council of Winchester had been decisive. The council had broken up on the same day that he arrived, on 1 September 1139. On the last day of the same month, Robert of Gloucester arrived in England, together with the empress.[213] Her coming to England was something of a gamble. Robert retained a base in the west country, for Stephen had not been able to capture Bristol. It was difficult, however, to find a port of entry, and a secure base on the south coast. The place chosen for the landing was Arundel, under the control of Henry I's widow Adeliza of Louvain and her second husband William d'Aubigny. This offered little security. While Robert of Gloucester rode to the west country to seek reinforcements, Arundel castle was soon surrounded by Stephen's forces, and the empress forced to withdraw. The best-known part of this story was that Matilda was given an escort of Waleran of Meulan and Henry of Winchester (across whose diocese the initial and most difficult part of the journey lay); thus protected and under a safe conduct she made her way to Bristol to join her brother. The king's misplaced chivalry was at the time, and has been since, a matter of remark. William of Malmesbury alludes to this, without emphasis, saying that it was a matter of etiquette for such an escort to be offered.[214] Neither party in fact was happy about what had happened at Arundel. For the Angevins, Henry I's widow Adeliza was seen to have broken, 'with a woman's fickleness', undertakings that she had made. Stephen's wrath fell upon those who had allowed the empress to get that far, the men who had control of the ports and had permitted her to land.[215] Thereafter Wareham in Dorset, to the west of the Solent, would provide the Angevins with a secure line of communication across the Channel.

The empress went first to Bristol, and then on to Gloucester, where she was received by Miles of Gloucester. In a charter, which regrettably survives only in a calendar copy, she speaks *viva voce*:[216]

[213] *HN* §31.
[214] 'quem cuilibet quis infestissimo inimico negare laudabilium militum mos non est': *HN* §31.
[215] JW iii. 268–9.   [216] *Regesta*, iii, no. 391.

I wish you to know that when I arrived in England after the death of my father, Miles of Gloucester, just as soon as he could, came to me at Bristol and received me as lady, and as she who was recognized as the rightful heir of the kingdom of England; and thence he brought me to Gloucester, and there did me liege homage against all men.

Miles was to become one of the empress's most important supporters. Later, when divisions had appeared in the Angevin camp, he would claim that the empress 'would not have eaten one day's meals nor had any provision for her table except through his munificence and stewardship'.[217] That claim is found in the Gloucester chronicle, an important source for the events of 1140 and 1141, which until recently has been difficult to use for want of a critical edition.[218] How Robert of Gloucester was viewed in the city from which he took his title is suggested by the description of him in this chronicle as 'the earl of Bristol', rather than 'the earl of Gloucester'.[219] It was from Bristol castle that evil spread over the whole of England. It is tempting to say that the Gloucester chronicle gives the story from the perspective of Miles of Gloucester, just as the *HN* gives the story from the perspective of Robert of Gloucester; but this would not be quite exact. The perspective is rather that of the monks and townspeople. It is critical of the lack of faith of both Robert and Miles, and it shows the empress claiming regal power: 'She received homage from all, and dispensed the laws of the kingdom of England according to her pleasure.'[220]

William of Malmesbury was now writing on the basis of immediate experience. The year 1140 was seen as overshadowed

[217] JW iii 298–9.

[218] This Gloucester 'chronicle' consists of interpolations within, and a continuation of, the G text of John of Worcester's *Chronicula* (Dublin, Trinity College MS 503, described in JW ii, pp. lix–lxiv), from which they were printed—but not separately distinguished—in Hardy's EHS edition of 1848–9. They were excluded from the text of John of Worcester's chronicle for the years 1118 to 1140 printed by Weaver in 1908. They are printed, and distinguished, in the new OMT edition: JW iii. The text printed by Weaver as undoubtedly the work of John of Worcester ends, imperfectly, in mid-1140, just before the execution of Robert Fitz Hubert (*HN* §39). The continuation up to autumn 1141, which also ends imperfectly, is mainly a Gloucester text, but it may—so Dr McGurk argues—include some material from John of Worcester. See ibid., iii, pp. xlviii–l, which Dr McGurk most kindly made available to me in typescript.

[219] JW iii. 252–3, 298–9, 302–3.   [220] JW iii. 270–1.

by the brutalities of war. 'There were many castles all over England, each defending its own district or, to be more truthful, plundering it.'[221] Mercenaries from Flanders and Brittany came to England, and lived off the land. The career of Robert Fitz Hubert, who had control for a time of the castle at Devizes, was selected as an example, 'the cruellest of all men in the recollection of our age'.[222] Against this stood the earl of Gloucester, sharing in regal power: it was he who urged the legate and the bishops to excommunicate offenders, he who created his brother Reginald earl of Cornwall, 'in view of the difficulties of the times'.[223] The king also acted vigorously, but was no more successful. Things went from bad to worse, 'for lack of justice'; and the coinage was devalued. We are presented with local tyranny, and a whole society that had become venal: 'erant igitur Angliae cuncta uenalia'.[224] In this context, Henry of Winchester sought to make peace. William of Malmesbury offers valuable clues as to the terms of agreement that were then worked out.[225] It was the king, seen as increasingly under the thumb of his courtiers, who rejected them. The legate at the end of book ii, just like Robert of Gloucester at the end of book i, was left to watch and to await developments.

Book iii deals with the years 1141 and 1142, at the end of which the text concludes. In 1141 the civil war seemingly came to a climax. The battle of Lincoln, fought outside the walls of the castle on 2 February 1141, led to King Stephen's capture and imprisonment. The empress, it appeared, stood poised at last to secure the position that her father had sought to arrange for her. Her failure came as a profound shock to Robert of Gloucester, and to all her supporters. They looked back, and William of Malmesbury can be seen in a 'recapitulation' looking back, to see what had gone wrong. There had been divided counsels in the Angevin camp, and mistakes had been made. William shows the Angevins coming to terms with these mistakes, and regrouping to fight again.

As soon as she received notice of the king's capture, the empress

---

[221] *HN* § 36.   [222] *HN* § 38.
[223] *HN* § 37.   [224] *HN* § 37.
[225] See further below, pp. lx–lxi.

sent messengers to Henry of Winchester, the papal legate, urging 'that she should be received without hesitation by church and state, since she was King Henry's daughter and the whole of England and Normandy was sworn to her'.[226] Envoys and letters went back and forth; a meeting was held 'on an open plain on the approach to Winchester' on 2 March 1141; and there an agreement was made. It was to be a conditional agreement, just like the one that Stephen had made with the Church over five years earlier. Again we read *quamdiu*, for as long as the empress kept the agreement, the legate would receive her as lady of England, 'in dominam Angliae recipere'. William of Malmesbury makes the focus of his attention the legatine council summoned at Winchester early in April,[227] which he also attended: 'my memory is very clear'.[228] This determined the succession. The legate needed to explain his authority to do this, and he felt it necessary also to exculpate his earlier behaviour. The clergy were now acting, he argued, just as they had acted earlier in December 1135, in the interests of peace. In the interests of peace, 'because it seemed tedious to wait for the lady', Stephen had been received. He had made an agreement with the Church, but had then broken it. He had done no justice, and in little over a year peace had broken down. It had been by the judgment of God that Stephen had been captured at Lincoln. The peace of the country was again in question, and it fell to the clergy, 'whose special prerogative it is to choose and consecrate a prince', to resolve the matter. They elected Matilda as 'lady of England and Normandy', and promised her fealty and support.[229]

By the summer of 1141, William of Malmesbury says a little later, 'the greater part of England had graciously accepted [the empress's] lordship'.[230] And yet by the end of the year, the Church would have withdrawn its support for her, and the area under her lordship would be only a little more extensive than it had been before the battle of Lincoln. The main sources for this critical

[226] *HN* §45.
[227] *HN* §46–51; *Councils and Synods*, i (2), no. 142, pp. 788–92.
[228] 'egregie quippe memini': *HN* §46.   [229] *HN* §47.
[230] *HN* §52.

year, in addition to the *HN*, are the *Gesta Stephani* (henceforth *GS*) and the Gloucester chronicle. These each identify—though they give a different weighting to—three elements in the empress's failure: first, a failure of temperament, in her dealings with her entourage and her use of patronage; second, her dealings with the Londoners; third, her attitude to the house of Blois. These will be considered in turn.

The author of the *GS* saw the personal failings of the empress as being of overriding importance. No sooner had Stephen been captured than:

She at once put on an extremely arrogant demeanour instead of the modest gait and bearing proper to the gentle sex, began to walk and speak and do all things more stiffly and more haughtily than she had been wont, to such a point that soon, in the capital of the land subject to her, she actually made herself queen of all England and gloried in being so called.[231]

All this occurred, according to the same source, even before her reception at Winchester by the legate, who is said subsequently to have 'bade the people, at a public meeting in the market-place of the town, salute her as their lady and their queen'.[232] William of Malmesbury's detailed description of the empress's reception at Winchester, and of the council which followed (which the *GS* does not mention), makes it most unlikely that Henry of Winchester ever gave the empress the title of queen. In the *HN* the empress is always called 'domina' and never 'regina'. It is equally unlikely that the precise distinctions of the clergy passed immediately into general use. Some phrase was needed for the authority which Matilda now exercised, and both the *GS* and the Gloucester chronicler refer to her *imperium*.[233]

That after Winchester the empress had a new authority as well as a new title was not in doubt. She need not have used, and probably did not use, the title *regina*.[234] Charters that she issued as

---

[231] *GS*, pp. 118–19.   [232] Ibid.
[233] *GS*, pp. 116–17; JW iii. 294–5. This can only have seemed a happy phrase, and it may have been one that enjoyed some currency around this time.
[234] J. C. Holt, review of *Regesta*, iii and iv, in *Economic History Review*, 2nd ser., xxiv (1971), 480–3; Chibnall, *Matilda*, pp. 102–4, and 'The charters of the Empress Matilda', *Law and Government*, pp. 276–98, at 279–80.

domina Anglorum granted estates to laymen and religious houses, bestowed earldoms and sheriffdoms and household offices, and assumed a routine control of the central administration, including the exchequer. On her coins she wore Stephen's lily-crown, and clutched Stephen's sceptre.[235] The rights that she claimed were royal, and this lay behind the further criticisms found in the *GS*: 'She arbitrarily annulled any grant fixed by the king's royal decree; she hastily snatched away and conferred on her own followers anything he had given in unshakeable perpetuity to churches or to his comrades in arms.'[236] If the adjectives are left on one side, there is nothing particularly remarkable in this passage. The empress's son after her would refuse to recognize Stephen's grants.[237] But this would be in terms of a settlement which recognized the integrity of those who had fought on the other side during the civil war.[238] The empress refused either to negotiate a settlement or to recognize that integrity. This is apparent in, and provides the broader context for, her dealings with the Londoners, and in the matter of Stephen's heir. The empress's failure was one of policy, not of personality.

William of Malmesbury sees the Londoners throughout the crucial months after the battle of Lincoln as an important political force. They attended the council at Winchester, and argued powerfully for the king's release. William listened with particular interest to the language which they used in speaking of themselves: 'they had been sent', they said, 'by what they call the commune of London (*missos se a communione quam uocant Londoniarum*)'.[239] The 'quam uocant' was intended to alert the listener then, and should alert the reader now, to William's unease at the claims made for the commune. A commune is a sworn association of the citizens,

---

[235] Mark Blackburn adduces strong arguments for identifying the much-discussed PERERIC coins as 'an official issue in the name of the empress produced and distributed from London during May or June 1141': 'Coinage and currency', in King, *Anarchy*, pp. 173–5, at 175. There are good reproductions in G. C. Boon, *Coins of the Anarchy 1135–54* (Cardiff, 1988), where two coins from the Cardiff mint, no. 4 of Stephen and no. 9 of the empress, may be compared.

[236] *GS*, pp. 120–1.

[237] This is a gross over-simplification of a complex matter, on which see J. C. Holt, '1153: The Treaty of Winchester', in King, *Anarchy*, pp. 291–316, esp. 302–4.

[238] *Regesta*, iii, no. 272.   [239] *HN* §49.

recognized by the public authority. That the Londoners had formed such an association is clear; that this was recognized by Stephen, at any time, should not be assumed.[240] With Stephen in captivity, Henry of Winchester was concerned to avoid giving even tacit encouragement to the 'new communal aspirations' of the Londoners.[241] He acknowledged the interest of the Londoners not because of their sworn association but because individually they were 'in effect magnates'. The Londoners would receive the empress only several weeks later, shortly before 24 June 1141,[242] and then after negotiation. According to the Gloucester chronicler, she was met at St Albans by a group of the leading citizens, 'and with them held various discussions concerning the surrender of the city'. They asked her for 'the laws of King Edward, which were excellent, and not those of Henry her father, which were severe'.[243] According to the *GS*, after she was received, the empress lost her temper with the Londoners when they protested against her levying an aid:

saying that many times the people of London had made very large contributions to the king, that they had lavished their wealth on strengthening him and weakening her, that they had previously conspired with her enemies for her hurt, and therefore it was not just to spare them in any respect or make the smallest reduction in the money demanded.[244]

The scene is well realized, and the empress's sentiments quite understandable. Behind the agreement there can have been no real basis of trust. The Londoners were closely identified with Stephen's cause; and that cause was still alive. The empress had been in London only a few days before she was driven out. It was a major setback.

If we look for what is distinctive in William of Malmesbury's account of events in the summer of 1141, a useful starting-point is

---

[240] Cf. Davis, *Stephen*, p. 54; C. N. L. Brooke and G. Keir, *London 800–1216: The Shaping of a City* (London, 1975), p. 36; and note the suggested amendment to the text, to provide a specific reference to the commune, in *GS*, pp. 6–7 and n. 1.

[241] M. McKisack, 'London and the succession to the crown during the middle ages', *Studies in Medieval History Presented to F. M. Powicke*, ed. R. W. Hunt *et al.* (Oxford, 1948), pp. 76–89, at 79.

[242] *HN* §52.   [243] JW iii. 294–7.   [244] *GS*, pp. 122–3.

his comment, after speaking of Robert of Gloucester's statesman-like behaviour, that 'if the other members of his party had trusted his restraint and wisdom, they would not afterwards have endured such a turn of ill-fortune'.[245] Chief among those criticized, as Round long ago pointed out,[246] can only have been the empress herself. And if we want to see the cause of division in the Angevin camp, we need to pick up William's narrative after the retreat from London. 'Not many days afterwards a quarrel arose between the legate and the empress, a mischance that I may truly call the origin of all the evils that followed in England.'[247] William is seldom so emphatic, and what he is here emphasizing is the importance of the arrangements that were to be made, while Stephen was in a captivity that was intended to be permanent, for his son Eustace. The legate wished him to have the counties of Boulogne and Mortain, which Stephen had controlled before his accession. 'The empress firmly refused, and, it may be, actually promised them to others.' The empress's refusal was understandable, just as her treatment of the Londoners had been. Even with the king in captivity, and the resources of the monarchy denied to it, the house of Blois remained a formidable opponent. Henry I had ensured that it would be so. He had given to Henry of Blois first the richest monastery in England (Glastonbury), and then one of the two richest dioceses (Winchester), which he was allowed to hold in plurality. He had given Stephen the county of Mortain in Normandy, the English lands once held by Roger the Poitevin (the honours of Eye and Lancaster), and in marriage the heiress to the honour of Boulogne.[248] This power-base remained intact after Stephen's capture.

In the summer of 1141 the legate and others were looking for a permanent settlement of the civil war. The provision for Eustace was just one part of a complex problem. For clues as to the terms of the discussion it is useful to go back to what

---

[245] *HN* § 52. [246] Round, *Geoffrey*, p. 114.
[247] *HN* § 53.
[248] This represented the resources of three amongst the first eleven of English estates in terms of their 1086 valuations (Hollister, *Anglo-Norman World*, p. 82 n. 2), aside from the honours of Eye and Lancaster, on which see C. P. Lewis, 'The king and Eye: A study in Anglo-Norman politics', *EHR* civ (1989), 569–89.

William of Malmesbury says about the peace discussions of the previous year.[249] There were two stages to this. First came the meeting near Bath, which involved representatives of the empress and of the king: 'they wasted both words and time and parted without making peace'. But, we are told, the two parties took up different positions. The empress's party were prepared to accept some form of clerical arbitration. The king's party declined to accept this, since they had the upper hand. After this meeting, the legate travelled to France, and there held discussions with 'the king of France, Count Theobald, and many churchmen'. He must have come back with precise peace terms, for 'the empress and the earl agreed at once'; but the king prevaricated, and in the end nothing came of it.

It would be interesting to know what those peace terms involved. We are offered no clear statement by William of Malmesbury, but a number of clues. The king of France was involved; and so clearly the discussions involved the succession to some of the continental lands feudally subject to the French monarchy. Theobald of Blois was involved, and his only standing would seem to be as the senior member of the house of Blois. It is at least a possible scenario that what was here proposed differed little from what would be accepted in 1153. This would have meant that the focus of attention was already in 1140 on the next generation, on the empress's eldest son Henry, and on Stephen's elder son Eustace. That Henry should take immediate control of Normandy, and Eustace of Boulogne and of Mortain, that control confirmed by the French king, might have been a corollary. On this hypothesis, Eustace would have been refused in 1141 lands promised to him in the previous year, in a settlement which the empress would have accepted. Henry of Winchester would have understood well enough, however, that after Stephen's capture the balance of advantage had changed. It had not, however, changed quite as much as the empress thought. This at least is the case that William of Malmesbury would seem to wish to see argued. There had been the possibility of a negotiated settlement in the summer

---

[249] *HN* §40.

of 1141, and the empress, ignoring advice, had thrown it away. William is not the only witness close to the Angevin camp at this time. The Gloucester chronicler, having mentioned the petition of the queen for her husband's release, of the legate for the *comitatus* of Eustace, and of the Londoners for the good old laws, commented: 'she would not listen to them . . . she did not listen to good advice but harshly rejected their petition'.[250] If there is so much emphasis on advice here, that is understandable. William of Malmesbury and the Gloucester chronicler reflect the positions respectively of Robert of Gloucester and Miles of Gloucester, the empress's two most senior advisers.

From London the empress went to Oxford, where William of Malmesbury says—possibly tongue in cheek—that she 'had long been in permanent quarters'.[251] Here the cracks that had already appeared in the Angevin strategy widened. What was being said can be seen in what is usually referred to as the empress's second charter for Geoffrey de Mandeville, which can be dated to this period at Oxford, in the last week of July 1141, with some confidence.[252] It is part charter, part agreement or *conuentio*. Geoffrey here asked for some security for the performance of what had been promised to him. Along with the grants of land and office, as his ancestors had best held them, there was the promise that the empress would make no agreement with the Londoners without his approval, 'for they were his mortal enemies'. That security he asked for from the empress's menfolk, from Geoffrey of Anjou her husband and from Henry their son, both of whom were to swear in the hand of Geoffrey to hold to this agreement. As neither of them was then in England this would need to be done by proxy; and the parallel charter offering an earldom to Aubrey de Vere was confirmed by the young Henry in the hand of Hugh of Ing, one of Geoffrey de Mandeville's vassals.[253] In this

[250] JW iii. 296–7.   [251] *HN* § 54.
[252] *Regesta*, iii, no. 275, there dated 25–31 July 1141: this date challenged by J. O. Prestwich in 'The treason of Geoffrey de Mandeville', *EHR* ciii (1988), 283–312, restated by R. H. C. Davis, ibid., pp. 313–17 (with a further exchange of views, ibid., pp. 960–8), and accepted by Chibnall, *Matilda*, pp. 108–11, and in 'Charters of the empress', *Law and Government*, pp. 282–3.
[253] *Regesta*, iii, nos. 634 (grant), 635 (confirmation); see Chibnall, *Matilda*, pp. 111–12, 143.

confirmation Henry described himself as 'the son of the daughter of King Henry and the rightful heir of England and Normandy'. Geoffrey de Mandeville had asked for the king of France to give a similar guarantee.

The empress would have been well advised to wait in Oxford and let the dust settle. Instead, however, she moved almost immediately to Winchester, where she had been first received as *domina Anglorum*. This was carrying battle to the enemy, and whatever the intention the effect was to unite Stephen's party, by giving them a focus, and further to divide her own. The Gloucester chronicler, here reflecting what he has been told by Miles of Gloucester, whom the empress had recently rewarded with the earldom of Hereford, says that she went to Winchester without Robert of Gloucester's knowledge.[254] William of Malmesbury in a few brushstrokes paints the picture of what became a siege, with men and provisions being brought in from the east to reinforce the queen's party, while the roads to the west leading from the west country became increasingly insecure.[255] The townsmen of Winchester and the religious of the city were caught, quite literally as reported, in the cross-fire. The Londoners, even further compromised in the eyes of the Angevins by the events of the previous few weeks, are represented as playing a crucial role, 'not letting slip a single thing that lay in their power whereby they might annoy the empress'. The empress's flight from Winchester became inevitable. Its route could be predicted, and it can have been no surprise that at one of its weak points, at the ford of Stockbridge, the rearguard was attacked and prisoners taken.[256]

One of the prisoners was Robert of Gloucester, who was taken immediately to the most secure fortress under the queen's control, the castle of Rochester in Kent.[257] William of Malmesbury is the best source for the negotiations that followed. Great promises were made to the earl. 'Let him abandon his sister and come over to the king's side', and he would be given, under the king, 'the lordship of the whole land'.[258] The Gloucester chronicle uses an

---

[254] 'ignorante fratre suo': JW iii. 298–9.   [255] *HN* §55.
[256] *HN* §56.   [257] *HN* §62.   [258] *HN* §64.

almost identical phrase: 'The king would be restored to his
kingdom, and the earl raised to the government of the whole of
England under him.'[259] The overtures were rejected: the earl
'could not be induced to allow negotiations for his release to
proceed behind his sister's back'.[260] Those negotiating for the king
were, however, able to secure that the king and the earl should be
released in a straight swap. The earl objected that he and the king
were not equals in rank. This was true, but his lands and his
prestige remained crucial to the empress's cause; and the king's
party had other captives also. The empress's agreeing to his
exchange for the king suggests she feared a further erosion of
her power-base should the earl remain in captivity.[261] A complicated arrangement was made for a series of exchanges of hostages
leading up to the exchange of the king for the earl.[262] William,
with a good eye for telling detail, notes that the two men met at
Winchester along the road. They talked with perfect courtesy, but
they had nothing to say to one another, and they went on their
way.[263]

All that had been agreed was that each of the protagonists
'should maintain his own cause to the best of his ability, as before'.
For the Angevins this was a bitter pill to swallow, for it took them
back to Stockbridge ford outside Winchester on 14 September
1141. Territorially they were on the retreat, and—much more
significant—they were divided in terms of their strategy. They
looked back to see what had gone wrong. This, it may be
suggested, is the significance of the 'recapitulation' which is
found in William of Malmesbury's text at this point.[264] The
year 1141, he says, 'whose tragedies I have briefly related, was
ill-omened and almost mortal for England'. By way of a prologue
to the final section of his work he would return to that year, and
link it with the events of 1142. A long paragraph in William's text
then started with Robert's oath in 1127, noted his conditional
homage to Stephen in 1136 which he later renounced, emphasized

---

[259] JW iii. 304–5.   [260] HN § 56.
[261] The empress's followers are represented as afraid that they would be picked off one
by one: HN § 66.
[262] HN § 57.   [263] HN § 69.   [264] HN § 60–2.

the sacrifices he had made in his sister's cause, and concluded with his imprisonment at Rochester. It was only at this point that the main details of the terms on which he was exchanged for Stephen were given. The recapitulation offers a justification of Robert of Gloucester's past behaviour, and at the same time of the Angevin cause.

Robert of Gloucester was not the only adherent of that cause who spent some time in 1142 reflecting on past history. One part of what must have been quite a lengthy exchange of letters between Brian Fitz Count and Henry of Winchester has survived.[265] The bishop's letter is only a fragment, but it included one of his texts for the times: 'Remember the wife of Lot, who on turning back was turned into a pillar of salt.' The lord of Wallingford stood accused of confiscating goods bound for the bishop's fair at Winchester. If you do not mend your ways, said the bishop, 'you will be numbered among the unfaithful men of England, which I have never believed you to be before'. Brian Fitz Count's reply offered a defence of his good faith, and a bitter criticism of the bishop's recent behaviour. Brian was proud to look back. He gave the bishop quite a lengthy history lesson, in which the good old days of Henry I, and the great deeds of the warriors of western Christendom on the First Crusade, loomed large.

When I look back to these great men, who obeyed the pope's command and left so much behind, who by assault and force of arms conquered Jerusalem like good knights, and established there a good and lawful king by the name of Godfrey; and when I look back to your command to help the daughter of King Henry with all my strength; then I have no fear that I am committing any crime, when I obey the commands of holy church.

'I look back to your command': the clergy had been instrumental in the acceptance of the Angevin claim. It was bad enough that they had changed their mind, insufferable that they now sought to lecture others on how to behave. Brian Fitz Count's letter concluded by challenging the bishop of Winchester to a duel,

[265] H. W. C. Davis, 'Henry of Blois and Brian Fitz-Count', *EHR* xxv (1910), 297–303, and for comment E. King, 'Economic development in the early twelfth century', *Progress and Problems in Medieval England: Essays in Honour of Edward Miller*, ed. R. Britnell and J. Hatcher (Cambridge, 1996), pp. 1–22, at 10–11.

while the reference to 'Theobald the so-called archbishop' offers a
pithy comment on his perceived role as a leader. It is not
surprising then that the two leaders of the clergy, the archbishop
and the legate, are shown after Robert of Gloucester's capture as
almost desperate to negotiate an exchange. They were even
prepared to offer themselves as hostages, to the earl, if the
king's party did not honour the undertakings they had made.
Each issued a sealed letter to this effect, which letters the earl 'put
in a safe place'.[266] William of Malmesbury reports faithfully, but
with little conviction, the Church's abandonment of the Angevin
cause and return to the allegiance of the king.[267]

The clergy's leadership had been found wanting. It was left to
the laymen, on both sides, to regroup, and to fight again. Just how
was the Angevin cause to be 'best maintained'? This was the
subject of a conference held at Devizes in the early weeks of
1142.[268] A first step was the struggle for Normandy. It was a
logical step, the control of Normandy a continuation of Angevin
policy that had probably been accepted in peace discussions from
1140 if not earlier. And yet, seen from the perspective of Robert of
Gloucester in England, the opening of another front by an army
that was already overstretched was something of a gamble. The
Devizes strategy group first asked Geoffrey of Anjou to come to
England. Only when he declined did Robert of Gloucester cross to
Normandy, and in return for substantial military help he obtained
only vague promises.[269] While he was away, Stephen's forces
managed to take Wareham castle, and with it threaten the Angevin
party's communications and supply lines.[270] On his return the earl
of Gloucester had to direct his energy to the recapture of Wareham and the establishment of a base in Dorset. This was
secured,[271] but in the meanwhile Stephen's forces had besieged
the empress in Oxford castle, and from here, as first from London
and then from Winchester she was forced to retreat.[272] Her escape,
said William of Malmesbury, was 'a manifest miracle of God'; and

[266] HN § 68-9.
[267] At a further council at Westminster in Dec. 1141: HN § 58-9; Councils and Synods, i (2), no. 143, pp. 792-4.
[268] HN § 71.   [269] HN § 73-4.   [270] HN § 75.
[271] HN § 76.   [272] HN § 78.

he promised to give further details of it as soon as he had them to hand.[273] The *HN* concludes with this episode.

The discussions at Devizes were not simply on matters of military strategy, but concerned the claims now to be made regarding the succession. This was the significance of the subsequent press-release, in which it was stated that all the empress's adherents 'approved sending for the count of Anjou, it being his duty to maintain the inheritance of his wife and children in England'.[274] This sentiment clearly lay behind Geoffrey de Mandeville's demand for security in July 1141. It now became Angevin policy, and it represented a change of policy. The empress's title, whatever it had been, was not abandoned, but now invariably it is associated with that of her sons.[275] And the focus of hope, in these dark days, lay in the person of her eldest son, 'the lawful heir'. William of Malmesbury, in sight of the time—long anticipated—when his life and his story would end together, now changed to prophetic mode. 'The boy is called Henry, recalling his grandfather's name, and would he may some day recall his prosperity and his power.' This is not quite William's final comment to his readers, for he would have liked to have taken the story on; but there was no need for him to do so. His judgement was exact, and subsequent events would neither alter the issues nor influence the outcome.

IV. THE MANUSCRIPTS

The *HN* was a tract for the times before it became a work of reference. It would be invaluable to know both where and when the text circulated during the civil war. There is no direct evidence. What clues there are come from the manuscripts; and one of the most interesting comes from a manuscript that has since been lost. Leland saw a copy at Glastonbury:[276] 'Praeter historiam quam de regibus scripsit Gulielmus Malmesb. uidi adiectos in fine

---

[273] *HN* §79. [274] *HN* §71.

[275] [Geoffrey of Anjou] 'the inheritance of his wife and sons', *HN* §71; [Robert of Gloucester] 'the inheritance of his sister and his nephews', *HN* §73.

[276] *English Benedictine Libraries: The Shorter Catalogues*, ed. R. Sharpe *et al.* (Corpus of Medieval British Library Catalogues, iv; London, 1996), B44.3.

ueteris codicis tres libellos titulo novellae historiae, id est tem-
porum Matildis imperatricis, ab ipso Malmesb. scriptos.' Much
turns on the translation of this passage. Here to a text of the *GR*
there had been added the three books of the *HN*. Now initially the
HN must have circulated independently of the *GR*. And it is
reasonable to surmise that Glastonbury would have acquired an
early copy of the *HN*. Here we may well see that copy, kept with
but distinct from the *GR*.[277] In addition to the Glastonbury copy,
Leland saw a copy of the *HN* at St Paul's, London.[278] Bale noted
six copies of the work, three of them apparently of the *HN*
alone,[279] and three of the *HN* as book vi of the *GR*.[280] None of
these can be identified with the manuscripts that have survived.

In all the surviving medieval manuscripts, the *HN* is found
together with the *GR*. While the *HN* is invariably found attached
to the *GR*, less than half the surviving manuscripts of the *GR*
contain the *HN*; and the earliest copies of the *GR* were made
before the *HN* was written. Where the *HN* is found, it is
sometimes in a later copy that has been added to the *GR*. These
points are important in indicating the bibliographical history of
the *HN*. The *GR* was always well known. The *HN* was a text that
each generation of historical scholarship would need to rediscover.
The connection of the *HN* with the *GR* has also—quite under-
standably, and no less importantly—determined its publication
history. The major editions of the *HN* have been editions of the
GR, and it has been with the manuscript history of the *GR* that
editors have been chiefly concerned.

No manuscripts of the *HN* have been found that were not

---

[277] The earlier Glastonbury catalogues fully support this hypothesis: (*i*) the *GR* was one
of the first books copied for Henry of Blois, probably before *c.*1137 (ibid., B37.22); (*ii*) this
(with the *HN* appended) would have been one of the two 'good copies' recorded in 1247/8
(ibid., B39.192), and (*iii*) probably also represents the two works (*Gesta Anglorum*, in 5
books, and *De Matilda imperatrice*, in 3 books) in the late medieval list recorded by John
Bale (ibid., B45.54–5).

[278] Leland, *Collectanea*, iv. 47.

[279] One was owned by Nicholas Lesse, one by Leland himself, and the third was held by
an unnamed stationer: Bale, *Index*, pp. xvii, xxviii, 135–6, 508.

[280] Two further copies were owned by Leland and by Thomas Keye, and a third was
noted from the catalogue of 'Boston of Bury': ibid., pp. xxvii, 135–6. 'Boston of Bury' was
Henry of Kirkstede of Bury St Edmunds (*c.*1346–78): R. H. Rouse, 'Bostonus Buriensis
and the author of the *Catalogus Scriptorum Ecclesiae*', *Speculum*, xli (1966), 471–99.

known to Stubbs, and it is his sigla (e.g. At, Ce) that have been followed here, as they were by Mynors. Stubbs's and Mynors's descriptions of the manuscripts are each masterly of their kind, and they have provided the foundation for the listing which is provided here.

Ag Oxford, Bodleian Library, MS Laud Misc. 548 fos. 194^r– 212^r (Newark, Surrey, s. xii^{ex})
This is possibly the earliest in date of writing of the manuscripts containing the *HN*.[281] The *ex libris* at the foot of fo. 3^r identifies this as a volume belonging to the Augustinian priory of Newark, near Guildford, Surrey, dioc. Winchester.[282] This house was founded *c*.1169 by Ruald de Calva; but, according to later tradition, this was a refoundation, and the house was first established by one of the bishops of Winchester.[283] The volume was purchased by Archbishop Laud in or before 1633 and given by him to the Bodleian Library in 1635.[284] It contains solely the *GR* (fos. 3^r–194^r) and the *HN*, in the A recension. The manuscript lacks all rubrics, but spaces left suggest the same rubrication as found in the other texts of the *HN* in this recension (see Plate 2). It lacks two leaves, between fo. 205 and fo. 206, dealing with events between Whitsun 1140 and Easter 1141.[285]

Ao Oxford, All Souls College, MS 35 fos. 138^r–153^v (English, s. xiii^{in})
A volume that has had an interesting history. It was written early in the thirteenth century, and letters copied in the margins of the

---

[281] The script bears a close resemblance to that of Cambridge, Corpus Christi College, MS 46, written 1159 × 1170: P. R. Robinson, *Catalogue of Dated and Datable Manuscripts c.737–1600 in Cambridge Libraries*, 2 vols. (Cambridge, 1988), no. 126 and plate 68.

[282] 'Hic liber est ecclesie sancte [Marie et beati Thome martiris de Nouo Loco. Quem qui furto] abstulerit, uel sine conscientia eiusdem ecclesie conuentus quocumque modo alienauerit, sit anathema maranatha. Amen'; for the identification see *Medieval Libraries of Great Britain*, ed. Ker, p. 133.

[283] *Heads*, p. 176; *VCH Surrey*, ii. 103.

[284] H. O. Coxe, *Bodleian Library Quarto Catalogues*, ii: *Laudian Manuscripts*, ed. R. W. Hunt (Oxford, 1973), pp. xix–xx, xxxv, col. 396; *A Summary Catalogue of Western Manuscripts in the Bodleian Library at Oxford*, i, ed. R. W. Hunt (Oxford, 1953), pp. 128–9.

[285] 'Eodem anno in Pentecoste resedit rex Lundonie in [fo. 205^v: *HN* § 40] . . . [fo. 206^r: *HN* § 47] fuisse, ita ut per uiuacitatem, animositatem, industriam eiusdem precellentissimi uiri.'

text relating to W. de Bernham in Paris and in Oxford are held to reflect his ownership.[286] By the fifteenth century it belonged to St Martin's priory, Louvain,[287] and further glosses reflect an interest in this region.[288] It seems then to have been acquired by Marquard Gude (1635–89), but was separated from his library before the bulk of his collection came to Wolfenbüttel in 1710. All Souls College bought this volume, along with two others which had followed the same route from Louvain,[289] in December 1768.[290] The volume is in two parts, the first containing the *GR* (fos. 1^r–138^r) and the *HN*, in Recension A, the second containing Geoffrey of Monmouth's *Historia regum Britannie* (hereafter *HRB*; fos. 154^v–182^v).[291] The rubrication identifies the *HN* as a separate work, in three books.[292]

At Cambridge, Trinity College, MS R. 7. 10 fos. 150^r–162^r (English, s. xii^{ex})

This is a significant copy of the *HN* for a number of reasons. It is the earliest complete text of the A recension. Its medieval provenance cannot be firmly established but it may have been close to Malmesbury itself. A fragment of an account of the late fifteenth or early sixteenth century, used as a binding leaf, refers to Marlborough, Ogbourne, and Snap in Aldbourne, in eastern Wiltshire. In the mid-sixteenth century the volume was used by Matthew Parker in his research on William of Malmesbury's

---

[286] N. R. Ker and W. A. Pantin, 'Letters of a Scottish student at Paris and Oxford c.1250', *Oxford Historical Society*, ns. 5 (1942), 472–91.

[287] W. Lourdaux and M. Haverals, *Bibliotheca Vallis Sancti Martini in Lovanio*, 2 vols. (Louvain, 1978–82), i. 691–6.

[288] Thus when Adeliza of Louvain is mentioned she is identified as 'Adela soror Godefridi cum barba ducis Brabant' (fo. 138^v).

[289] MS 34 contains the *GP* of William of Malmesbury (s. xii med.), and MS 36 the *Historia Anglorum* of Henry of Huntingdon (s. xii. ex.).

[290] See correspondence between Sir Edmund Craster, Librarian of All Souls College, and Sir Roger Mynors in 1947, filed with MS. A. G. Watson, *A Descriptive Catalogue of the Medieval Manuscripts of All Souls College Oxford* (Oxford, 1997), pp. 69–71, contains a full description and discussion of the manuscript history.

[291] J. C. Crick, *The Historia Regum Britannie of Geoffrey of Monmouth*, iii: *A Summary Catalogue of the Manuscripts* (Cambridge, 1989), no. 132, pp. 215–16.

[292] 'Incipit prologus Willelmi monachi. in nouella historia Anglorum ad Robertum comitem Gloecestrie' (fo. 138^r); 'Explicit prologus. Incipit liber .i.' (fo. 138^v); 'Explicit liber primus. Incipit secundus' (fo. 143^r); 'Explicit liber .ii. Incipit liber .iii. nouelle historie' (fo. 147^r).

historical texts. His belief that a proper collection of these should contain the *HN* led to two copies of the *HN* being made from this manuscript, the first added to an early copy of the *GP*, to make up a set of William of Malmesbury's historical works to be presented to the Cambridge University Library, the second added to a late copy of the *GR*.[293] The volume was given to Trinity College by Whitgift in 1604.[294] It contains the *GR* (fos. 1^r–150^r) and the *HN* in the A recension; it was considered by Mynors to be a twin of MS Ao, and contains the same rubrication.

Bc London, BL, Royal MS 13. B. xix fos. 71^r–83^r (English, s. xiv)

A case where a 'set' of the *GR* and the *HN* has been made up. The manuscript of the *GR* is from the early thirteenth century, and the copy of the *HN* has been added later. The manuscript belonged in 1650 to John Theyer. There is a possible clue here to medieval provenance, for Theyer's collections were based on the library of Llanthony secunda, Gloucestershire. The extensive surviving collections of this important Augustinian house do not otherwise contain any of the works of William of Malmesbury.[295] Charles Theyer, the grandson of John, sold his manuscripts to Robert Scot, a London bookseller, from whom they were purchased by Charles II.[296] The volume contains the *GR* (fos. 1^r–71^r) and the *HN* in the B recension, and the *Description of the Holy Land* by Burchard (fos. 84^r–91^r). The only rubrication in the *HN* comes at the beginning and at the end of the work: at the beginning the *HN* is identified as being book vi of the *GR* ('Liber vj', fo. 71^r), but at the end we find 'Explicit nouella historia Anglorum' (fo. 83^r).

---

[293] Cambridge University Library, MS Ff. 1. 25 (the *GP* books i–iv is part 1, s. xii; book v is supplied as part 2, and the *HN* as part 3); Trinity College, MS R. 5. 34 (the *HN* supplied as part 6). For discussion and reference to full manuscript descriptions see below, pp. cvi–cvii.

[294] M. R. James, *The Western Manuscripts in the Library of Trinity College, Cambridge: A Descriptive Catalogue*, 4 vols. (Cambridge, 1900–4), ii. 224–5 (no. 748); P. Gaskell, *Trinity College Library: The First 150 Years* (Cambridge, 1980), pp. 80–1.

[295] *Medieval Libraries of Great Britain*, ed. Ker, pp. 108–12; ibid., *Supplement to the Second Edition*, ed. A. G. Watson, pp. 41–3; the attribution to Llanthony was suggested by Stubbs, i, p. lxxviii.

[296] G. F. Warner and J. P. Gilson, *Catalogue of Western Manuscripts in the Old Royal and King's Collections*, 4 vols. (London, 1921), ii. 100–1.

Bk Oxford, Bodleian Library, Bodley MS 712 fos. 186ᵛ–198ʳ (Salisbury, s. xiv)

One of two surviving collections of historical works made in the mid-fourteenth century for Robert Wyvill, bishop of Salisbury (1330–75). It contains the bishop's arms on the first page and on the fore-edge. The study of the second volume, Oxford, Worcester College, MS 285, led Neil Ker to conclude: 'it appears probable that the contents of the book were drawn from different volumes and that the exemplars dated from the twelfth century'; and he suggested also that those exemplars came from Salisbury.[297] These conclusions would seem to hold good, in the same terms, for the exemplars used for the Bodleian volume, which contains the *GR* and the *HN*: the scribe, for example, did not recognize the distinctive abbreviation that William of Malmesbury used for *enim*,[298] and he retains the *punctus elevatus*. The volume was owned in the fifteenth century by Roger Wormesley, in the sixteenth century by Roger Savile, and in 1604 it was presented to the Bodleian Library by Thomas Kerry, clerk of the Privy Seal.[299] This substantial collection contains Bede's *Ecclesiastical History* (fos. 1ʳ–88ᵛ), William of Malmesbury's *GR* (fos. 89ʳ–186ʳ) and the *HN* in the B recension, the *Chronicon pontificum et imperatorum* of Martinus Polonus (fos. 199ʳ–248ʳ), and chronicles from 449 to 1269 under the name *Historia post obitum Bedae* (fos. 249ʳ–371ᵛ). This manuscript views the *HN* as book vi of the *GR* without equivocation, all traces of its independence having disappeared.[300]

---

[297] R. W. Hunt, 'A manuscript belonging to Robert Wivill, bishop of Salisbury', *Bodleian Library Record*, vii (1962–7), 23–7 and plate IV.

[298] Stubbs, i, p. cxxxiii.

[299] F. Madan and H. H. E. Craster, *A Summary Catalogue of Western Manuscripts in the Bodleian Library at Oxford*, ii (1) (Oxford, 1922), pp. 453–4; O. Pächt and J. J. G. Alexander, *Illuminated Manuscripts in the Bodleian Library Oxford*, 3 vols. (Oxford, 1966–73), iii, no. 587; M. B. Parkes, *English Cursive Book Hand, 1250–1500* (Oxford, 1969), p. xviii and plate 7(i).

[300] 'Incipit liber sextus de gestis Anglorum' (fo. 186ᵛ); 'Explicit liber sextus et ultimus de gestis Anglorum secundum Willelmum Malmesberiensem monachum' (fo. 198ʳ, reproduced as Plate 3).

Bq Cambridge, Trinity College, MS R. 7. 1 fos. 132^r–147^v (English, s. xiii)

A thirteenth-century manuscript bearing no marks of ownership, which came to Trinity College as a gift of Thomas Neville c.1611.[301] It was the view of M. R. James that it bears resemblance to MS R. 5. 16 in the same collection, which comes from Glastonbury; but 'these two manuscripts were not written at the same time',[302] and it is difficult to find a match with the description in the Glastonbury catalogues.[303] The manuscript contains the *GR* (fos. 1^r–132^r) and the *HN* in the B recension. Its chief distinguishing feature is the doubt that was introduced during the sixteenth century as to the status of the *HN* as a separate work. The manuscript was originally rubricated as the A texts, though lacking any rubric after book i, but the rubrics were altered to make book i into book vi, and book iii into book vii.[304]

Cd London, BL, Royal MS 13. D. v fos. 132^v–142^r (St Albans, s. xiii^{in})

A collection of writings on British history made for the abbey of St Albans early in the thirteenth century. Rodney Thomson suggests that the volume was copied not long after the *terminus post quem* of 2 November 1206, given by the *Visio Thurkilli*, and notes that this is one of a group of volumes used by, and possibly made for, Roger of Wendover; and he suggests also that 'the contents were presumably copied from a collection or collections made not much later than c.1150'.[305] The volume was seen and used by

---

[301] James, *The Western Manuscripts in the Library of Trinity College, Cambridge*, ii. 215–16 (no. 739); Gaskell, *Trinity College Library: The First 150 Years*, pp. 81–2.

[302] J. P. Carley, 'John Leland and the contents of English pre-Dissolution libraries: Glastonbury Abbey', *Scriptorium*, xl (1986), 107–20, at p. 113.

[303] If this is a Glastonbury manuscript, it cannot have been that seen by Leland (see above, pp. lxvii–lxviii), but could have been the second 'good copy' recorded in 1247/8 (*English Benedictine Libraries: The Shorter Catalogues*, ed. R. Sharpe et al., B39.192).

[304] 'Incipit prologus Willelmi monachi in nouella historia Anglorum ad Robertum comitem Gloucestrie' (fo. 132^r); 'Explicit prologus. Incipit liber vj' [the vj is overwritten, originally .i.] (fo. 132^r); 'Liber secundus' [in a later hand] (fo. 137^r); 'Explicit liber vj. Incipit vij nouelle historie' [the vj and the vij are overwritten, originally .ii. and .iii.; and subsequently the whole rubric has been crossed out, possibly by the same individual who inserted liber secundus] (fo. 141^r).

[305] R. M. Thomson, *Manuscripts from St Albans Abbey 1066–1235*, 2 vols. (Woodbridge, 1982), i. 73–5 (discussion), 98–9 (description; no. 35).

Polydore Vergil shortly before the Dissolution; it came thereafter to John, Lord Lumley, and was in the Royal Library by 1666.[306] The main contents of a substantial volume are: (i) Geoffrey of Monmouth's *HRB* (fos. 1^r–37^v),[307] (ii) the *Visio Thurkilli* (fos. 45^r–50^v), (iii) William of Malmesbury's *GR* (fos. 51^r–132^v) and the *HN*, (iv) Ailred of Rievaulx's *Genealogia regum Anglorum* (fos. 142^r–151^v),[308] and finally (v) William of Malmesbury's *GP* (fos. 153^r–200^v). The *GR* text follows the C recension, but this is not distinct in the *HN* texts other than in Ce. The *HN* text is difficult to categorize: it mainly follows B variants, but at times follows A, and at other times goes its own way. It follows the drift of the B recension in identifying the *HN* as book vi of the *GR*, and the initials .G. and .R. provide headers to each page.[309]

Ce^1 London, BL, Royal MS 13. D. ii fos. 110^r–123^v (Margam, S. Wales, s. xii^{ex} or later)

This manuscript has been taken as the basis of the printed editions of the *GR* and the *HN* since Hardy in 1840. It is an early, but not the earliest, surviving manuscript containing these works. Its status comes not from its age but from its association with Robert earl of Gloucester. The three works which it contains, the *GR* (fos. 4^r–110^r) and the *HN*, and additionally Geoffrey of Monmouth's *HRB* (fos. 124^r–173^v),[310] all bear dedications to Robert of Gloucester. The volume is securely attributed from *ex libris* and from other evidence to the library of Margam Abbey. Margam was a Cistercian house in south Wales, which had been founded by Robert of Gloucester in 1147. This copy seems not to have been known to scholars in the sixteenth century; and it came to the Royal Library by 1666.[311] The Ce recension derives from A

---

[306] Warner and Gilson, *Catalogue of Western Manuscripts in the Old Royal and King's Collections*, ii. 110.

[307] Crick, *Manuscripts of Geoffrey of Monmouth*, no. 113, pp. 184–6.

[308] On this work, a particularly intelligent choice to follow on from the *HN*, see *The Life of Ailred of Rievaulx by Walter Daniel*, ed. F. M. Powicke (NMT, 1950), pp. xci–xcii.

[309] The only rubric, however, is 'Incipit liber sextus', supplied before the prologue, and fitting somewhat awkwardly into the space left for it (Plate 1).

[310] Crick, *Manuscripts of Geoffrey of Monmouth*, no. 112, pp. 183–4.

[311] Warner and Gilson, *Catalogue of Western Manuscripts in the Old Royal and King's Collections*, ii. 109.

and not from B in its rubrication of the books,[312] seeing the *HN* as a work distinct from the *GR*. The differences from both A and B texts, which include the rubrication of many of the paragraphs, and the introduction of new material, are substantial. The manuscript is fully examined in the following section, where it is argued that the Ce tradition represents a 'second edition' of the *HN*, which is not from the pen of William of Malmesbury.

Ce² London, BL, Additional MS 38129 fos. 180ᵛ–200ʳ (English, s. xvⁱⁿ)

A late copy, whose interest derives from the fact that it very closely resembles, though it is not an exact copy of, MS Ce¹. On fo. 1ʳ there is an obliterated *ex libris*, 'liber hospitalis . . .'. Its movements can be fully documented from the early seventeenth century. In 1635 it belonged to Sir Roger Twysden; it came thereafter to the Sebright family, and at the sale of part of Sir John Sebright's library in 1807 it was bought by Richard Heber; at the sale of Heber's library in 1836 it was purchased by the great bibliophile Sir Thomas Phillipps. It was bought by the British Museum in the Phillipps sale of 1911.[313] The volume contains solely the *GR* (fos. 1ʳ–180ʳ) and the *HN*. Six leaves are missing towards the end of the *HN* text, dealing with events from April 1141 until summer 1142.[314] The beginning of the *HN* was not marked by the scribe, but thereafter the rubrication of the books follows what is found in the A recension.[315] The main point of

[312] The rubrics which follow should be compared with those of the A recension, above p. lxx n. 292. It will be seen that they follow these closely but not exactly: the Explicit for Book III is not found elsewhere. 'Incipit prologus Willelmi Malmesberiensis in libros nouelle historie missos Roberto comiti Gloecestrie' (fo. 110ʳ); 'Explicit prologus. Incipit liber primus nouelle historie' (fo. 110ʳ); 'Explicit liber .i. nouelle historie. Incipit secundus' (fo. 114ʳ); 'Explicit liber .ii. nouelle historie. Incipit prologus tercii' (fo. 118ʳ); 'Explicit liber .iiii. (*sic.*) nouelle historie' (fo. 123ᵛ).
[313] *Catalogue of Additions to the Manuscripts in the British Museum 1911–1915* (London, 1925), p. 30.
[314] '. . . legatis et litteris causas cur non uenissent dederunt [fo. 194ᵛ: *HN* §46] . . . [fo. 199ʳ: *HN* §74] et ea multa obiecit . . .'. The missing portion of text was supplied in print on fos. 195-8 from Hardy's edition of 1840, with four printed folios making a quire of eight leaves. This was done whilst the manuscript was in the Phillipps collection.
[315] [At head of page in modern hand: *Hist.Nouellae. Lib.1.*, fo. 180ᵛ);] 'Explicit epistola. Incipit liber primus nouelle historie' (fo. 180ᵛ)); 'Explicit liber .i. nouelle historie. Incipit .ii.' (fo. 187ʳ); 'Explicit liber .ii. Incipit liber tercius nouelle historie' (fo. 193ʳ).

difference from Ce¹ is that the full, not the abbreviated text of the final paragraph is given, along with the distinctive ending of Ce¹.[316]

Cm London, BL, Arundel MS 161 fos. 121ᵛ–135ʳ (English, s. xiv)

A copy of items (iii), the *GR* (fos. 2r-121ʳ) and the *HN*, and (iv) Ailred of Rievaulx's *Genealogia regum Anglorum* (fos. 135ʳ–148ᵛ), from the St Albans manuscript Cd. One of the manuscripts of Thomas Howard, earl of Arundel (1585–1646), it was presented to the Royal Society in 1678, and from them purchased by the British Museum in 1831.[317]

V. THE ESTABLISHMENT OF
THE TEXT

William of Malmesbury was one of the last of the medieval chroniclers to go into print. All three of his major historical works, the *GR*, the *HN*, and the *GP*, appeared in a large composite volume, which included also Henry of Huntingdon's *Historia Anglorum* and Roger of Howden's *Chronica*, edited by Henry Savile and published in 1596.[318] Savile's principal manuscript source for the *HN*, in the view of Mynors, was MS Bq Cambridge, Trinity College, MS R. 7. 1.[319] The first critical text, of the *GR* and the *HN* alone, was produced by Sir Thomas Duffus Hardy for the English Historical Society in 1840.[320] Hardy's edition was reprinted by Migne in *Patrologia Latina*; and relevant extracts appear also in the series *Monumenta Germaniae Historica*

---

[316] ' . . . ab his qui interfuere ueritatem accepero. Sed hec in uolumine sequenti Deo uolente latius expedientur [fo. 200ʳ]'.

[317] British Museum, *Catalogue of Manuscripts in the British Museum, ns. 1, pt 1, The Arundel Manuscripts* (London, 1834), p. 44.

[318] *Rerum Anglicarum Scriptores Post Bedam Praecipui, ex vetustissimis codicibus manuscriptis nunc primum in lucem editi*, ed. H. Savile (London, 1596; reset and repr. Frankfurt, 1601): *HN* text, fos. 98vᵛ–110ᵛ (1596), pp. 174–95 (1601). *HN* is here printed in two books, the beginning of Book III, at fo. 105ᵛ (1596) and p. 186 (1601), not being noted.

[319] Mynors, p. xl; M. McKisack, *Medieval History in the Tudor Age* (Oxford, 1971), pp. 63–5.

[320] *Willelmi Malmesbiriensis Monachi Gesta Regum Anglorum, atque Historia Novella*, ed. T. D. Hardy, 2 vols. (EHS: London, 1840): *HN* text, ii. 685–769.

and *Receuil des Historiens des Gaules et de la France* (*RHGF*).[321]
These early editions provided also the basis of the first English
translation of the *GR* and the *HN*, that of John Sharpe in 1815,
which was revised and reprinted by Joseph Stevenson in 1854.[322]
In 1889 Bishop Stubbs produced a new edition of the *GR* and the
HN for the Rolls Series, providing in his introductions to these
volumes the first major study of William of Malmesbury's life and
historical writings.[323] Finally, when the Nelson's Medieval Texts
series was established, the *HN* was one of the first texts to be
printed, appearing apart from the *GR* for the first time. The editor
of this volume—as of the *Gesta Stephani*, which appeared in the
same series at the same time—was K. R. Potter.[324] The Latin text,
however, was established by Sir Roger Mynors, joint-editor of the
series, on the basis of a new collation of the manuscripts. Hardy,
Stubbs, and Mynors were the most distinguished editors of their
day, and a new editor who is able to draw on their work is
fortunate indeed.

In establishing the text to be printed in the present edition the
essential starting-points are the relevant sections of the RS
(Stubbs) and the NMT (Mynors) editions, as noted above.[325]
They showed that the text in the Margam Abbey manuscript
(Ce¹) and the volume closely related to it (Ce²) was different in
several respects from that found in all the A, all the B, and in the
other C texts (cited hereafter as AB). As Mynors put it: 'There are
not three stages of the text, as in the *Gesta Regum*; there are two.
Ce represents a text different in details from that found alike in
A and B.'[326] Neither Stubbs nor Mynors professed himself

---

[321] *Willelmi Malmesburiensis Monachi Opera Omnia*, ed. J. P. Migne (*PL* clxxix, 1855):
HN text, cols. 1391–1440; *Ex Willelmi Malmsburiensis Scriptis Historicis*, ed. D. G. Waitz
(*MGH SS* xii, 1852), pp. 484–5; *Ex Willelmi Malmesburiensis Historiae Novellae*, ed. M.
Bouquet (*RHGF* xiii, 1738), pp. 20–30.

[322] *The History of the Kings of England, and the Modern History of William of Malmesbury*, trans. J. Sharpe (London, 1815), from Savile's text, and revised by J. Stevenson,
from Hardy's text, *The History of the Kings of England, and of his Own Times, by William of
Malmesbury* (Church Historians of England, iii (1); London, 1854), pp. 381–422, and repr.
in *Contemporary Chronicles of the Middle Ages* (Llanerch, 1988), pp. 11–52.

[323] *Willelmi Malmesbiriensis Monachi de Gestis Regum Anglorum libri quinque; Historiae
Novellae libri tres*, ed. W. Stubbs, 2 vols. (RS xc, 1887–9): *HN* text, ii. 523–96.

[324] *Willelmi Malmesbiriensis Monachi Historia Novella*, ed. K. R. Potter (NMT, 1955).

[325] Stubbs, i, pp. lxii–lxv; Mynors, pp. xxxviii–xliii.   [326] Mynors, p. xli.

completely sure whether Ce came after AB or before it. The main
concern of these editors was with whether the Ce text was the
work of William of Malmesbury. Each saw some difficulties, but
each concluded that it was his work. Stubbs set out the matter as
follows: 'We will suppose, and, without some such hypothesis, an
argument of the kind is impossible, that the great Margam MS.
which presents the earliest and best form of the third recension
(C.), and likewise contains, in immediate continuity and without
change of hand, the *Historia Novella* also, does represent to us
most nearly the author's final revision.'[327] It will be noted that the
hypothesis of Stubbs establishes a text for both the *GR* and the
HN, even though he seems to have recognized that the *HN* had a
distinct textual history. It does this by giving priority to a single
manuscript.

Each of the main editors went out of his way to praise BM (now
BL), Royal MS 13 D. ii: a 'magnificent manuscript', said Hardy, a
'splendid folio', said both Stubbs and Mynors, while for Stubbs it
was simply 'the great Margam manuscript'.[328] This manuscript
gained a particular authority because it came from Margam
Abbey, and that abbey was founded by Robert earl of Gloucester,
to whom both the *GR* and the *HN* were dedicated. It could thus
be identified as 'the standard text of the work', namely of the *GR*
and the *HN* combined.[329] Stubbs gave a mid-twelfth century date
to the manuscript, which permitted him the additional comment:
'It is, however, at least, not impossible, or even probable, that [it]
may have been copied for the abbey at the cost of the founder, or
even bequeathed by him to the library of the new house.'[330] Later
palaeographers have not given so early a date for the script, and so
this particular suggestion must be put to one side; but the Margam
is none the less one of the earliest surviving manuscripts, and
Mynors's discussion left its primacy unchallenged:

For the textual critic of the *Historia Novella* the moral is clear. Hardy
and Stubbs were right in taking as their basic text Ce, that is to say, Ce[1]
checked by the later but independent evidence of Ce[2], and it is from Ce[1]

---

[327] Stubbs, i, pp. lxii–lxiii.
[328] Hardy, ii, p. xxii; Stubbs, i, pp. lxii–lxiii, lxxx; Mynors, p. xl.
[329] Stubbs, i, p. lxxxi.   [330] Stubbs, i, p. lxxxi.

that we have taken our text, our chapter divisions and headings, and our spelling, recording all its variations from our printed text, but not the variants of Ce². . . . The variations of AB from the supposed 'final revision' have been fully reported, even though rarely of any historical significance, because they *may* come from the author's hand at an earlier stage of the work; they may contain evidence for the stylistic habits of a writer who deserves our respect not only as an historian but as a scholar and a man of letters.[331]

The present edition prints a different text from that of Stubbs and Mynors. It is not a 'basic text' based on a single manuscript, but the foundation is provided by the AB readings, with all the variants of Ce being annotated. The new text comes from a new hypothesis, which contradicts that of Stubbs: he had, however, seen the problems, and so what follows could well be termed Stubbs's alternative hypothesis. That hypothesis is that the AB text *does* come from the hand of William of Malmesbury; while the Ce text, where it differs from AB, *may* be the work of William of Malmesbury, but more likely represents a revision of his work made some time after his death. The case for this hypothesis will now be argued. At times the argument must go into some detail, for which the defence—if defence is felt to be necessary—comes best from the pen of Stubbs: 'I feel that I have gone into dry minutiae which only [the *HN*'s] importance in English historiography can justify.'[332]

The changes made as between the AB and the Ce texts are substantial, a good deal more extensive than earlier editors have recognized. They will be considered under three main headings: first, the addition of new material; second, changes in emphasis; and third, changes in presentation and layout. It will be immediately apparent—and the discussion will demonstrate—that no firm lines can be drawn between these different categories. Under each heading, enough examples must be given, 'so that the reader may judge'. The changes considered all together are sufficiently substantial for it to be argued that the Ce text should be seen as a new edition. A final section, of necessity more speculative than

---

[331] Mynors, pp. xlii–xliii.   [332] Stubbs, i, p. lxv.

those that have gone before, will consider when and why the new edition was made.

1. *The New Material*

Throughout the Ce text there are short paragraphs, sentences, and phrases not in the AB text; and these must be viewed as additions to it. The total number of additions is not great, but there is enough to challenge the reader to find a pattern in them. The first passage singled out by earlier editors is a short paragraph on the deeds of Robert Fitz Hubert, who in October 1139 occupied the castle of Malmesbury, but was thereafter driven out by the king, who turned then to attack Trowbridge.[333] A little later, in the description of the horrors of the civil war, there is first a sentence on the kidnapping and torturing of the common people,[334] and then detail of the fortifications which Robert of Gloucester captured from the king in 1140.[335] In the latter instance, the new material has been introduced in mid-sentence, and so it has also in what is in many ways the most interesting of the new passages, which notes the appearance of Geoffrey de Mandeville alongside the Londoners in helping drive the empress from Winchester in early August 1141.[336] The Ce text has the names of the two castles surrendered by Alexander of Lincoln after 'the arrest of the bishops' in 1139;[337] and it lists the castles in Normandy taken by Geoffrey of Anjou with the assistance of Robert of Gloucester in 1142.[338] John 'the marshal', castellan of Marlborough, is given his patronymic when he appears and inflicts exemplary punishment on Robert Fitz Hubert;[339] and the castellan of Lulworth, who deserted the empress, is also named.[340]

Mynors followed Stubbs both in his selection of the relevant new material and in his interpretation of it:

These are hardly the changes of a later reader of the *Historia*, much less a copyist, nor the longer draft of a work later cut down; they convey the impression that the author is putting further touches to his work here

---

[333] *HN* §31.
[334] *HN* §36.
[335] *HN* §37.
[336] *HN* §55.
[337] *HN* §23.
[338] *HN* §74.
[339] *HN* §39.
[340] *HN* §78.

and there in the light of further information. We seem to have, as Stubbs
supposes, the author's 'final revision'.[341]

In this interpretation, the new material allowed the text to be
brought up to date. 'In the course of writing, William added
"stop-press" news arriving too late for inclusion in the original
text.'[342] There are problems with this explanation. It might serve
for interpolations to the final section of text within book iii, such
as the names of the Norman castles captured in 1142. It is much
more problematic for changes that were made in book ii. The
first of these, in the above list, deals with the atrocities
committed at Malmesbury by the mercenary Robert Fitz
Hubert. This short paragraph is clearly interpolated: the previous paragraph had taken the empress, after her landing in
1139, via Bristol to Gloucester; the following paragraph continued, 'and so the whole district around Gloucester' went over
to the empress in the later months of the year. Robert Fitz
Hubert in the AB text was first introduced a little later, when he
captured Devizes castle on 26 March 1140.[343] Events in and
around Malmesbury late in 1139 can hardly be seen as 'later
news', reaching there only in 1142 or 1143. Just as clearly
interpolated is the passage about Geoffrey de Mandeville at
the siege of Winchester. AB reads here:

Ab occidente itaque raro et anguste importabantur necessaria, uiatoribus
nonnullis interceptis et uel occisis uel parte membrorum mutilatis. Ab
oriente uero toto tramite uersus Lundoniam constipabantur semitae
multitudine commeatuum, episcopo et suis importandorum; et Lundoniensibus maxime annitentibus, nichilque omnino quod possent pretermittentibus quo imperatricem contristarent.

The Margam manuscript reads here (new material in italic):

Ab occidente itaque raro et anguste importabantur necessaria, uiatoribus
nonnullis interceptis et uel occisis uel parte membrorum mutilatis: *ab
oriente uero toto tramite uersus Lundoniam constipabantur semitae*

---

[341] Mynors, p. xlii.

[342] Gransden, *Historical Writing*, i. 183.

[343] *HN* § 39. Robert was introduced in the AB text here as 'immanis et barbarus'; in Ce
these epithets were taken forward to § 31, and in § 39 he was simply 'prefatus'.

multitudine commeatuum, episcopo et suis importandorum; *Gaufrido de Mandeuilla, qui iam iterum auxilio eorum cesserat, antea enim post captionem regis imperatrici fidelitatem iurauerat*, et Lundoniensibus maxime annitentibus, nichilque omnino quod possent pretermittentibus quo imperatricem contristarent.

It seems most likely that the gist of the new material originated as a gloss to an earlier copy. The editor (in this analysis) has found the short passage almost impossible to insert, and the insertion makes for a loss of coherence and of narrative drive. Geoffrey de Mandeville is not mentioned in the AB text. He is introduced here as it were without introduction; and there is just too much to be fitted in. That William of Malmesbury was responsible for this botched interpolation to his carefully balanced text is most unlikely. In other cases also the 'new material' might have been thought well enough known to William of Malmesbury had he wished to use it.[344] Mynors discounted the possibility that these were 'changes of a later reader',[345] but he gave no reason for this opinion; and the alterations seem most unlikely to have come from William of Malmesbury's pen.

2. *Changes of Emphasis*

No clear line can be drawn between this and the previous category, but here we are dealing with changes of words and phrases. Some of the passages already discussed may have originated in glosses to a text, for none is so substantial as to preclude this possibility. The same explanation may serve for some of the passages which follow, but, if so, they come from a single hand.

Every word and nuance of what was written in the *HN* about Robert of Gloucester has been subject to the very closest attention. Not just the earl himself, but also his family and his *familia* are consistently written up. The AB texts frequently refer to Robert of

---

[344] E.g. *HN* at end of §23, the names of the castles of Newark and Sleaford have been added, even though Newark had been mentioned earlier; *HN* §39, 'quendam Johannem ... qui apud Merleberge castellum habebat', now becomes John Fitz Gilbert, but he had been properly introduced and identified, and the patronymic of an important castellan who lived a day's ride from Malmesbury can hardly have been 'news' to William.

[345] Mynors, p. xlii.

Gloucester simply as *comes*; and at times in such cases Ce provides the name for additional emphasis.[346] The earl's wife comes in for similar attention. Robert of Gloucester is introduced, on his taking the oath to the empress in 1127, as the king's son, whom he made earl of Gloucester. Ce continued, 'giving him to wife Mabel, a lovely and noble woman, a lady who was both obedient to her husband and blessed in being the mother of numerous and very fair offspring'. The beautiful Mabel is mentioned twice thereafter, and in each case the text has been touched up to provide additional emphasis.[347] None of these were mentioned by Stubbs as among 'the changes that can be thought to have any significance',[348] nor did Mynors draw attention to them.

A further set of passages concern the earl's military household. The earl's knights are introduced during the listing of the castles recaptured in 1140, the first of these being Harptree, which Stephen had earlier taken 'a quibusdam militibus comitis'.[349] The valour of these same knights was shown in better light by the strengthening of the king's party at the battle of Lincoln: in AB it was stated that a few barons of outstanding loyalty—'pauci barones predicandi fidei'—had been taken with the king, while in Ce 'pauci' was altered to 'plures', and prefaced to this was the statement that six earls had fought for the king in the battle.[350] The knights went with the earl to Normandy in 1142, and they helped him capture the ten castles, which are named in Ce;[351] and it may even be that we hear them speak, for we have the French forms of the place-names.[352] These were not men to abandon their post, and so at Wareham later in the year the fortress once deserted ('uacuum') is now inadequately munitioned ('non bene munitum').[353] The passages relating to chivalric custom might

---

[346] Thus in *HN* § 37, 'comes' in AB becomes 'comes Gloecestre Robertus'; in § 56, 'comes' becomes 'comes Gloecestre'; and in § 76, 'comes Robertus' becomes 'comes Gloecestre Robertus'.

[347] In *HN* § 63, 'uiri sui' in AB becomes 'uiri sui dilecti', and shortly thereafter in § 65, 'uxoris suae' becomes 'uxoris suae scilicet'.

[348] Stubbs, i, p. lxiv.

[349] *HN* § 37.

[350] *HN* § 43.

[351] *HN* § 74.

[352] There are some indications elsewhere that vernacular forms have made their way into the Ce text, e.g. 'Reinnulfus' for 'Rannulfus', *HN* § 54, and 'Liuns' for 'Leonas', *HN* § 11.

[353] *HN* § 75.

almost be seen as addressed specifically to them, and to serve as a kind of running gag.[354]

There is a clear pattern in these changes concerning members of the earl's military household, just as there had been in the changes concerning the earl and his wife. In the light of these changes—and of all the arguments about the Ce text so far—we may consider some changes made in Ce, which Stubbs thought not beyond the capacity of a good copyist. Mynors commented at this point:

If Ce is a final revision of the text, the question at once arises whether we are to ascribe to the author, and not (as Stubbs perhaps rather illogically suggests) to 'copyists', the changes in vocabulary, in phrasing, and in word order which equally distinguish Ce from AB. This is a point which we should prefer for the present to leave in suspense, for it can only be usefully considered in the light of such comparable information as may be derived from the *Gesta Regum* in its three editions.[355]

It is far from clear that the textual history of the *GR* is relevant to this discussion, and in any event there is enough in our own text to form a judgement. Thus, thinking Ce to be the earlier text, Stubbs postulated a change from 'periuros' to 'peruersos' in the prologue, as those who would be subject to divine retribution. These are close enough to be alternative readings, but the AB texts are quite consistent on 'peruersos', and this is what William of Malmesbury wrote. The perjury is an editorial change, and chief among the perjurers was Stephen himself.[356] Another change is made when Henry I's son William died in the *White Ship*: here the judgement is softened, 'quanto dampno patriae' has become 'quanto incommodo patriae', the disaster of William's death has become a misfortune.[357] Both Stubbs and Mynors were right to point to the significance of the changes made from 'ciues' (citizens) in AB to 'burgenses' (burgesses) in Ce in describing the townspeople of Lincoln (on two occasions) and of Southampton.[358] This change

---

[354] See above, p. xlviii and n. 188. [355] *HN*, p. xlii.

[356] The Angevin party charged Stephen with perjury at the Lateran Council in 1139: John of Salisbury, *Historia Pontificalis*, ed. Chibnall, p. 83.

[357] *HN* § 2.

[358] The men of Lincoln are described as citizens in the AB text, while in Ce they have become burgesses: 'ciues interim Lincoliae ciuitatis' at §41 are replaced by 'burgenses'; and we then have 'burgensium' for 'ciuium' for the men of Lincoln, at §43, while the men of

takes us into the world of urban aspiration, on the one hand, and, on the other, the feelings of the Angevin party about the towns-people and the support they had offered to Stephen's cause. William noted that many of the inhabitants of Lincoln had died in the sack of the city after the battle, and that neither side had any sympathy for them, 'since it was they who by their instigation had given rise to this calamity'. It is difficult none the less to see William of Malmesbury as it were correcting himself, and writing 'burgess' for 'citizen'. Bede,[359] the other chroniclers,[360] and William's usage elsewhere, all argue for 'ciues' in his own text.[361] It is easier to see one of his readers glossing or marking up his copy for alteration. These changes should be seen as editorial, not simply the work of copyists; and perhaps there are others also.[362]

3. *Changes in Presentation*

It was primarily the addition of new material and secondarily the changes in emphasis that attracted the attention of earlier editors of the *HN*. This is not, however, the main point of difference between the AB and the Ce texts that confronts a reader of the manuscripts. This concerns rather how the text is ordered and presented on the page. The main divisions of the text are first into three books, and then within the books into paragraphs. The only rubrication in the majority of the AB texts served to identify the divisions between the books: there was no rubrication of individual paragraphs. The beginning of each book was noted by an *incipit*, and the end of the book by an *explicit*: thus to divide book i from book ii we have first 'explicit liber primus', and then 'incipit liber secundus'.

Southampton, perhaps less entitled to the dignity, have suffered the same fate with the making of the same change in § 77. In consequence the Ce text has been stripped of all its citizens other than the Londoners.

[359] J. Campbell, 'Bede's words for places', *Names, Words and Graves: Early Medieval Settlement*, ed. P. H. Sawyer (Leeds, 1979), pp. 34–54.

[360] Henry of Huntingdon has Robert of Gloucester refer to the citizens of Lincoln in his imagined address before the battle: HH, pp. 728–9. They are 'ciues' also in OV vi. 538–47; John of Hexham, in SD ii. 308; *GS* 110–13.

[361] In his collection on miracles, indeed, William appears to be 'under the spell of cities': P. Carter, 'The historical content of William of Malmesbury's Miracles of the Virgin Mary', *The Writing of History in the Middle Ages: Essays Presented to Richard William Southern*, ed. R. H. C. Davis and J. M. Wallace-Hadrill (Oxford, 1981), pp. 127–65, at 161.

[362] Below, p. xciv n. 398.

The evidence of other manuscripts from the scriptorium at Malmesbury, and of the manuscripts of the *GR* and the *HN* considered together, suggest that this 'skeletal rubrication' (as it will be referred to in the discussion which follows) was all that was found in the original texts of these works. Amongst the other manuscripts we may note Bodleian MS, Arch. Seld. B. 16, a collection of Roman history. Here the rubrication looks to be in the same hand as those parts of the text identified as being written by William himself;[363] and we find, for example: (fo. 48ᵛ) 'Explicit liber .v. Incipit prologus libri sexti'; (fo. 49ʳ) 'Explicit prologus. Incipit liber sextus'; (fo.134ᵛ) 'Incipit adbreviatio Willelmi'.[364] This rubrication corresponds closely with what is found in the earliest manuscripts of the *HN*. There are, however, many variations in the surviving manuscripts of the *HN*: some have this skeletal rubrication, dividing the three books; others have this rubrication and rubrication of many of the paragraphs; and some show the *HN* as book vi of the *GR*. These variations led Stubbs to cite as one of the reasons for printing as his standard text Ceⁱ, 'the great Margam manuscript', that it was 'the authority for entitling the *Historia Novella* as a separate work with proper numbering of the books'.[365] Stubbs very shrewdly noted the problem, but his conclusion in this case was wrong. The full evidence is set out in the manuscript descriptions.[366] It is not just in the Ce texts, but in the two rubricated A texts (Ao, At), that the skeletal rubrication is found; and there are indications that a third A text was intended to be rubricated in this way (Ag). There are traces of this rubrication in one of the B texts also (Bq), but in most thirteenth-century and later copies the *HN* has come to be viewed as book vi of the *GR* (Bc, Bk, Cd, Cm). This might be termed the 'third edition' of the *HN*, but it has no authority.

The rubrication of Ce, however, provides the clearest evidence that we are dealing with a second edition. Here, in addition to the rubrication which distinguishes the three books, fifty-four of the

---

[363] Thomson, pp. 92–3.

[364] A reproduction of fo. 73ʳ of this manuscript is given in A. G. Watson, *Catalogue of Dated and Datable Manuscripts c.435–1600 in Oxford Libraries*, 2 vols. (Oxford, 1984), ii, plate 48.

[365] Stubbs, i, p. lxiii.

[366] Above, pp. lxix–lxxvi.

paragraphs—about two-thirds of the total—have been rubricated. In the printed texts these rubrics are a prominent feature. They provide the structure of the work, and they tell the story. In the choice of paragraphs to rubricate, and in the rubrics themselves, particular elements of the text are highlighted. The pattern is exactly the same as was seen when the textual changes were examined.[367] Robert of Gloucester is the focus of attention. His arrival in England is emphasized by the creation of a new paragraph, which is not in the AB texts, headed: *The arrival in England of Robert earl of Gloucester.*[368] These headings can be at times a rather partial reading of the text which follows on from them. A short paragraph on the Norman expedition in 1137 is headed, perfectly fairly: *The crossing of King Stephen and Robert earl of Gloucester to Normandy and the ambush that the king laid for the earl.*[369] The Battle of Lincoln, however, is seen as the story of *The earl of Gloucester's fight and the king's capture.*[370] The ill-fated campaign at Winchester in August 1141, where clearly the empress took the lead, is headed: *How the earl of Gloucester, with the empress and their supporters, summoned the legate.*[371] And the penultimate paragraph, the last one to be rubricated, describes how *The earl of Gloucester collected an army and marched to relieve the empress*, even though the text explains that she had escaped before the army could set out.[372] The effect of the rubrication is that where the earl of Gloucester is on stage, which is for most of the action, then he is thrust to centre-stage.

It has been noted that a new paragraph was supplied to highlight the earl of Gloucester's arrival in England in 1136. There was similarly an extra paragraph put in half way through the description of the council at London on 1 January 1127, to emphasize *The oath that the chief men of England took to the empress.*[373] A final series of changes have been put in place in the latter part of book iii of the *HN*. This, the last of the three stages

---

[367] Above, pp. lxxxii–lxxxiv.
[368] *HN* § 17.   [369] *HN* § 20.
[370] *HN* § 43; while for a tenant of the earl of Chester it was 'the battle between King Stephen and Ranulf earl of Chester': Sir Frank Stenton, *The First Century of English Feudalism 1066–1166*, 2nd edn. (Oxford, 1961), p. 243.
[371] *HN* § 54.   [372] *HN* § 78.   [373] *HN* § 3.

of composition,[374] deals with the events of 1142, starting with a *recapitulatio* which stresses the consistency of Robert of Gloucester, and supplies some further details of the negotiations which resulted in him and Stephen being released in November 1141. From this point on the Ce texts have twenty-two paragraphs.[375] Of these, A and the other C texts have only ten paragraphs, while the B texts have either three or four paragraphs. These last paragraphs in the B manuscripts are certainly longer than those found earlier, in this and the other recensions. This may provide one further indication that this part of the text lacked the author's final revision.

The ending of the *HN*, however, which is more often cited as showing that William of Malmesbury left the *HN* unfinished, may have a different interpretation. What is in all manuscripts the final paragraph of the *HN* is found with three distinct endings, that in Ce[1], that in Ce[2], and that in all the other manuscripts. The paragraph in all manuscripts starts: 'I should certainly be pleased to add the manner of the empress's escape if I had sure knowledge of it, for it is a manifest miracle of God.' It then continues with brief details of her escape from Oxford castle to Abingdon and thence to Wallingford. All but the Ce manuscripts conclude: 'I am, however, disposed to go into this more thoroughly if ever by the gift of God I learn the truth from those who were present (*ab his qui interfuere ueritatem accepero*).' The Ce[1] text omits all that happens after Oxford, and concludes: 'But these matters will be more fully set forth, God willing, in the next book.' Ce[2] adds this final sentence to the full text found in the other manuscripts, and so has both the alternative endings;[376] and it is this text that was printed by Stubbs and by Mynors. There are a number of ways in which this complicated textual history could be elucidated. Mynors followed earlier editors in seeing the ending as strong evidence that Ce represented the author's 'final revise'.[377] It needs to be noted, however, that the text as abbreviated in Ce[1] exactly

---

[374] Above, p. xxxii.   [375] *HN* §60–79.

[376] It is thus clear that the scribe of Ce[2] had in front of him an AB as well as a Ce manuscript.

[377] Mynors, p. xliii.

fills the verso of a folio, which unabbreviated would have run on to a new folio for just a few lines (see Plate 4); and that this is also the end of a quire. The last sentence may be a final editorial change, made to fit the matter into the space available.[378]

4. *The Making of the New Edition*

It is not in dispute that Ce is a distinctive version of the text of the *HN*. What is in question is its status. The answer to this question turns on when and where it was made. It was a version later than the AB text: this had to be made as an assertion at the beginning of the discussion of the two versions, and it is hoped that by now it has been proved. Note has been made in particular of the way new material cuts into William of Malmesbury's sentences and inter-rupts the development of his ideas, of the layout and the rubrication of the Ce text, and of the introduction of words and phrases—which may originate as glosses—that in a number of places modify the judgements made. It is a later version. The changes made in this later version are systematic, and they are consistent. Ce represents not just a distinct stage in the evolution of the text of the *HN*, but a new edition. So where was it made? There would appear to be two possibilities: either it was made at Malmesbury, during or after the author's lifetime, or it was made in one of the centres in which the *HN* circulated.

If it was made at Malmesbury, could it have been, as the most recent editors have argued, the author's 'final revise'? William is known to have been a great reviser of his own work.[379] There is nothing inherently improbable in his having revised his last work, the *HN*, but there are none the less considerable difficulties in accepting that he did so. The work is a short tract. It was written over little more than two years. It shows signs that it was unfinished: it has been rounded off at the chronological point that had been reached (December 1142), but it was intended to be continued. It was the categorical opinion of Stubbs, who was very cautious on most points of difficulty, that it was 'impossible' that

---

[378] Stubbs, who missed nothing, alluded to this possibility, speaking at this point of 'the author, or the transcriber of the Margam MS': Stubbs, i, p. lxv.

[379] Gransden, *Historical Writing*, i. 180–2, and references there cited.

William of Malmesbury issued a second edition of the *HN*.[380] All the discussion so far tends to support this judgement, in which case it must be AB that is William's text while Ce is not his. Could it then have been revised at Malmesbury after William's death? Had the *HN* been a history of the monastery, its continuation might have been viewed as a communal duty. But the *HN* was not such a text, rather it was an individual commission. William founded no school at Malmesbury; there was no continuity of historical writing in this house; and his own memory was not kept alive there.[381] A copy of *HN*, however, remained on the shelf in the library at Malmesbury, and while the copy does not survive it is possible to identify its recension. This is because, in the mid-fourteenth century, one of the monks of Malmesbury used the library to write a work entitled *Eulogium Historiarum*. He copied almost verbatim from the *HN* the two paragraphs that dealt with the empress's return to England, and the oaths sworn in her support. He happily chose material that has a particularly rich harvest of textual variations,[382] and these leave no doubt that it was a text of the B recension that he found on the shelves. This provides an additional strong, though not conclusive, argument against identifying the Ce text with Malmesbury. And it was an A text that was found at Winchester cathedral priory in the mid-fifteenth century,[383] so that if we are looking for a route of transmission for Ce via Henry of Winchester, who had been William's main clerical patron, we also come to a dead-end.

The strongest argument, however, against William as the author

---

[380] Stubbs, i, p. lxiii.

[381] Gransden, *Historical Writing*, i. 166: at Malmesbury before William's day, 'the level of culture was low, and after it the monks relapsed into mediocrity, scarcely remembering the work of their greatest brother'; Gransden, *Historical Writing*, ii. 103; J. Leland, *Commentarii de scriptoribus Britannicis*, ed. A. Hall, 2 vols. (Oxford, 1709), i. 195–6.

[382] In *HN* §2, 3, there are five distinct readings where AB differs from Ce, all of them found in *Eulogium*, iii. 59–60. These include the phrase about Edward the Confessor being buried at Westminster, left out in Ce, and the additional emphasis on the empress's descent from the Scottish royal house. There are a further seven verbal differences where B differs from ACe, all of them followed in *Eulogium*. The addition of *proceres*, in Ce but not in AB, is prima facie an exception to this rule, but *Eulogium* has the word several times earlier where *GR* does not, and it seems to have been supplied here again. *Eulogium*, iii. 62–3, dealing with Henry I's last visit to Normandy, following *HN* §10, has also some distinctive AB readings.

[383] See below, pp. ciii–civ.

and Malmesbury as the place of writing of the Ce text is that its distinctive features seem to show a strong secular bias. The text has gone outside 'professional' historical circles. It shows clear signs of having been read in the circles to which it was addressed. Those circles, to use a convenient shorthand phrase, were Angevin circles. As Stubbs put it, in the *HN* William 'wrote for the ear of great men'.[384] And for one great man above all. Following the example of William, and using the phrase of the rubricator of the Ce version, let us attempt a 'recapitulation':

(a) William of Malmesbury dedicated the *HN* to Robert of Gloucester; he obtained much information from him; he saw him as a figure of true nobility.

(b) The changes made in Ce, particularly the rubrication, served to heighten the earl's already high importance.

(c) The changes show not just a pride in the earl, but in his wife also, and in their progeny.

(d) The changes also show an interest in, and some signs of protectiveness towards, the knights of the earl's household.

In sum, as has become clear as the different facets of the Ce version have been examined, the new text brings out the importance of the earl of Gloucester, of his family, and of his *familiares*. We seem to see here a particular interest in the contents and in the judgements of the *HN* being shown by the family of the great man to whom the work was dedicated.

The hypothesis which follows is based on the clues as to the authorship of the new edition that have been examined. The first major editorial change was in the fuller description of Robert of Gloucester's spouse, the mother of 'numerous and very fair offspring'. Now the youngest of the offspring of Robert of Gloucester, and his father's particular favourite, so we are told on the authority of Thomas Becket,[385] was Roger. He occurs in the foundation charter of Margam Abbey, issued shortly before his father's death on 31 October 1147;[386] and other charters show him

---

[384] Stubbs, ii, p. cxlii.

[385] *Materials for the History of Thomas Becket*, ed. J. C. Robertson and J. B. Sheppard, 7 vols. (RS lxvii, 1875–85), vii. 258–61.

[386] *Gloucester Charters*, no. 119.

fully involved in his family's affairs. He became a clerk, studied in Paris, and in 1163 was elected bishop of Worcester, possibly a few months before his thirtieth birthday. He died in 1179. He was a man universally admired by contemporaries, his nobility of mind matching his nobility of character according to Gerald of Wales, who was no ready flatterer of diocesan bishops.[387]

The historiography of the Becket dispute has left some valuable information on Roger of Worcester's early career, not least his pride in his family, and this has been very sensitively handled by Mary Cheney in her study of the bishop.[388] Roger of Worcester was the cousin of Henry II. This gave him a particular standing among the members of the English episcopate, and a particular independence, which Henry might have resented but never questioned. In 1170 a bitter dispute arose when Roger refused to attend the coronation of the young king. The exchanges were well reported, and they are of particular interest here. The bishop, said the king, was a traitor and certainly no true son of Robert of Gloucester, 'the good earl, my uncle, who brought us up together in that castle, and had us instructed in the first elements of learning and good behaviour'. The castle was Bristol, where Henry had stayed on his first visit to England.[389] Roger's reply to this last charge revealed a cleric well able to adapt to the language of the court. 'You say I am not Earl Robert's son. How do I know? But I was the son of my mother, with whom my father received the inheritance of the whole earldom and honour.'[390] The obligations of kinship worked both ways:

As for you, you never showed by due reward that Earl Robert was your uncle, that he maintained you with fitting honour, that he fought King Stephen for you for sixteen years and was even taken prisoner in battle. If you had remembered my father's services, you would not have reduced my brothers to poverty and exile. My brother the earl[391] should have a

---

[387] Gerald of Wales, *Opera*, ed. J. S. Brewer *et al.*, 8 vols. (RS xxi, 1861–91), vii. 62–7.

[388] M. Cheney, *Roger, Bishop of Worcester 1164–1179* (Oxford, 1980), pp. 1–16.

[389] *HN* § 74 notes simply the stay in England; the references to Bristol are in *Regesta*, iii. p. xlvi and nos. 126, 996.

[390] *Materials for the History of Thomas Becket*, iii. 104–5; trans. Cheney, *Roger of Worcester*, p. 48.

[391] William, earl of Gloucester, 1147–83: *CP* v. 687–9.

fee of a thousand knights, which King Henry your grandfather gave my father; you have diminished it by two hundred and forty knights. Another younger brother, said to be a good knight, you left so poor and so hopeless that he gave himself for ever to the Hospital of Jerusalem.[392] This is how you reward your friends and repay them.

Roger of Worcester did not just refer to his father's past service, he quoted chapter and verse on the size of his father's military establishment. Was he even for a time part of it?[393]

There is every sign that the Ce version was the work of single editor. There is a temptation—which has not been totally resisted here—to provide him with a name. Ralph Davis did this for the *Gesta Stephani*, saying that it was the work of Robert of Lewes, bishop of Bath, and this view has gained a measure of acceptance.[394] With the Ce version of the *HN* there is a good deal less to go on. But the Ce version has an immediacy, an involvement with the issues of the civil war, that is unmistakable. This helps explain why it was long seen as the work of William himself. And there was a 'bookish' side to the revision that also must be taken account of here. The new editor of the *HN* needed not just a good memory, but some classified correspondence,[395] and some chronicles also.[396] The Ce tradition is not well developed, but

[392] This is most likely Philip, the empress's custodian of Cricklade, who went over to Stephen's party, and is last heard of going on pilgrimage to Jerusalem: *GS*, pp. 180–1, 186–7, 190–1. When the future Henry II, at the age of fourteen, mounted an abortive campaign in England in 1147, he made directly for Cricklade; this suggests a specific reaction to his cousin's defection, and would in turn explain a particular animus against him: *GS*, pp. 204–9.

[393] Becket said that Roger was 'dedicated from the first to God' (*Materials for the History of Thomas Becket*, vii. 258, trans. Cheney, *Roger of Worcester*, p. 6 n. 7), but charter attestations in his teens show him in a family context. He attested his father's foundation charter for Margam Abbey in 1147, and three charters of his brother William as earl, one of them after the birth of his brother's heir, which cannot have been earlier than 1151: *Gloucester Charters*, nos. 34, 35, 119, 280; Cheney, *Roger of Worcester*, p. 8. He witnessed a royal charter of Jan. 1156 as an unbeneficed clerk: W. Dugdale, *Monasticon Anglicanum*, ed. J. Caley *et al.*, 8 vols. (London, 1817–30), iv. 538–9.

[394] R. H. C. Davis, 'The authorship of the *Gesta Stephani*', *EHR* lxxvii (1962), 209–32, revised and reprinted in *GS*, pp. xviii–xl; doubts have been voiced by Gransden, *Historical Writing*, i. 188–93, at p. 190, and F. Barlow, *The English Church 1066–1154* (London, 1979), p. 21 and n. 83.

[395] The list of ten Norman castles taken in 1142, given in §74, is more likely to be based on a contemporary letter than on later memory.

[396] There are indications that the author of the new edition had at least Henry of Huntingdon and John of Worcester to hand. At the battle of Lincoln, 'sex enim cum rege

Ce¹ and Ce² derive from Ce.[397] If we are looking to place Ce, a rather better case can be made for Worcester, with its tradition of historical writing, than for Margam: both centres have appropriate links with Robert of Gloucester. It is even possible that there were two stages in the making of Ce: the annotation of an AB (probably a B text), and its subsequent writing-up in this new edition. In such case, the annotator could even be Robert of Gloucester himself;[398] the writer-up could be a clerk in the service of Roger of Worcester. As to particular individual and particular place, all this is speculative; but as to intellectual milieu, the case may be thought a good deal stronger. And this leads in to an area of some importance. Contemporary historians in their prefaces will often ask for corrections and observations to be sent to them, for use in a subsequent edition. There is every indication that in the mid-twelfth century one of William of Malmesbury's readers took him at his word, and did precisely that.

VI. THE LATER USE OF THE TEXT

It was the complaint of Roger of Worcester in 1170 that the king had too soon forgotten the service of Robert of Gloucester to the empress's cause. Irrespective of whether Roger had any involvement in the revision of the *HN*, by this date the issues of the civil war had faded from view, and there was no continuing market for the text which provided the most subtle analysis of those issues. In the decade after it was written, the *HN* must have circulated quite narrowly. After 1154 there remained a continuing interest in the

comites bellum inierant', *HN* §43, and their names are found in HH, pp. 736–7; the reference to Alexander of Lincoln's castles at Newark and Sleaford at *HN* §23 may also be from the same source, HH, pp. 720–3. The interpolated passage on Robert Fitz Hubert, *HN* §31, seems to draw in part on JW iii. 284–7, and the revision in *HN* §39 ('patibulo appensus'), may draw on JW iii. 288–9 ('patibuli suspensione').

[397] 'Ce²' is very close indeed to Ce¹, but it is not descended from it, being sometimes right where Ce¹ is wrong. It must be derived from a twin of Ce¹, and provides a useful check. Their common ancestor shall be called Ce': Mynors, p. xli.

[398] Thus, it could be argued, there are some signs of patrician judgement, or at very least a concern for precedence, in the addition of 'proceribus' at *HN* §3, and the deletion of 'primatum' at §61; while at §2, the toning-down of the judgement on the *White Ship* disaster, the loss of a son being a misfortune rather than a tragedy, would be intriguing if it came—at whatever remove—from another of the king's sons.

eventful period of history which our text covers, but there were others, who wrote for a wider market, and who had the good fortune to survive throughout the reign, who better met the need for information on it. The two most important of these historians were Henry of Huntingdon in England and Robert of Torigni in Normandy. These for their immediate successors were the main sources for a narrative of history in the first half of the twelfth century. The *HN* came to be valued not primarily as a record but rather as part of the *œuvre* of a major historian.

In his preface to the *GR*, Stubbs noted that this work 'seems to have sprung at once into the position of a popular and standard history'. He was able to demonstrate that all the major British historians of the later twelfth century, including Ralph de Diceto and Roger of Howden, made use of the *GR*.[399] From the references he gave, however, it is clear that it was the Anglo-Saxon material that William of Malmesbury's successors most valued. The few direct borrowings that have been identified from the *HN* are each of them in some way problematic. The earliest and most intriguing is the possible use of the Latin text of the *HN* by the monk of Peterborough who wrote the 'E' text of the *Anglo-Saxon Chronicle* (henceforth *ASC*). There seem to be 'verbal parallels', as Dorothy Whitelock noted,[400] between the *HN* description of the anarchy and the more famous passage in the *ASC*. This last comprises the annal for 1137, but it is evident that it was written only at the end of the civil war: 'these things we suffered nineteen years for our sins'. This means that any relationship posited with what we have termed the first edition of *HN*, i.e. William of Malmesbury's own text, would have to involve use of the *HN* in *ASC*. It is, intriguingly, possible not just to postulate a link but to provide the name of an intermediary. The *ASC* concludes with the election of William de Waterville as abbot of Peterborough, 'a good cleric and a good man, and well loved by the king and by all good men'.[401] The Waterville family were hereditary stewards of the abbey of Peterborough; a younger

---

[399] Stubbs, i, pp. xci–xcii (quotation p. xci).

[400] *The Anglo-Saxon Chronicle*, trans. D. Whitelock (London, 1961), p. 199 n. 3; *HN* §36; *ASC* E, s.a. 1137.

[401] *ASC* E, s.a. 1154.

brother of the contemporary tenant of the abbey fee was Geoffrey
de Waterville; and Geoffrey de Waterville was the steward of
Robert earl of Gloucester.[402] The matter is complicated, however,
because the most substantial passage which seems to echo the *ASC*
is not in William of Malmesbury's text, but is an interpolation in
the second edition. This passage reads in the *HN*: 'Under-tenants,
peasants, any who were thought wealthy, they kidnapped and
compelled to promise anything by the severity of their tortures.'
This may be compared with the *ASC*: 'They took those people
they thought had any goods—men and women—and put them in
prison and tortured them with indescribable torture to extort gold
and silver.' William of Malmesbury also stated of the wrongdoers
that 'they spared neither churches nor graveyards',[403] and that
excommunication proved futile; and these points are made also by
the *ASC*. These are most easily explained as echoes of a familiar
phrase from conciliar legislation, which had a long history in the
Peace of God. There is not enough to support the view that the
HN was used by the writer of the *ASC*.[404] It is more likely that
what we are dealing with here, and in descriptions of the anarchy
from other authors, are independently produced variations on a
number of common themes.[405]

Among the Latin writers cited by Stubbs as making use of the
GR in the later twelfth century, Ralph de Diceto is the one who
took the closest interest in the Angevin succession. In the

---

[402] E. King, *Peterborough Abbey 1086–1310: A Study in the Land Market* (Cambridge,
1973), pp. 32–3; idem, 'Dispute settlement in Anglo-Norman England', *ANS*, xiv (1992),
115–30, at p. 115.

[403] 'nec aecclesiis nec cimiteriis parcentes', and the later reference to the excommunication of 'omnes effractores cimiteriorum et uiolatores aecclesiarum': *HN* § 36; and he had
earlier written of mercenaries as men ready 'uel cimiteria frangere uel aecclesias expolire':
HN § 17. Henry of Huntingdon has the following couplet in his poem on the anarchy,
'Contio predonum cimiteria, templa refringit / Iamque sacerdotes (res miseranda!) rapit':
HH, pp. 724–5 (s.a. 1140); The Annals of Waverley, s.a. 1143, adds to a short passage
seemingly based on Robert of Torigni a reference to those who 'res ecclesiasticas et
cemiteria fregebant': *Ann. Mon.*, ii. 229; Roger of Wendover refers to the condemnation of
anyone 'qui ecclesiam cimiteriumque uiolauerit': *Chronica*, ed. H. O. Coxe, 4 vols. (EHS,
1841–2), ii. 232; and valuable discussion in *Councils and Synods*, i (2), p. 795 n. 1.

[404] I have changed my mind on this: cf. E. King, 'Introduction', in King, *Anarchy*,
pp. 1–36, at 1–2.

[405] Note in particular the range of texts cited in the admirable apparatus to this passage
in *The Peterborough Chronicle 1070–1154*, ed. Cecily Clark, 2nd edn. (Oxford, 1970),
pp. 106–9.

Ymagines historiarum he starts a new era with the knighting of the future Henry II at Carlisle in 1149.[406] In the *Abbreviationes chronicorum*, which precede his history proper, he makes particular use of Henry of Huntingdon (often at second-hand through Robert of Torigni) and John of Worcester.[407] The editor, Stubbs, suggested the *HN* as the source for the entry on the oaths sworn to the empress at the Christmas court of 1126/7: 'primates Angliae regnum jurauerunt imperatrici, et primus inter omnes Stephanus comes Boloniae'.[408] The earlier annals for 1126, however, are taken from John of Worcester, and this passage also might ultimately derive from the same source.[409] Ralph gives a fuller and more circumstantial account of the oaths to the empress under the year 1133, the only chronicler to do so. This reads:

Mense Martio natus est Cenomannis Henricus, primogenitus Gaufridi Plantegenest comitis Andegauorum et Matildis imperatricis. Quod cum rex Henricus audisset, conuocatis regni sui principibus, filiam suam et heredes filiae suae sibi successuros instituit. Dispositionem suam omnes obseruaturos astrinxit sacramento corporaliter praestito. Stephanus filius Alae sororis suae primus praestitit sacramentum apud Westmustier.[410]

Here the passage italicized is from Robert of Torigni, and what follows is from Ralph de Diceto. It is not impossible that the oaths were renewed in 1133, consequent upon this event, but both the late date and the textual history cause problems.[411] There are similar problems, as Marjorie Chibnall has pointed out, in using

---

[406] Diceto, i. 291.

[407] It is Robert of Torigni whom he acknowledges as his main source for the period from 1123 to 1147: ibid., i. 23.

[408] Ibid., i. 245; and thence in Roger of Wendover, *Chronica*, ed. H. O. Coxe, ii. 207, and in Matthew Paris, *Chronica maiora*, ii. 153.

[409] JW iii. 176–81.   [410] Diceto, i. 246–7.

[411] This passage is not in all the manuscripts. It appears in the AC text, but not in the BD text: the manuscripts are described by Stubbs in Diceto, i, pp. lxxxviii–xcii, and their relationship is discussed ibid., i, pp. xciii–xcvi. He concluded that the AC text had 'the latest alterations which the compiler thought it worth his while to make' (ibid., i, p. xcvi). Why did Ralph de Diceto make this alteration? He might have been drawing on a fresh written or oral source: he has original material on events in London, and there was a meeting of the royal court at Westminster early in 1133, at which Stephen was present (*Regesta*, ii, no. 1761). He clearly wished to highlight the significance of Henry's birth, however, and the new oath may have been supplied for additional effect.

Roger of Howden's *Chronica* as authority for a further oath around this time.[412] There is no mention of an 1133 oath in the *HN*.

In the early thirteenth century the *HN* was slightly more fully used, but it still had to compete in a crowded market-place, and those who did have knowledge of it found that its literary style made it at times difficult to follow. The use made by the St Albans chroniclers is particularly interesting, both because of the importance of this centre of historical writing, and because the key manuscripts relating to the transmission of the text there have survived. The first of these is BL, Royal MS 13. D. v, copies of the *GR* and the *HN* and of Geoffrey of Monmouth's *HRB* made for Roger of Wendover. In his *Flores historiarum* (*FH*), Roger noted that William concluded his 'history of the English' in 1142.[413] It is thus clear that he knew the text of the *HN*, but there are no signs that he used it. The *FH* was the main source of the *Chronica maiora* (*CM*) of Matthew Paris, up to the year 1236.[414] The text of this latter work up to 1188 is found in Cambridge, Corpus Christi College MS 26, produced under the supervision of Matthew Paris, and with marginalia giving additional material that are in his own hand.[415] Some of the more substantial amongst these are taken from the *HN*. The first of these takes in short order Stephen's landing in England after Henry I's death, his coronation, and his taking over Henry's treasure.[416]

Die quo applicuit idem Stephanus, contra naturam hiemis horrendum intonuit super omnem terram tonitruum cum fulgure horribili, ita ut mundus in antiquum chaos redigi uideretur. Stephanus quoque rex, praesentibus archiepiscopo cum duobus episcopis, scilicet, Wintoniensi et Sarisberiensi, totum thesaurum, quem auunculus suus congesserat, occupauit, scilicet centum milia libras, exceptis uasis aureis et argenteis et gemmis.

---

[412] '[Henry I] fecit archiepiscopos et comites et barones totius sue dominationis jurare fidelitates Matildae imperatrici filiae suae et Henrico filio eius adhuc minimo, et constituit eum regem post se': Roger of Howden, *Chronica*, i. 187, s.a. 1134, discussed Chibnall, *Matilda*, p. 61.

[413] 'Hoc quoque anno magister Willelmus, Malmesberiensis monachus, Anglorum historiam terminavit': Roger of Wendover, *Chronica*, ed. Coxe, ii. 234–5.

[414] On the relationship between Roger of Wendover and Matthew Paris see R. Vaughan, *Matthew Paris* (Cambridge, 1958), pp. 21–34.

[415] Ibid., pp. 103–9.

[416] Cambridge, Corpus Christi College, MS 26, fo. 113ᵛᵃ; *Chronica maiora*, ii. 163–4.

This section of text reworks four distinct passages in the *HN*, three of them close together, and the fourth taken from the description of the eclipse of 1140.[417] Matthew had to pull in this later text because the phrase that William used at this point, 'ita ut mundus solui putaretur', he had already applied to the storms which accompanied Stephen's landing.[418] Another passage from the *HN* follows almost immediately.[419]

[1136] Eodem anno post Pascha comes Glouerniae Robertus nomine uenit in Angliam, cuius prudentiam et potentiam rex Stephanus uerebatur; post cuius aduentum episcopi jurauerunt fidelitatem regi, et rex jurauit libertates ecclesiasticas et bonas leges se obseruaturam, et inde cartam suam fecit, et comes Robertus sibi homagium fecit sub conditione, scilicet si dignitatem suam sibi seruaret illibatam, secundum illud antiquum prouerbiam: 'Quamdiu habebis me pro senatore, et ego te pro imperatore.'

As a précis of the relevant text from the *HN* this could hardly be improved upon,[420] and the Latin tag which Matthew has supplied himself is a neat one. A further passage then deals with the council of Winchester in 1139:[421]

Eodem anno Wintoniensis episcopus frater regis Stephani, apostolicae sedis legatus in Anglia, pro eo quod rex inuitatos ad prandium quosdam nobiles coegit ad deditionem aliquorum castrorum indignans, cum Theobaldo archiepiscopo et aliis episcopis et prelatis Angliae concilium apud Wintoniam celebrauit, tertio kalendas Septembris, ad quod regem fratrem suum uocari fecit; qui comitem Albericum de Ver, in causarum uarietatibus exercitatum, misit ad concilium, de captione dictorum episcoporum, super qua erat impetitus, se sic de iure facere posse allegantem, et factum regis defendentem; et licet aliter uisum est concilio super querelis in episcopis motis, et uerbis hinc inde propositis, kalendis Septembris solutum est concilium.

---

[417] *HN* § 14 (Stephen's landing), § 15 (three bishops), § 17 (Henry I's treasure), § 38 (end of the world).
[418] Cambridge, Corpus Christi College, MS 26, fo. 113rb; *Chronica maiora*, ii. 161 and n. 5.
[419] Cambridge, Corpus Christi College, MS 26, fo. 113va; *Chronica maiora*, ii. 164.
[420] *HN* § 17 (comes to England), § 18 (freedom of church).
[421] Cambridge, Corpus Christi College, MS 26, fo. 114va; *Chronica maiora*, ii. 171; cf. *HN* § 24–5 (council summoned), § 26 (Aubrey de Vere), § 31 (council dissolved).

This almost achieves the impossible task of telling the story of the council in a single sentence.

These marginal entries in the *CM* were then taken into the main text of Matthew Paris's own *Flores historiarum* (henceforth *FH*). This was not a question of simple transcription, however, for the new material (such as the passages above), was used by Matthew Paris independently in the writing of the *FH*.[422] At this point he took in a number of new passages from the *HN*. William of Malmesbury's original text on the great storm of 1135 was restored.[423] The story of Robert of Gloucester's homage in 1136, left hanging in the margins of the text in the *CM*, was developed, the *FH* noting briefly the plot laid against the earl in Normandy in 1137, and his renunciation of homage in 1138.[424] There are more substantial borrowings under 1140, tied to the eclipse of that year: first the dreadful deeds of the mercenary Robert (here Ralph) Fitz Hubert, and then, jumping over the description of the anarchy, a note of the peace discussions later in the year.[425] As a result of this process of assimilation and reworking, the *HN*, while it featured not at all in Roger of Wendover, had become one of the main sources of the *FH* of Matthew Paris, for the period between Henry I's death and the battle of Lincoln. This helped to disseminate some of William of Malmesbury's material on the early part of Stephen's reign, for it was through the *FH* that Matthew Paris's work was later best known.

Matthew Paris was very interested in eclipses and in natural phenomena of all kinds.[426] This may be one of the reasons why he made use of the *HN* while Roger of Wendover did not, even though we know that he had a text of the work to hand. A similar interest, in the storms and eclipses which William of Malmesbury records, is found in the use made of the *HN* in two thirteenth-century annals, those of Margam and Winchester. The Margam annals are brief.[427] They pick up the text of the *HN* in 1131,

[422] Vaughan, *Matthew Paris*, pp. 103–7.

[423] *Flores Historiarum, per Matthaeum Westmonasteriensem collecti*, ed. H. R. Luard, 3 vols. (RS xcv, 1890), ii. 58.   [424] Ibid., ii. 58–9.

[425] Ibid., ii. 61–2.   [426] Vaughan, *Matthew Paris*, pp. 253–8.

[427] The relevant annals are found in only two pages of the printed text, *Ann. Mon.*, i. 13–14; *HN* is identified as a source ibid., i, p. xiii.

noting under that year the plague of animals, and the dispute between the dioceses of Llandaff and St Davids, in each case in direct quotation; and similarly, under 1132, there is noted the storm and the eclipse which preceded Henry I's last crossing to Normandy, following the *HN* in misdating this. The later eclipse, in 1140, is also noted, as are simply the dates of Henry I's death and Stephen's coronation; but otherwise the text is not used. An interest in Robert of Gloucester might have been expected, but it is no more than a token one: he is mentioned when he is captured in 1141, and not otherwise until his death in 1147. There are a couple of hints that, as might have been suspected, it is the surviving Margam manuscript that has been used by the compiler of the Margam annals.[428]

In the Winchester annals there is found a more detailed and more comprehensive use of a copy of the first edition of the *HN*. This provides the main, though not the exclusive, source for these annals between 1126, when the empress returned from Germany, and the end of 1142, when she escaped from the siege of Oxford.[429] There are occasional sentences taken from the *HN*: thus the summary of the horrors of war in 1140, and a brief mention of the peace negotiations of the same year.[430] Also, and most usefully, there can be seen direct use of the passage which describes the empress's escape with four knights from the siege of Oxford, a passage not found in the Margam text. Aside from this, the Winchester annals for the most part paraphrase the *HN*, with individual phrases picked out sufficiently frequently to make the derivation of the text from the *HN* indisputable. A single passage may serve for many. This concerns Robert of Gloucester in Normandy in 1137:[431]

Hoc anno rex Stephanus in Normanniam euectus nauigio est, ubi nihil memorabile fecit, nisi quod Roberto fratri imperatricis *insidias* parauit; et

---

[428] It has two distinctive Ce readings, 'sui defectione' regarding the eclipse of 1132 (correctly 1133), and the form 'Liuns' for Lyons-la-Forêt, in *HN* § 11.

[429] *Ann. Mon.*, ii. 48–53; William is identified as a source ibid., ii, p. xvi.

[430] 'Hic annus totus guerrae asperitate inhorruit', and the two following sentences, leading immediately to 'mediante legato factum est colloquium inter regem et imperatricem': *HN* § 36, 40; *Ann. Mon.*, ii. 52.

[431] *Ann. Mon.*, ii. 50–1.

ut eum cautius deciperet, *missa manu Hugonis Rothomagensis archiepiscopi in manu Roberti*, ipse rex amicitiam ei spondebat cum sacramento; sed hoc nec illi nec aliquibus aliis tenuit. Habebat itaque uterque suspectum alium; unde rege reuerso in Angliam, abnegauit ei comes homagium et fidelitatem, et amicitiam ab eo abscidit, et nuntio suo uerba plena odii atque discordiae mandauit. Hoc rex audito, fecit eum disseisiare de *omnibus* quae habebat *in Anglia* excepta Bristoa.

The affidation *in manu* alone is taken from the *HN*, but what has been supplied additionally is supplied with good sense. An original passage emphasizes the castle-building in 1138.[432] The Winchester annals give a straightforward account of the first phase of the civil war, the set pieces boiled down to their essentials, and all literary embellishment taken out. One reason for this taste for simplicity may have been that the author found the copy of the text of the *HN* that he was using difficult to read. The reference to Miles of Gloucester as *Milo subcomite* abbreviates a passage of text,[433] while the statement that the nine-year-old Henry arrived on his first visit in 1142 with 350 knights is almost certainly a misreading.[434]

In the mid-fourteenth century, the work of writing a general history was again taken up at Malmesbury, by one of the cloister monks, to relieve his boredom, 'because of the length of the lessons and the monotony of the prayers'. He entitled his work the *Eulogium historiarum*, and one of those eulogized was William of Malmesbury, whom he cited as an authority and sought to defend against criticism.[435] The *Eulogium* uses William's *GR* almost exclusively for its history of the Norman kings, and it uses the *HN* also.[436] It quotes the two paragraphs dealing with the empress's return to England, and the oaths sworn to her, almost

---

[432] *Ann. Mon.*, ii. 51.

[433] Robert of Gloucester and the empress came to England, 'susceptique sunt in Glocestria a Milone subcomite': *Ann. Mon.*, ii. 51; cf. 'recepit illam [the empress] postea in Gloucestram Milo qui castellum eiusdem urbis sub comite [Robert of Gloucester] habebat': *HN* § 31.

[434] Geoffrey of Anjou, 'occupatus circa multa misit pro se puerum Henricum filium suum cum cccl. militibus': *Ann. Mon.*, ii. 53; cf. 'filium suum ex imperatrice progenitum auunculo concessit in Angliam deducendum, cuius intuitu proceres . . . animarentur', where 'cuius intuitu' is possibly the passage misread: *HN* § 74.   [435] *Eulogium*, i. 3.

[436] This was noted by the editor, *Eulogium*, iii, pp. iv–vii, but the printed text does not distinguish the authorities used.

verbatim, which allows the text used to be identified as one of the B recension.[437] It then summarizes the entries concerning Henry I.[438] The date of Stephen's coronation is also taken from the *HN*,[439] but the story of his reign is not told, other than to say that this king was a usurper and had no peace in his time.[440] The use the monk made of the *HN* was thoroughly mechanical, and he even managed to get the earl of Gloucester's Christian name wrong.[441]

The most influential chronicler of the fourteenth century was Ranulf Higden, monk of Chester. He had been one of those who had taken issue with William of Malmesbury, for he found it hard to credit that early in the twelfth century Chester had been less well developed than it was in his day: 'he must have been dreaming' was the only explanation he could suggest.[442] Higden made extensive and intelligent use of both the *GR* and the *GP* in his *Polychronicon*.[443] His autograph manuscript, now in the Huntington Library, shows him late in life adding several passages from the *GR*, including a long section on the life of Henry I.[444] This interest in the *GR*, taken with the lack of material from the *HN*, might suggest that the copy of the *GR* that Higden used did not include the *HN*.

In the mid-fifteenth century, Thomas Rudborne, a monk of St Swithun's, Winchester, wrote a history of the church in his home city. This was later entitled, with reference to other works presumed to have been written by him, his *Historia major*.[445]

[437] *Eulogium*, iii. 59–61; *HN* §2, 3; for the identification of the recension see above, p. **.

[438] *Eulogium*, iii. 62–3; *HN* §4–5, 8–11, 13, 16.   [439] *Eulogium*, iii. 65; *HN* §15.

[440] *Eulogium*, iii. 65. The later material in the *HN* has, however, at least been glanced at, for the reference to Roger of Salisbury's castle at Malmesbury, 'a turri ecclesiae quantum est iactus lapidis', at *Eulogium*, iii. 61, picks up the phrase in *HN* §22, and the treatment of the earl of Gloucester and the count of Anjou, at *Eulogium*, iii. 65, seems to draw on *HN* §71 ff.

[441] In *Eulogium*, iii. 59, he leaves out the reference to the succession, which provides the context for the discussion; and, while the earl of Gloucester is introduced as Robert, ibid., p. 60, he is thereafter Henry, ibid., pp. 61, 65.

[442] *Polychronicon Ranulphi Higden Monachi Cestrensis*, ed. C. Babington and J. R. Lumby, 9 vols. (RS xli, 1865–86), ii. 78; Gransden, *Historical Writing*, ii. 50–2, 104.

[443] J. Taylor, *The Universal Chronicle of Ranulf Higden* (Oxford, 1966), pp. 62–3, 85–6.

[444] Ibid., pp. 82–3, 103, 175–6.

[445] A valuable discussion, noting the sources and the problems in their interpretation, is found in Gransden, *Historical Writing*, ii. 394–8, 493–4.

civ INTRODUCTION

What survives now of this work covers the period from AD 164 to 1141. The manuscripts break off in mid-sentence,[446] and it is clear that material has been lost, though how much can only be surmised.[447] Rudborne's prime interest was Winchester, but his work 'also includes much general history'.[448] In the *HN* he found a text in which the history of the nation seemed to revolve around Winchester, and the diocesan bishop, as papal legate, took a leading role. There was only one way to do justice to so material a text from so prestigious an authority: he copied out the lot.[449] He had other material to hand, in particular, for the period with which the *HN* is concerned, the *FH* of Matthew Paris. There is a measure of editing,[450] but for the most part the different authorities are laid end to end.[451] Thus when the story is broken off the king's supporters are mustering at Winchester in 1141, but the earl of Gloucester's capture, and his exchange for the king, which followed later in the year, had already been noted from Matthew Paris. The survival of a full text provides additional evidence that the Ce tradition did not originate from Winchester: Rudborne copied faithfully from an A text of the *HN*.[452]

---

[446] After 'preterea plures illorum': *HN* § 54.

[447] The two manuscripts are Lambeth Palace MS 183, and (copied from this) Cambridge, Corpus Christi College, MS 350: M. R. James and C. Jenkins, *A Descriptive Catalogue of the Manuscripts in the Library of Lambeth Palace* (Cambridge, 1930–2), pp. 286–7 (no. 183), and (more summarily), M. R. James, *A Descriptive Catalogue of the Manuscripts in the Library of Corpus Christi College, Cambridge*, 2 vols. (Cambridge, 1912), ii. 184 (no. 350).

[448] Gransden, *Historical Writing*, ii. 395.

[449] The only printed edition of the *Historia maior* is in *Anglia Sacra sive Collectio Historiarum de Archiepiscopis et Episcopis Anglie ad Annum 1540*, ed. H. Wharton, 2 vols. (London, 1691), i. 179–286. Wharton declined to transcribe material that Rudborne had copied verbatim from standard authorities, and for the *HN* he refers by folio and by line to the 1596 edition of Savile. These references indicate, and the manuscripts confirm, that Rudborne provides a full text of the *HN* up to the point when the manuscripts break off in the middle of § 54.

[450] The text of Stephen's 'charter of liberties' is copied at the end of § 14, when it is first mentioned, rather than in § 18, as in the *HN*. The material on the French monarchy is omitted in § 8, but not the long treatment of the papal schism of 1130 which is found in § 5–7.

[451] This was characteristic of his methodology. 'He names [his sources] meticulously, and often cites long passages *verbatim*': Gransden, *Historical Writing*, ii. 396.

[452] The manuscripts have not been fully collated towards this edition, but samples taken over the full range of surviving text invariably show AB rather than Ce readings, and A rather than B where the two diverge.

It was the work of the Tudor historians and bibliophiles to survey for the first time the full range of William of Malmesbury's work, to preserve texts as the great monastic libraries were dispersed, and finally to see his main historical works into print. William of Malmesbury's reputation came before him, but its basis was far from secure, and the survival of individual manuscripts remained significant even for a middle-ranking work such as the *HN*. The St Albans copy made for Roger of Wendover, and used by Matthew Paris, was now taken in hand and annotated by Polydore Vergil.[453] In his preparations for writing the history of England, the *Anglica historia*, Polydore Vergil surveyed the full range of earlier writers, and found them for the most part wanting, 'bald, uncouth, chaotic and deceitful'.[454] He exempted from these strictures Bede, 'than whom nothing more truthful could be found', William of Malmesbury, and Matthew Paris. Here was the Great Tradition of medieval historical scholarship, and in identifying it Polydore Vergil claimed a place within it. After the Norman Conquest, possibly following the pattern set in the *GR*, Polydore Vergil told the story of each reign in a single book. In his treatment of Stephen's reign, Polydore Vergil more than once indicates that he is drawing on a number of sources, and that at times their accounts differed.[455] Some passages hint at an awareness of the *HN*,[456] but it was not an important source for him, as were, for example, Henry of Huntingdon, directly or at second-hand,[457] and John of Worcester, who is used heavily in the account of the period with which the *HN* is concerned.[458]

[453] D. Hay, *Polydore Vergil: Renaissance Historian and Man of Letters* (Oxford, 1952), p. 86.

[454] Ibid., pp. 152–3, citing the dedication of the manuscript copy in the Vatican Library.

[455] Polydore Vergil, *Anglicae Historiae* (Basle, 1555), where Stephen's reign is book xii, pp. 197–210: *cuncti Anglici testantur annales*, p. 198 ll. 20–1; *hic non consentiunt scriptores*, p. 202 l. 41.

[456] The introduction of Stephen as Henry I's *nepos ex sorore Adela* (*Anglicae Historiae*, p. 197 l. 5), uses the same phrase as the *HN* § 3; the treatment of 'the arrest of the bishops' is placed in the context of reports of the empress being about to land (*Anglicae Historiae*, p. 201 l. 46), as in the *HN* § 22; and when she does land, although some said that Matilda brought a great army with her into England, *alii scribunt, quibus cum magis stamus, eam cum parua manu uenisse* (*Anglicae Historiae*, p. 202 ll. 44–5), as in the *HN* § 31.

[457] The description of Stephen's 'charter of liberties' (*Anglicae Historiae*, p. 197 ll. 29–34), as in HH, pp. 704–5.

[458] The statement that Stephen took 40,000 marks from the treasure of Roger of

The final, and a significant, stage in the pre-publication history of the *GR* and the *HN* comes in the work of Matthew Parker, 'a mighty collector of books'.[459] Parker had in his hands, at one time or another, at least three copies of the *GR*, and he knew of at least four others. He 'not only collected manuscripts but used them: reading, cross-referencing, and commenting upon them'.[460] He knew that the *HN* was a work distinct from the *GR*, and he believed that a proper library of William of Malmesbury's historical works should contain both these texts, as well as the *GP*. His scholarship is seen most clearly in two related manuscripts which he presented in 1574 to the University Library at Cambridge, where they are MSS Ff. 1. 25 and Ii. 2. 3.[461] MS Ii. 2. 3 was a good twelfth-century copy of the *GR*, which left his hands largely as he found it, save that he supplied unnecessarily a copy of the prefatory letter to Robert of Gloucester.[462] The core of MS Ff. 1. 25 was an early copy of the first four books of the *GP*; to this were added on supply leaves the final book of the *GP*, the Life of Aldhelm, and the *HN*, from a manuscript in the possession of John Whitgift.[463] Parker had two other copies of the *GR*, neither of which originally contained the *HN*. One copy had the *HN* supplied, and came eventually to Trinity College, Cambridge;[464]

Salisbury (*Anglicae Historiae*, p. 202 l. 10), is from the 'Gloucester' text of John of Worcester (JW iii. 258–9), while the account of the empress (*ipsa Augusta*) in 1141 (*Anglicae Historiae*, p. 204 ll. 11–23), relies heavily on the same source (JW iii. 294–7).

[459] J. Strype, *The Life and Acts of Matthew Parker* (London, 1711), p. 535; McKisack, *Medieval History in the Tudor Age*, pp. 26–49; R. I. Page, *Matthew Parker and his Books* (Kalamazoo, Mich., 1993).

[460] Page, *Matthew Parker and his Books*, p. 55.

[461] A common feature of the two volumes is that they contain illuminated initials incorporating Parker's arms as archbishop: J. C. T. Oates, *Cambridge University Library: A History*, [i:] *from the Beginnings to the Copyright Act of Queen Anne* (Cambridge, 1986), pp. 97–108, at 108.

[462] Stubbs, i, pp. lxxxvi–lxxxvii (MS Cs). The letter does not occur in A manuscripts; it occurs at the beginning of book i in B manuscripts; and at the end of book iii in C manuscripts: ibid., ii, p. 355 n. 1. It is 'supplied in a Parkerian hand' to Trinity College, MS R. 7. 10 (Ms At): James, *The Western Manuscripts in the Library of Trinity College, Cambridge*, ii. 224–5 (no. 748). The only B text that can be associated with Parker's circle is Trinity College, MS R. 5. 34, on which see further below, n. 464.

[463] *A Catalogue of the Manuscripts Preserved in the Library of the University of Cambridge*, ii, pp. 315–18.

[464] Trinity College, Cambridge, MS R. 5. 34. It was a gift of Whitgift, and had formerly been in the library of John Parker: James, *The Western Manuscripts in the Library of Trinity College, Cambridge*, no. 725, ii. 203–4; S. Strongman, 'John Parker's manuscripts: An

the other, which contains a note in the archbishop's own hand that the *HN* was lacking, may have been intended for Corpus Christi College, Cambridge.[465] Another text known to Parker and his circle was a comparatively ordinary thirteenth-century copy of the *GR* and the *HN*, which came to Trinity College, Cambridge from Thomas Nevile.[466] This has been identified as the chief source of the first printed edition, that of Savile in 1596.[467] If Savile chose this from among a number of copies, and variant readings show that he knew of at least one other, it can only have been for its legibility. After the uncertainty as to whether the *HN* was book vi of the *GR*, or a separate work in three books, it appeared in print for the first time as a separate work in two books.

VII. EDITORIAL PRINCIPLES

It was established by Mynors, following the work of Stubbs, that there are two main stages of the text, AB and Ce. It has been argued above that these two stages represent two distinct editions of the text, that Ce is definitely later than AB, and that only AB is text from the distinctive pen of William of Malmesbury. It follows that the AB text should provide the basis of the present edition. It is printed in full, in normal type, with the book divisions in capitals. All the variant readings of Ce—i.e. where Ce^1 and Ce^2 agree[468]—are printed in the apparatus. In the English translation some of the Ce readings have been included in square brackets. This has been done with all new material, ranging in length from

edition of the lists in Lambeth Palace MS 737', *Trans. of Cambridge Bibliographical Soc.*, vii (1) (1977), 1–27, at p. 15.

[465] Princeton University, Scheide MS 159, formerly Phillipps MS 26641, whence cited by Stubbs, in *GR*, i, pp. lxxiv–lxxv (MS Aa³). On this see C. T. Berkhout, 'The Parkerian legacy of a Scheide manuscript: William of Malmesbury's *Gesta regum Anglorum*', *Princeton University Library Chronicle*, lv (1994), 277–86, illustrating Parker's annotation at p. 283.

[466] Trinity College, Cambridge, MS R. 7. 1; James, *The Western Manuscripts in the Library of Trinity College, Cambridge*, no. 739, ii, pp. 215–16.

[467] Mynors, p. xl; McKisack, *Medieval History in the Tudor Age*, pp. 64–5; and see further above, p. lxxvi.

[468] On a number of occasions the Ce^1 text printed by Stubbs and Mynors was not confirmed by Ce^2, which had the same reading as AB. These are not noted in the present edition. The text of Ce^2 is missing between §47 and §74, and in the absence of this check all Ce^1 readings have been given, even though some of them are manifestly corrupt.

the short paragraph dealing with events late in 1140 to individual words (such as the substitution of 'burgesses' for 'citizens'). It has not been done in any case where the change may result from a corruption of the text, or where the changes seem to be more of emphasis than of fact or judgement. The most difficult decision has been on how to treat the Ce rubrics. These are significant, but also highly intrusive. They appear, with all the other Ce readings, in the apparatus to the Latin text, but they have been excluded from the English translation, on the grounds that they represent highlighting or changes in emphasis rather than new material. The net effect of these decisions will be to leave a text that looks unfamiliar, and possibly a little austere, to readers who are familiar with the Stubbs and the Mynors–Potter editions. The intention is to confront the reader with William of Malmesbury's own text.

Within the three books the main subdivisions of the text are the paragraphs. The stripping-out of the rubrics from the main text allows a fresh view to be taken of the paragraphing. Here the main traditions show some variation, and particularly in book iii it is difficult to feel that these represent the author's final view. And so they have been revised, some of the longer paragraphs being split up, and some of the shorter amalgamated. These changes do not make much difference overall: Stubbs, followed exactly by Mynors, had seventy-five paragraphs, while this edition has seventy-nine paragraphs. The *HN* is, however, a distinct work, and so there is no reason for the paragraphs to be numbered consecutively on from the *GR*. The first paragraph in this edition is, therefore, no. 1, not no. 450; but for convenience of reference the RS and NMT paragraphing and numbering is indicated in the margin of the Latin text.

Within the AB text—i.e. the textual tradition that excludes the distinctive voice of Ce—there are additional variations as between A and B, mainly in the forms of individual words, sometimes in word order. Neither of the two traditions is manifestly superior, and each case has been considered on its merits. The concordances to William of Malmesbury's usage in the *GR* and the *GP* have been invaluable here, and might have helped produce a definitive text in more experienced hands. The *GP* is particularly useful in

attempting to establish the forms of place- and personal names. Here the earliest manuscripts, which are of the A recension, correspond most closely to the usage of *GP*. A single form of each place- and personal name has been chosen on this basis, and is used throughout, no variants being noted. On the basis of the *GP* autograph also, the editors of the OMT edition of the *GR* have been able to establish William of Malmesbury's orthography.[469] I have attempted to follow this.

---

[469] *GR*, i, pp. xxvi–xxviii.

SIGLA

THE '1st EDITION'

Ag Oxford, Bodleian Library, MS Laud Misc. 548
Ao Oxford, All Souls College, MS 35
At Cambridge, Trinity College, MS R. 7. 10
A agreement of Ag, Ao, At

Bc London, BL., Royal MS 13. B. xix
Bk Oxford, Bodleian Library, Bodley MS 712
Bq Cambridge, Trinity College, MS R. 7. 1
B agreement of Bc, Bk, Bq

Cd London, BL, Royal MS 13. D. v

AB agreement of A, B, Cd

THE '2nd EDITION'

Ce^1 London, BL, Royal MS 13. D. ii
Ce^2 London, BL, Additional MS 38129

1. BL, Royal MS 13. D. v (Cd), fo. 132ᵛ: *GR* §449, *HN* prologue and § 1, 2. This manuscript, made for St Albans Abbey and used by Matthew Paris, sees the *HN* as book vi of the *GR*: see above, pp. lxxiii–lxxiv.

2. Bodleian Library, MS Laud Misc. 548 (Ag), fo. 200ᵛ: *HN* § 21, 22. A space has been left for rubrication to mark the division of the books, here between book i and book ii: see above, p. lxix.

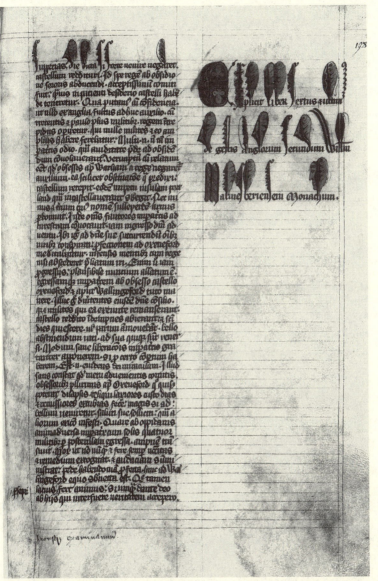

3. Bodleian Library, MS Bodley 712 (Bk), fo. 198^r: *HN* §77–79. The conclusion of the *HN*, in a volume made in the mid-fourteenth century, has an ornate *explicit*, which identifies the *HN* as book vi of the *GR*: see above, p. lxxii.

4. BL, Royal MS 13. D. ii (Ce¹) fo. 123ᵛ: *HN* §75–79. The conclusion of the text in the Margam Abbey copy of the *HN*, which may have been abbreviated so as not to overrun this folio: see above, pp. lxxxviii–lxxxix.

TEXT AND TRANSLATION

PROLOGVS

Domino amantissimo Rotberto filio regis Henrici et consuli Gloecestrensi, Willelmus bibliothecarius Malmesberiae, post emerita trophea in terris triumphare in caelis. Pleraque gestorum precellentis memoriae patris uestri stilo opponere non neglexi, et in quinto libro regalium actuum*a* et in tribus libellis quibus Cronica dedi uocabulum. Nunc ea quae moderno tempore magno miraculo Dei acciderunt in Anglia, ut mandentur posteris, desiderat animus uestrae serenitatis. Pulcherrimum plane*b* desiderium, et uestrorum omnium simile. Quid enim plus ad honestatis spectat commodum, quid magis conducit*c* aequitati, quam diuinam *d*agnoscere circa bonos*d* indulgentiam, et erga peruersos*e* uindictam? Quid porro iocundius quam fortium facta uirorum monimentis tradere litterarum,[1] quorum exemplo ceteri exuant ignauiam, et ad defendendam armentur patriam? Quod quia offitio stili mei preceptum est fieri, ordinatius puto posse historiam transigi, si paulo altius repetens a reditu imperatricis in Angliam post uiri*f* decessum seriem *g*contexam annorum.*g* Itaque primo uocata *h*in auxilium ut decet*h* Diuinitate, rerum ueritatem scripturus, nichilque offense daturus aut gratiae, ita incipiam.

a om. B   *b* plene B   *c* conducibilius Ce   *d-d* circa bonos agnoscere A
e periuros Ce   *f* sui add. Ce   *g-g* annorum contexam Ce   *h-h* ut decet in auxilium Ce

PROLOGUE

To his well-beloved lord Robert, son of King Henry and earl of Gloucester, William the librarian of Malmesbury sends the wish that he may triumph in heaven when he has ended his victories on earth. Most of the achievements of your father of illustrious memory I have not failed to set down, both in the fifth book of the *Deeds of the Kings* and in the three little books to which I have given the name of *Chronicles*. Now your highness's mind desires the transmission to posterity of those things that, by a wonderful dispensation of God, have happened in England in recent times: indeed a very noble desire, and like everything in you. For what is more to the advantage of virtue or more conducive to justice than recognizing the divine pleasure in the good and punishment of those who have gone astray [**Ce** perjurers]? Further, what is more pleasant than consigning to historical record the deeds of brave men,[1] so that following their example the others may cast off cowardice and arm themselves to defend their country? And since I am bidden to do this by the service of my pen, I think the history may be related in more orderly sequence if I go a little further back and open my annals with the empress's return to England after her husband's death. Therefore, first, as is fitting, calling God to my aid and intending to write the truth of things without any concession to dislike or favour, thus will I begin.

---

[1] Virgil, *Aen.* x. 369; Bede, *HE*, prologue.

LIBER PRIMVS

450 1.[a] Anno Henrici regis Anglorum uicesimo sexto, qui fuit incarnationis Dominicae millesimus centesimus uicesimus sextus, Henricus imperator Alemannorum, cui prefati regis filia Mathildis nupserat, in ipso aetatis et uictoriarum flore obiit.[b][2] Morabatur eo tempore rex noster Normanniae, ad[c] pacificandos si qui in his partibus fierent motus. Qui, ubi primum obitum generi accepit, non multo post honoratis uiris a se missis filiam reuocauit. Inuita ut aiunt imperatrix rediit, quod dotalibus regionibus consueta esset, et multas ibidem possessiones haberet.[3] Constat certe aliquos Lotharingorum et Longobardorum principes succedentibus annis plus quam semel Angliam uenisse, ut eam sibi dominam requirerent, sed[d] fructu laborum caruisse,[4] cogitante rege ut filiae conubio inter se et Andegauensem comitem pacem componeret. Mirum enim in modum uir ille, omnium regum quos nostra et etiam patrum nostrorum tenet memoria maximus, suspectam tamen semper habuit Andegauensium potentiam. Hinc est quod sponsalitia quae Willelmus nepos suus, comes postea Flandriae, cum filia comitis Andegauensis Fulconis, postea regis Ierosolimorum, contracturus esse dicebatur,[e] dissoluit et cassauit.[5] Hinc est quod aliam eiusdem filiam filio suo Willelmo impubi uixdum adolescenti coniunxit.[6] Hinc est quod hanc filiam

[a] *Rubric* Quibus de causis imperatricem rex Henricus ab Alemannia reuocauerit *Ce*   [b] obierat uel obiit *A*   [c] ob *Ce*   [d] ueruntamen *Ce*   [e] uidebatur *Ce*

[2] Henry V, emperor of Germany, was born 11 Aug. 1086, married Matilda on 7 Jan. 1114, and died at Utrecht on 23 May 1125: *Frutolfs und Ekkehards Chroniken und die Anonyme Kaiserchronik*, ed. F. J. Schmale and I. Schmale-Ott (Darmstadt, 1972), pp. 262–3 (marriage), 374–5 (death); OV v. 200–1 (marriage), vi. 360–1 (death).

[3] According to Orderic, the empress 'preferred to live among her own people though she was greatly loved abroad': OV v. 200–1.

[4] Robert of Torigni confirms this, saying that 'the eminent princes of the Roman court . . . followed her to her father's court making this petition': *GND* ii. 240–1; also RT i. 173, and discussion in Chibnall, *Matilda*, pp. 43–4.

[5] William Clito, son of Robert of Normandy, born 25 Oct. 1102 (Hollister, *Anglo-Norman World*, p. 92 n. 6), elected count of Flanders 23 Mar. 1127, died 27 or 28 July 1128 (F. Vercauteren, *Actes des comtes de Flandre 1071–1128* (Brussels, 1938), p. xix). He

BOOK I

1. In the twenty-sixth year of Henry, king of England, which was the year of the Lord's incarnation 1126, Henry, emperor of Germany, whom the aforesaid king's daughter Matilda had married, died in the very flower of his age and victories.[2] At that time our king was staying in Normandy, to calm any disturbances that might arise in those regions. On hearing of his son-in-law's death, he not long afterwards sent men of distinction and called his daughter home. The empress, they say, was reluctant to return, because she had grown accustomed to the lands into which she was married, and had many possessions in them.[3] At any rate there is no doubt that some princes of the Lombards and Lotharingians came to England more than once in the following years to ask for her as their lady; but they gained nothing by their efforts,[4] the king being minded to establish peace between himself and the count of Anjou by his daughter's marriage. For strangely enough that great man, though the mightiest of all kings in our recollection or that of our fathers, yet always regarded the power of the Angevins with suspicion. For this reason he broke off and brought to nothing the alliance that William, his nephew, afterwards count of Flanders, was said to be about to contract with the daughter of Fulk, count of Anjou, afterwards king of Jerusalem.[5] For this reason he married another daughter of that same count to his own son William, who was then a mere boy, hardly yet a youth.[6] For this reason he married this daughter of his own, of

married Sibyl the daughter of Fulk of Anjou in 1123. Henry I's diplomacy secured the marriage's annulment, announced in a papal bull dated 26 Aug. 1124, and confirmed after appeal in the following year: OV vi. 164–7, 332–3; Chartrou, *Anjou*, pp. 16–18, 174–5; *Councils and Synods*, i (2), pp. 730–2; S. B. Hicks, 'The Anglo-papal bargain of 1125: The legatine mission of John of Crema', *Albion*, viii (1976), 301–10.

[6] William was born in 1103, was betrothed to Matilda the daughter of Fulk of Anjou in Feb. 1113, and married her at Lisieux in June 1119, the year before his death in the *White Ship*. In writing of William as 'impubis' William of Malmesbury is thinking of him (and echoing the language which he used of him) at the time of his betrothal: *GR* §419. The marriage is referred to in *ASC* E, s.a. 1119; JW iii. 144–5; OV vi. 224–5; Suger, pp. 194–7; SD ii. 257–8; *Chroniques des comtes d'Anjou et des seigneurs d'Amboise*, ed. L. Halphen and

suam, de qua incepimus loqui, post imperatorium thorum, eiusdem Fulconis filio nuptum collocauit, sicut sermo procedens dicere perget.[7]

451   2.[a] Anno uicesimo septimo regni sui, rex Henricus Angliam uenit mense Septembri, adducens secum filiam suam.[8] Proximo uero Natali Domini conuocato apud Lundoniam magno cleri et optimatum numero,[9] uxori suae, filiae ducis Louannensis,[10] quam post obitum Mathildis duxerat, comitatum Salopesberiae dedit.[11] Quam uidelicet feminam dolens non concipere, dum et perpetuo sterilem fore timeret, de successore regni merito anxius cogitabat. De qua re antea multum diuque deliberato[b] consilio, tunc in eodem concilio omnes totius Angliae optimates, episcopos etiam et abbates, sacramento adegit et obstrinxit, ut, si ipse sine herede masculo decederet, Mathildam filiam suam quondam imperatricem incunctanter et sine ulla retractatione[c] dominam reciperent.[d] Prefatus quanto dampno[e] patriae fortuna Willelmum filium[f] sibi surripuisset, cui iure regnum competeret. Nunc superesse filiam, cui soli legitima debeatur successio, ab auo, auunculo, et patre regibus;[g] a materno genere, multis retro seculis. Siquidem ab Egbirhto rege[h] Westsaxonum, qui primus ceteros insulae reges uel expulit uel subegit, anno Dominicae incarnationis octingentesimo, sub quattuordecim regibus, usque ad eiusdem incarnationis annum millesimum quadragesimum tertium, quo rex Eduardus [i]qui apud Westmonasterium iacet[i] in regnum sullimatus est, nec umquam eiusdem regalis sanguinis linea defecit, nec in successione regni claudicauit. Porro Eduardus illius progeniei ultimus, idemque et preclarissimus, proneptem suam Margaretam ex fratre

---

[a] *Rubric* De concilio habito Londoniis *Ce*[1]   [b] considerato *ACe*, desiderato *Cd*   [c] retractione *AgAtB*   [d] susciperent *ACe*   [e] incommodo *Ce*   [f] suum *add. B*   [g] et *add. B*   [h] *om. B*   [i-i] *om. Ce*

R. Poupardin (Paris, 1913), p. 161; Chartrou, *Anjou*, p. 13; C. W. Hollister and T. K. Keefe, 'The making of the Angevin Empire', in Hollister, *Anglo-Norman World*, pp. 247–71, at 254–6.

[7] *HN* §3.

[8] 11 Sept. 1126 (SD ii. 281); 'between 8 Sept. and 29 Sept. [Michaelmas]' (*ASC* E, s.a. 1126); 'about Michaelmas' (HH, pp. 476–7).

[9] The court met at Windsor at Christmas 1126, and then transferred to London where the oaths were sworn on 1 Jan. 1127: JW iii. 166–7; SD ii. 281; Hugh the Chanter,

whom I have begun to speak, to the son of that same Fulk after she
had been married to the Emperor, as the narrative will relate in
due course.[7]

2. In the twenty-seventh year of his reign King Henry came to
England in the month of September, bringing his daughter with
him.[8] Next Christmas, summoning a great number of the clergy
and nobility to London,[9] he gave to his wife, the daughter of the
duke of Louvain,[10] whom he had married after Matilda's death,
the county of Shropshire.[11] In grief that the woman did not
conceive, and fearing that she would always be barren, he was,
with good cause, thinking anxiously about the successor to his
throne. After deliberating long and deeply on this matter he then,
at this same council, bound the nobles of all England, also the
bishops and abbots, by the obligation of an oath that, if he himself
died without a male heir, they would immediately and without
hesitation accept his daughter Matilda, formerly empress, as their
lady. He said first what a disaster [**Ce** an inconvenience] it had
been for the country that fortune had deprived him of his son
William, who would have claimed the kingdom as of right. As it
was, he said, his daughter remained, in whom alone lay the
legitimate succession, since her grandfather, uncle and father
had been kings, while on her mother's side the royal lineage
went back for many centuries. And furthermore from Ecgberht,
king of Wessex, who first drove out or subdued the other kings of
the island, in the year of the Lord's Incarnation 800, through
fourteen kings, up to the year of His Incarnation 1043, when King
Edward who lies at Westminster was raised to the throne, the line of
that same royal blood never failed or suffered impediment in
succession to the monarchy. Then Edward, last and most illustrious
of that race, married his great-niece Margaret, descended from his

pp. 218–19; the *Anglo-Saxon Chronicle* refers to Windsor only (*ASC* E, s.a. 1126); Round,
Geoffrey, p. 31.
   [10] Adeliza, daughter of Godfrey VII, count of Louvain, married (first), on 29 Jan. 1121,
Henry I (d. 1135), (second), in 1138, William d'Aubigny (by whom she had children), d.
23 Apr. 1151: *Handbook of Chronology*, p. 35; *CP* i. 233–5.
   [11] This was a grant not of the earldom but the 'comitatus' of Shropshire, the king's
lands and rights in the county, and the income therefrom: P. Latimer, 'Grants of "Totus
Comitatus" in twelfth-century England: their origins and meaning', *Bulletin of the Institute
of Historical Research*, lix (1986), 137–45 at p. 140; *VCH Shropshire*, iii. 10–11.

Edmundo Ireneside Malcolmi regis Scottorum nuptiis copulauit.[12]
Quorum *filia Mathildis huius imperatricis mater extitit.*[13]

452 3.[b] Iurauerunt ergo cuncti, quicumque in eodem concilio alicuius
uiderentur[c] esse momenti. Primo Willelmus Cantuariae archiepiscopus,[14] mox ceteri episcopi, nec minus abbates. Laicorum primus
iurauit Dauid rex Scottiae, eiusdem imperatricis auunculus.[15]
Tunc Stephanus *comes Moritonii*[d] et Bononiae, nepos Henrici
regis ex sorore Adala.[16] Mox Rotbertus filius regis, quem ante
regnum susceperat, et comitem Gloecestriae fecerat.[e][17] Notabile
fuit ut fertur[f] certamen inter Rotbertum et Stephanum, dum
emula laude uirtutum inter se contenderent quis eorum prior
iuraret, illo priuilegium filii, isto dignitatem nepotis spectante.[19]
Ita obstrictis[g] omnibus fide et sacramento,[20] tunc quidem a
quoque in sua discessum est. Post Pentecosten uero misit rex
filiam suam[h] in Normanniam, iubens eam per Rotomagensem
archiepiscopum desponsari filio predicti Fulconis,[21] adolescenti

---

[a] filiam fuisse Matildem huius imperatricis matrem constat *Ce*   [b] *Rubric* De
sacramento quod primates Anglie fecerunt imperatrici *Ce*   [c] uidentur *A*
[d-d] Moritonii comes *B*   [e] data ei in matrimonium Mabilia, spectabili et excellenti
femina, domina tum uiro morigera, tum etiam fecunditate numerose et pulcherrime prolis
beata *add. Ce*   [f-f] ut dicitur fuit *Ce*   [g] proceribus *add. Ce*   [h] *om. Ce*

---

[12] Margaret of Scotland, granddaughter of Edmund Ironside, born 1046, married 1069
Malcolm III, king of Scots, died 1093, canonized *c.*1249: D. H. Farmer, *The Oxford
Dictionary of Saints* (Oxford, 1978), pp. 262–3; D. Baker, ' "A nursery of saints": St
Margaret of Scotland reconsidered', *Medieval Women*, ed. D. Baker (Studies in Church
History. Subsidia i; Oxford, 1978), pp. 119–41. Her sanctity and lineage were emphasized
by William in *GR* §228, 418 ('ex antiqua et illustri regum stirpe'), and in his dedicatory
letter to David, king of Scots (*GR*, epistola i. 2: 'antecessorum uestrorum prosapiam'); as
also by Orderic (OV iv. 272–3) and Robert of Torigni (*GND* ii. 240–3, drawing on the *Vita
Margaretae*, ibid., i, pp. lxxxvii–lxxxviii, on which see L. L. Huneycutt, 'The idea of the
perfect princess: The *Life of St Margaret* in the reign of Matilda II (1100–1118)', *ANS*, xii
(1990), 81–97).
[13] Edith-Matilda, born *c.*1080, married to Henry I on 11 Nov. 1100, died 1 May 1118:
Handbook of Chronology, p. 35.
[14] William of Corbeil, archbishop of Canterbury 1123–36: *Fasti*, ed. Greenway, ii. 4; D.
Bethell, 'William of Corbeil and the Canterbury York dispute', *Journal of Ecclesiastical
History*, xix (1968), 145–59; for the king's benevolence to the archbishop at the time of the
council, see Hollister, *Anglo-Norman World*, pp. 159–60.
[15] David, son of Malcolm III and Margaret of Scotland, was born *c.*1085, became king
of Scots in 1124, and died in 1153: *Handbook of Chronology*, p. 57; J. A. Green, 'David I
and Henry I', *Scottish Historical Review*, lxxv (1996), 1–19.
[16] Adela, daughter of William the Conqueror, born 1067, married Stephen count of
Blois (d. 1102) *c.*1081, died 8 Mar. 1137: *GND* ii. 262–3; K. A. LoPrete, 'The Anglo-

brother Edmund Ironside, to Malcolm, king of Scots.[12] [Ce It is well known that] Matilda, the mother of this empress, was their daughter.[13]

3. So all in that council took the oath who were regarded as carrying any weight. First William, archbishop of Canterbury,[14] then the other bishops, and lastly the abbots. Of the laity David, king of Scots, the empress's uncle,[15] swore first; next Stephen, count of Mortain and Boulogne, King Henry's nephew by his sister Adela;[16] then Robert the king's son, whom he had recognized as his before he came to the throne and made earl of Gloucester[17] [Ce *adds* giving him to wife Mabel, a lovely and noble woman, a lady who was both obedient to her husband and blessed in being the mother of numerous and very fair offspring].[18] There was a noteworthy contest, it is said, between Robert and Stephen, who as rivals in distinction strove with each other for the honour of swearing first, the one claiming the prerogative of a son, the other the rank of a nephew.[19] When all [Ce the chief] men had thus been bound by faith and oath they departed, each to his own home.[20] After Whitsuntide the king sent his daughter to Normandy with orders that she be betrothed by the archbishop of Rouen to the son of the aforesaid Fulk,[21] a young man of very high

---

Norman card of Adela of Blois', *Albion*, xxii (1990), 569–89. Stephen was their third surviving son, born in the early 1090s; on his tenure of the counties of Mortain and Boulogne, see further below, *HN* § 53.

[17] Robert was named by Robert of Torigni as the eldest of Henry's illegitimate children (*GND* ii. 248–9; *CP* xi, App. D, pp. 105–6); he was made earl of Gloucester in 1121 or 1122 (Round, *Geoffrey*, pp. 420–36; *CP* v. 683–6).

[18] Mabel, the daughter of Robert Fitz Hamon, married Robert between 1107 when her father died and 1113/14: *Gloucester Charters*, pp. 151–2. Robert of Torigni says that they had five sons and one daughter: *GND* ii. 248–9; for their names, *CP* v. 686.

[19] John of Worcester states that Robert, sitting at the king's left, gave precedence to Stephen, who sat on the king's right, he being the elder: JW iii. 178–9. William of Malmesbury states in his 'recapitulation' that Robert swore first: *HN* § 61.

[20] The *Anglo-Saxon Chronicle* says the oath was sworn by 'archbishops, bishops, abbots, earls and all those thegns present' (*ASC* E, s.a. 1127); John of Worcester refers to the archbishop of Canterbury, the bishops 'Anglice regionis', and 'principibus terre ipsius' (JW iii. 166–7); Symeon of Durham notes the clergy, David, king of Scots, and 'comites et barones totius Anglie' (SD ii. 281).

[21] The empress leaving for Normandy after Whitsun (22 May) is confirmed by Henry of Huntingdon (HH, pp. 476–7); she was accompanied by Robert of Gloucester and Brian Fitz Count (*ASC* E, s.a. 1127); and was betrothed at Rouen at a date unrecorded in the summer of 1127 (Chartrou, *Anjou*, pp. 21–2).

magnae nobilitatis et predicandi roboris.[22] Nec distulit quin ipse
quoque Normanniam nauigaret, eosque matrimonio coniungeret.[23]
Quo facto, quodam uaticinio omnes predicabant ut post mortem
eius a sacramento desciscerent. Ego Rogerium Salesberiensem
episcopum sepe *audiui dicentem,*[a] [24] solutum se a[b] sacramento
quod imperatrici fecerat. Eo enim pacto se iurasse, ne rex preter
consilium suum et ceterorum procerum filiam cuiquam nuptum
daret extra regnum. Eius matrimonii nullum auctorem, nullum
fuisse conscium, nisi Rotbertum comitem Gloecestriae, et Bria-
num filium comitis,[25] et episcopum Luxouiensem.[26] Nec uero haec
iccirco dixerim quod credam uera fuisse uerba hominis, qui se
unicuique tempori pro uolubilitate fortunae accommodare nosset;
sed sicut uerax historicus opinionem prouintialium scriptis
appono.

453 4.[c] Reliquos annos uitae et regni Henrici[d] breuiter percensere libet,
ut nec rerum cognitione fraudenter posteri, nec in[e] his quae minus
ad hanc historiam pertinent prolixus[f] immorari uidear. Anno
uicesimo octauo rediit in Angliam [g]rex a Normannia.[g] [27] Anno
uicesimo nono quiddam accidit in Anglia quod mirum uideatur
crinitis nostris, qui, obliti quod[h] nati sunt, [i]in muliebris sexus
habitum capillorum longitudine se ipsos[i] transformant. Quidam
prouintialium militum, magno crinium luxu superbiens, conscien-
tiaque stimulante perterritus, uisus est sibi uidere in somnis quasi
aliquis eum capillorum suorum criniculis suffocaret. Quare,
somno excussus,[28] quicquid superfluebat comarum cito abscidit.
Concurrit exemplum per Angliam, et, sicut recens pena mentem

a–a dicentem audiui *Ce*   *b* om. *Ce*   *c* *Rubrics* De obitu Honorii pape et de
contentione eligendi apostolici *Ce¹*, De obitu Honorii pape *Ce²*   *d* regis *add. Ce*
e om. *Ce*   *f* prolixius *Ce*   *g–g* a Normannia rex *BcBqCd*   *h* quid
Ce   *i–i* libenter se in muliebris sexus habitum *Ce*

²² Geoffrey, son of Fulk V, count of Anjou, born 1113, count of Anjou 1129, duke of
Normandy 1144, died 14 Sept. 1151. The reference to the count's 'high birth' was
intended to counter any suggestion of disparagement in the empress's marriage, 'post
imperatorium thorum' (*HN* § 1), to the son of a count; see further *GND* i, p. lxxxviii, and
Chibnall, *Matilda*, p. 55.
²³ Henry left for Normandy on 26 Aug. 1127 (SD ii. 282; 'in August', HH, pp. 476–7),
and the marriage was on 17 June 1128 (Chartrou, *Anjou*, pp. 21–2).
²⁴ Roger, bishop of Salisbury 1102–39; on his career, see below, *HN* § 33–4.

birth and remarkable strength.[22] He did not delay sailing to
Normandy himself and joining them in matrimony.[23] When this
had been done all men began to assert, as though by some
prophetic spirit, that after his death they would fail to keep
their oath. I myself have often heard Roger, bishop of Salisbury,[24]
saying that he was released from the oath he had taken to the
empress, because he had sworn only on condition that the king
should not give his daughter in marriage to anyone outside the
kingdom without consulting himself and the other chief men, and
that no one had been involved in arranging that marriage, or had
been aware that it would take place, except Robert, earl of
Gloucester, and Brian Fitz Count,[25] and the bishop of Lisieux.[26]
In saying this I would not wish it to be thought that I accepted the
word of a man who knew how to adapt himself to any occasion
according as the wheel of fortune turned; I merely, like a faithful
historian, add to my narrative what was thought by people in my
part of the country.

4. I wish to review the remaining years of Henry's life and reign in
brief, so that posterity may not be deprived of the knowledge of
events, and yet I may not appear to dwell too long on matters
irrelevant to this history. In the twenty-eighth year of his reign the
king returned from Normandy to England.[27] In the twenty-ninth
year something occurred in England that may cause wonder to our
long-haired friends who, forgetting what they were born, grow
their hair long and make themselves look like women. One of the
knights of the provinces, proud of his very luxuriant hair but
alarmed by the stings of conscience, imagined in his sleep that he
saw someone strangling him with his own tresses. And so, on
waking up,[28] he promptly cut off all the excess of hair. Word of
this quickly made its way through England, and, as a penalty just

[25] Brian Fitz Count was son of Alan Fergant, count of Brittany. For an outline of his
career, see J. H. Round in *Dictionary of National Biography*; Green, *Henry I*, pp. 247–8.
[26] John, bishop of Lisieux (1107–41), served under Henry I as the head of the Norman
administration: OV vi. 142–5; Haskins, pp. 87–100; and for his family, *The Letters of
Arnulf of Lisieux*, ed. F. Barlow (Camden Soc., 3rd ser. lxi, 1939), pp. xi–xxv.
[27] Henry returned to England on 15 July 1129 (i.e. towards the end of his twenty-ninth
year): SD ii. 283; 'in July', JW iii. 186–7; 'in autumn', *ASC* E, s.a. 1129.
[28] Ovid, *Fasti*, i. 547.

mouere solet, omnes pene milites ad iustum*a* modum crines suos recidi equanimiter tulerunt. Sed non *b*diu stetit*b* haec sanctitas. Vix enim*c* anno elapso, cuncti, qui sibi curiales esse uidebantur, in prius uitium reciderunt. Longitudine capillorum cum feminis certabant, et, ubi crines deficiunt, inuolucra quaedam innodabant, obliti uel potius ignari sententiae apostolicae, 'Vir si comam nutrierit, ignominia est illi'.[29]

5. Anno tricesimo rex Henricus transiit in Normanniam.[30] Eo anno defuncto papa Honorio magna contentione eligendi apostolici Romana fluctuauit aecclesia.[31] Erant tunc in eadem urbe duo famosissimi cardinales, Gregorius diaconus sancti Angeli,[32] et Petrus presbiter cardinalis filius Leonis Romanorum principis.[33] Ambo litteris et industria insignes; nec erat facile discernere populo quisnam eorum iustius eligeretur a clero. Preuenit tamen pars quae fauebat Gregorio ut pontifex ordinatus uocaretur Innocentius. Sparsus est etiam rumor in plebem quod adhuc Honorius spiraret, et ita fieri preciperet. Auctores fuerunt huius ordinationis Willelmus Prenestinus episcopus,[34] Matheus Albanensis,[35] Cuonradus Sabinensis,[36] Iohannes Hostiensis,[37] Petrus Cremensis de titulo sancti Crisogoni,[38] Haimericus cancellarius.[39] At uero pars altera, sepulto iam Honorio, annitentibus fratribus

---

  a istum *A*   *b–b* stetit diu *A* *c om. B*

[29] 1 Cor. 11: 14.

[30] The king sailed from Portsmouth (*Pipe Roll 31 Henry I*, p. 125) either late August or early September, and was at Bec on 8 Sept. 1130: RT, p. 317; cf. HH, pp. 486–7 ('at Michaelmas'), *ASC* E, s.a. 1130 ('in autumn').

[31] On the papal schism of 1130 there is an extensive literature, summarized in *Councils and Synods*, i (2), pp. 754–7, and surveyed in Robinson, *Papacy*, pp. 69–78. H. Bloch, 'The schism of Anacletus II and the Glanfeuil forgeries of Peter the Deacon of Monte Cassino', *Traditio*, viii (1952), 159–264, at p. 168 n. 34, says that William of Malmesbury's 'whole treatment of the schism is remarkable for its objectivity'.

[32] Gregory, cardinal deacon of S. Angelo in Pescheria, elected as Pope Innocent II on 14 Feb. 1130, died 24 Sept. 1143: Hüls, *Kardinäle*, pp. 223–4; Boso, *Vita Innocentii*, in *Le Liber Pontificalis*, ed. L. Duchesne and C. Vogel, 3 vols. (Paris, 1886–1957), ii. 379–85.

[33] Peter Pierleone, cardinal deacon of SS. Cosma e Damiano 1111/12–20, cardinal priest of S. Maria in Trastevere 1120–30, elected as Pope Anacletus II on 14 Feb. 1130, died 25 Jan. 1138 (OV vi. 508–9): Hüls, *Kardinäle*, pp. 189–91, 225.

[34] William, cardinal bishop of Palestrina 1123–*c*.1137: Hüls, *Kardinäle*, pp. 116–17; Schmale, *Schisma*, p. 48.

suffered is wont to influence the mind, almost all the knights had no objection to their hair being cut to a reasonable length. But such strict observance did not last for long. Scarcely had a year passed before all who regarded themselves as courtiers relapsed into their old fault. They vied with women in the length of their locks, and, when the hair was inadequate, they fastened on a kind of hair-piece, forgetting, or rather not knowing, the Apostle's judgement, 'If a man have long hair it is a shame unto him.'[29]

5. In his thirtieth year King Henry crossed to Normandy.[30] On the death of Pope Honorius in that year the Church at Rome was agitated by a great dispute about the papal election.[31] There were then in that city two most celebrated cardinals, Gregory, deacon of S. Angelo,[32] and Peter, a cardinal priest, son of Leo a prince of the Romans.[33] Both were eminent for learning and zeal, nor was it easy for the people to distinguish which of them would more properly be elected by the clergy. However, the partisans of Gregory anticipated their rivals and ordained him pope giving him the name of Innocent. A story was even spread among the common people that Honorius was still alive and bade this be done. Those who brought about this ordination were William, bishop of Palestrina,[34] Matthew of Albano,[35] Conrad of Sabina,[36] John of Ostia,[37] Peter [recte John] of Crema,[38] whose title-church was S. Grisogono, and Haimeric the chancellor.[39] But after Honorius's burial the other side, supported by the efforts of Peter's brothers,

[35] Matthew, cardinal bishop of Albano 1126–35, previously prior of St Martin-des-Champs, Paris, and a relative of Hugh, archbishop of Rouen: Hüls, *Kardinäle*, pp. 96–8; U. Berlière, *Mélanges d'histoire bénédictine*, 4 vols. (Maredsous, 1897–1902), iv. 1–51; *Peter the Venerable*, ii. 96–7.

[36] Conrad, cardinal priest of S. Pudenziana 1110–26, cardinal bishop of Sabina 1126–53, Pope Anastasius IV 1153–4: Hüls, *Kardinäle*, pp. 128–9, 201–2; P. Classen, 'Zur Geschichte Papst Anastasius IV', *Quellen und Forschungen aus italienischen Archiven und Bibliotheken*, xlviii (1968), 36–63.

[37] John III, cardinal bishop of Ostia 1126–c.1133, previously prior of Camaldoli: Hüls, *Kardinäle*, p. 108; Schmale, *Schisma*, pp. 53–4.

[38] John of Crema, appointed cardinal priest of S. Grisogono by Pope Paschal c.1116, active as a papal legate in England, France, and the Empire, died c.1136: Hüls, *Kardinäle*, pp. 176–8; Schmale, *Schisma*, pp. 34–8; *Councils and Synods*, i (2), pp. 730–2, with further references.

[39] Haimeric, cardinal deacon of S. Maria Nuova and papal chancellor 1123–41: Schmale, *Schisma*, pp. 93–191; Robinson, *Papacy*, pp. 94–5, and *passim*.

Petri, locupletissimis Romanorum et potentissimis, eum electum et sacratum uocauit Anacletum. Maximus huius ordinationis hortator et auctor Petrus Portuensis episcopus fuit.[40] Cuius epistolam si posuero, ea omnem controuersiam aperiet, pronior tamen in Anacletum.

454 6.[a] 'Petrus Portuensis episcopus, quattuor episcopis Willelmo Prenestino, Matheo Albanensi, Cuonrado Sabinensi, Iohanni Hostiensi.[41]

Quanta sit pro uobis tribulatio cordis mei, ille solus nouit qui omnia nouit. Vobis quoque meis litteris cognitum saltem iam ex parte fuisset, nisi aecclesiae sententia et communis auctoritas prohiberet. De commendatione seu uituperatione personarum de quibus nunc sermonum uarietas agitatur, non est huius temporis iudicare. Est qui querat et iudicet. Si tamen quisquam presto fuerit accusare, presto erit et qui debeat respondere, presertim cum in uestro et meo, immo in totius aecclesiae conspectu, uterque sapienter uixerit et honeste, et quae offitii sui erant plena hucusque exercuerint libertate. Abstinere uos potius conuenit a sermonibus otiosis et uerbis precipitationis. Si de rumoribus agitur, longe se aliter habent res quam uestrae apud me litterae protestantur. Ad haec, si uerba quae posuistis,[b] si ordinis rationem attenditis, ut salua reuerentia uestra loquar, factionem illam uestram qua confidentia, qua fronte, electionem uocare presumitis? Cur illum uestrum dicitis ordinatum, cum prorsus in causa eius ordo non fuerit? Siccine didicistis papam eligere, in angulo, in abscondito, in tenebrosis et umbra mortis?[42] Si mortuo pape uiuum succedere uolebatis,[c] cur mortuum uiuere predicabatis? Multo melius erat mortuo humanitatem impendere, et sic de uiui solatio cogitare. Sed ecce dum de mortuo solatium uiuo requiritis, et uiuum et mortuum pariter suffocatis.[d] Postremo nec uestrum,

---

[a] *Rubric* Epistola Petri Portuensis de eadem contentione *Ce*[1]   [b] proposuistis *A*   [c] uoluistis *AgAtCd*, uoluistis uel uolebatis *Ao*   [d] suffocastis *Ce*

[40] Peter *Senex*, cardinal bishop of Porto 1111–33/4: Hüls, *Kardinäle*, pp. 122–4; Schmale, *Schisma*, pp. 57–9.

[41] This letter is found also in BL, Royal MS 5. A. xiii, fo. 198[r-v] (from Worcester), and Oxford, Corpus Christi College MS 137, fo. 86[v]. These two copies vary slightly one from

the richest and most powerful of the Romans, elected him and consecrated him by the name of Anacletus. He who chiefly urged and brought about this ordination was Peter, bishop of Porto.[40] If I quote his letter it will explain the whole dispute, though it is too favourable to Anacletus.

6. 'Peter Bishop of Porto to the four bishops William of Palestrina, Matthew of Albano, Conrad of Sabina, John of Ostia.[41]

How great is the affliction of my heart for you He alone knows Who knows all things. You also would already have learnt of it, at least in part, through a letter from me, did not the judgment of the Church and its universal decision forbid. With regard to praise or blame of the persons about whom differing opinions are now being expressed this is not the time to judge. There is one who seeks and judges. If, however, anyone comes forward to accuse, one also will come forward whose duty it is to answer, especially as in your sight and mine, and indeed in that of the whole Church, each of the two has lived in wisdom and righteousness, and has up to now discharged fully and freely all the duties of his office. You would do well to refrain from idle speech and rash words. As to these rumours, the facts of the matter are quite different from what you assert in your letter to me. And indeed, going by your own account and what you say of the procedure, with respect, by what brazen impudence do you presume to call that plot of yours an election? Why do you say your man was ordained, when there was no order at all in his case? Is this the way you have learned to elect a pope, in a corner, in secret, in darkness and the shadow of death?[42] If you wished a living pope to succeed a dead one, why did you say that the dead man was alive? It would have been much better to show respect for the dead, and in this way provide succour for the living; but, behold, in seeking succour from the dead for the living you strangle living and dead alike. Finally, it was neither for you

another, and more markedly from the text found here in *HN*. The variants have not been noted.

[42] Honorius II died in the monastery of S. Gregorio during the night of 13–14 Feb. 1130, was buried there before dawn, and an electoral commission elected Gregory of S. Angelo, who was enthroned as Innocent II in the Lateran palace early the following morning. The allusion is to Job 3:5.

sicut nec meum, fuit eligere, sed potius electum a fratribus
spernere uel approbare.[43] Quod igitur, neglecto ordine, contempto
canone, spreto etiam ipso a uobis condito anathemate, me inconsulto priore uestro, inconsultis etiam fratribus maioribus et
prioribus, nec etiam uocatis aut expectatis, cum essetis nouitii et
in numero breui paucissimi,[44] facere presumpsistis, pro infecto
habendum esse, et nichil omnino existere, ex ipsa uestra estima-
tione potestis aduertere. Cito autem nobis Dominus affuit, et uiam
qua errori[a] uestro contraire possemus ostendit; fratres siquidem
nostri cardinales, quorum precipua est in electione potestas, cum
clero uniuerso, expetente populo, cum honoratorum consensu, [b]in
luce, in manifesto,[b] unanimi uoto et desiderio, elegerunt dominum
Petrum cardinalem in Romanum pontificem Anacletum. Hanc ego
electionem canonice celebratam conspexi, et auctore Deo con-
firmaui.[45] Hunc aecclesia suscipit et ueneratur; hunc per Dei
gratiam episcopi, abbates, principes, capitanei, et barones,
quidam per se ipsos, quidam per nuntios suos, uidentibus nobis
frequentant. Depredationem illam et crudelitatem, quam preten-
ditis, non uidemus. Quicumque ad eum pro responsis seu negotiis
suis ueniunt benigne suscipiuntur,[c] benignius reuertuntur. Redite,
iam redite ad cor.[46] Nolite scisma in aecclesia facere ad animarum
subuersionem. Nolite ulterius laborare. Teneat uos timor Dei,[d]
non pudor seculi. Numquid qui dormit non adiciet[e] ut resurgat?[47]
Desistite iam mendatiis, in quibus impii spem suam ponere
consuerunt. Dominus Tiburtius in scriptis suis cum sacramento[f]
testificatus est,[48] dicens quod ego diaconum sancti Angeli solum
idoneum iudicaui ad pontificatus ordinem. Videat ipse quid
dixerit. Ego in occulto locutus sum nichil. Non est aliquis qui
hoc uerbum ab ore meo umquam audierit. Haec fuit sententia mea

---

[43] The view that the election was the responsibility of the cardinal priests and cardinal
deacons, not the cardinal bishops, was expressed by Cardinal Deusdedit in his Collectio
canonum of c.1086, and revived by the Anacletan party: Robinson, Papacy, pp. 75–6; Bloch,
'The schism of Anacletus II', p. 165 n. 18.

[44] On the composition of the two parties, see Robinson, Papacy, pp. 70–6; and see
further here, M. Stroll, The Jewish Pope: Ideology and Politics in the Papal Schism of 1130
(Leiden, 1987), pp. 102–10. The older among the cardinals (appointed by Pascal II, 1099–

nor me to elect, but rather to reject or approve him who had been elected by our brethren.[43] You can therefore perceive by your own judgement that the thing must be regarded as altogether null and void which you presumed to carry out, although you were novices and very few in number,[44] ignoring the procedure, despising the canon law, showing contempt even for the very interdict that you yourselves had drawn up, not consulting me your senior or your brethren of greater age and seniority, or so much as summoning us or waiting for us. But the Lord speedily came to our aid and showed us a way whereby we might counteract your error, for our brother cardinals, who have chief power to elect, together with the entire clergy, at the request of the people, with the agreement of the nobles, in the open light of day, by the wish and desire of all, have elected Lord Cardinal Peter to be Anacletus, pope of Rome. This election I saw performed according to the canon law, and by God's authority I ratified it.[45] This man the Church accepts and reveres; I have seen that by the grace of God bishops, abbots, princes, captains and barons, some in person, some by messenger, come flocking to him. I do not see the plundering and cruelty that you allege. All who come to him for decisions or on matters of business are received graciously and are courteously sent on their way. Return, return now to understanding.[46] Do not make a schism in the Church for the ruin of souls. Labour no longer. Let the fear of God be upon you, not the shame of the world. Shall he who sleeps not rise again?[47] Cease now from lies, in which the wicked are wont to put their trust. The bishop of Tivoli,[48] in his letter, bore witness on oath, saying that I judged the deacon of S. Angelo alone fitting the dignity of pope. Let him take heed to his own words. I spoke nothing in secret. There is no man who has ever heard this saying from my lips. This was always my opinion,

---

1118) tended to support Anacletus, and the younger (appointed by Calixtus II, 1119–24, and Honorius II, 1124–30) tended to Innocent.

[45] When news of Innocent II's election became known, a majority of the cardinals assembled in S. Marco, elected Peter Pierleoni, who was enthroned as Anacletus II in S. Pietro, all during the day of 14 Feb.

[46] Isa. 46: 8.

[47] Ps. 58: 3.

[48] Guy, cardinal bishop of Tivoli, 1123–39, previously archdeacon of Pisa: Hüls, *Kardinäle*, p. 138; Schmale, *Schisma*, pp. 50–1; Hugh the Chanter, p. 138 n. 1.

semper, ut non nisi sepulto papa de successoris persona mentio haberetur. Vnitatem aecclesiae tenui et tenebo. Veritati et iustitiae adherere curabo, confidenter sperans quia iustitia et ueritas liberabit me.'

7. Sic predictus Petrus Portuensis ^aepiscopus in Petrum Leonis filium^a pronior scripsit. Nec uero pars altera cessabat quin et ipsum Petrum catulum leonis diceret,[49] et fautores eius factionis complices nominaret. Et illi quidem uaria inter se dubiis de rebus agebant.[50] Innocentius uero exclusus Roma, transcensis Alpibus, Galliam contendit.[51] Ibi ab omni citramontana aecclesia incunctanter susceptus est. Quin etiam et rex Henricus, qui non leuiter a sententia quam semel proposuisset deici nosset, illi apud Carnotum ultro manus dedit, et apud Rotomagum non modo suis sed et optimatum et etiam Iudeorum muneribus eum dignatus est.[52] Nec uero Innocentius, quanuis ab Anglorum et Francorum regibus, simul et ab imperatore Alemannorum,[53] ualde iuuaretur, numquam tamen quiete potiri potuit, quod Anacletus Romanae ^baecclesiae sedem teneret.^b At uero ipso Anacleto ^coctauo presumpti ut dicebatur sui episcopatus anno defuncto,^c [54] dominus Innocentius inconcussa ad hoc tempus pace apostolica fruitur dignitate.

455 8. Anno tricesimo primo regni sui ^drex Henricus rediit^d in Angliam.[55] Imperatrix quoque eodem anno natali solo aduentum suum exhibuit; habitoque non paruo procerum conuentu apud Northamtonam, priscam fidem apud eos qui dederant nouauit, ab

---

^{a–a} Petro Leoni *Ce*   ^{b–b} sedem teneret ecclesie *Ce*   ^{c–c} defuncto ... anno *Ce*   ^{d–d} rediit rex *Ce*

---

⁴⁹ Ps. 34: 10.
⁵⁰ Virgil, *Aen.* xi. 445.
⁵¹ Innocent II was recognized by a council of the French Church which met at Étampes on 25 May 1130: *Actes de Louis VI*, ii, no. 291; iii. 215; T. Reuter, 'Zur Anerkennung Papst Innocenz II', *Deutsches Archiv*, xxxix (1983), 395–416. He settled at Cluny in Sept. 1130, and from there summoned a council to meet at Clermont on 18 Nov. 1130: Suger, pp. 256–61; A. Graboïs, 'Le schisme de 1130 et la France', *Revue d'histoire ecclésiastique*, lxxvi (1981), 593–612.
⁵² The meeting at Chartres was on 13 Jan. 1131: OV vi. 420–1. A major church council

that until the pope was buried nothing should be said about the person to succeed him. I have maintained, and will maintain, the unity of the Church. I shall take care to cling to truth and justice, in the sure hope that justice and truth will set me free.'

7. Thus wrote the aforesaid Peter of Porto, too much favouring Peter son of Leo. Nor did the other side refrain from calling Peter himself the lion-cub[49] and his supporters accomplices in a plot. And they for their part were contending about matters that lay in doubt.[50] Innocent, banished from Rome, crossed the Alps and hastened to France.[51] There he was immediately recognized by the entire Church on this side of the Alps. Moreover King Henry, who could not lightly be moved from a decision he had once made, paid him reverence voluntarily at Chartres, and at Rouen honoured him with gifts not only from himself but also from the nobles and even from the Jews.[52] Innocent, however, though strongly supported by the kings of England and France, as also by the emperor of Germany,[53] still could not obtain a tranquil life, because Anacletus held the capital city of the Roman Church. But since the death of Anacletus in the eighth year of what was alleged to be his episcopate,[54] the Lord Innocent has enjoyed the position of pope in peace undisturbed to this day.

8. In the thirty-first year of his reign King Henry returned to England.[55] That year the empress also arrived on her native soil, and holding no small gathering of the nobles at Northampton received an oath of fealty from those who had not given one before

met at Rouen on 9/10 May 1131: *GND* ii. 250–1; RT i. 185; *Councils and Synods*, i (2), pp. 754–7. The mention of the Jews would seem to be an allusion to the Jewish ancestry of Anacletus II: Graboïs, 'Le schisme de 1130', pp. 609–11; for the Jewish community at Rouen, see N. Golb, *Les Juifs de Rouen au moyen âge: Portrait d'une culture oubliée* (Rouen, 1985), discussing this passage at pp. 127–9, 427 (no. 41).

[53] When Innocent II was at Clermont in Nov. 1130 messengers arrived to say that a meeting at Würzburg had accepted him, and the Emperor Lothair III met him at Liège on 22 Mar. 1131: OV vi. 420–1; Schmale, *Schisma*, pp. 238–47; Robinson, *Papacy*, pp. 444–6, with further references.

[54] Anacletus still controlled Rome, but had little support outside the city, at the time of his death on 25 Jan. 1138.

[55] Henry returned to England with the empress 'in summer' (HH, pp. 486–7), 'before autumn, after 29 June' 1131 (*ASC* E, s.a. 1131).

his qui non dederant accepit.[56] Eodem anno Ludouicus rex
Francorum, et in senium uergens[57] et nimia corpulentia grauis,
filium coronari iussit ut regni successorem. Quo non multo post casu
equi exanimato, alterum per manum pontificis Romani[a] diademate
insigniuit.[58] Is, ut fertur, ab antiqua Francorum fortitudine non
degenerans, etiam Aquitaniam iuri suo per uxoris dotale fedus
adquisiuit;[59] quam post Ludouicum, Karoli Magni filium, in
proprio dominatu Francorum reges non habuisse noscuntur.

456　9.[b] Anno tricesimo primo regni Henrici, infesta lues domesticorum
animalium totam peruagata est Angliam. Plene porcorum arae
subito uacuabantur; integra boum presepia repente destitueban-
tur.[60] Durauit sequentibus annis eadem pestis, ut nulla omnino
totius regni uilla, huius miseriae immunis, alterius incommoda
ridere posset. Tunc etiam contentio inter Bernardum episcopum
Meneuensem et Vrbanum Landauensem de iure parrochiarum,
quas idem Vrbanus illicite usurpauerat, aeterno fine sopita est.[61]
Tot enim ad curiam Romanam appellationibus, tot iterum expensis,
tot causidicorum conflictibus multis annis uentilata, tandem ali-
quando morte Vrbani apud Romam soluta uel potius decisa est.[62]
Nam et apostolicus, aequitate rei perpensa, religioni et iustitiae
Meneuensis episcopi qua decebat sententia satisfecit. Eodem etiam[c]
anno Willelmus archiepiscopus Cantuariae legationem in Anglia
Romanae sedis indulgentia personaliter impetrauit.[63]

　　[a] Remensis Ce　　　　[b] Rubric De lue pecorum Ce　　　[c] om. A

[56] Henry of Huntingdon gives the date 8 Sept. 1131 (HH, p. 486–7). The scale of the
gathering is indicated by the witness-list to Regesta, ii, no. 1715.
[57] Statius, Theb. i. 391.
[58] The two coronations were in fact separated by more than two years. Philip son of
Louis VI was crowned on 14 Apr. 1129 by Reginald, archbishop of Reims, and died on 13
Oct. 1131; the second son Louis (VII) was crowned on 25 Oct. 1131 by Innocent II: Actes
de Louis VI, iii. 215–16; OV vi. 390–1 (1129), 446–7 (1131).
[59] Louis VII married Eleanor of Aquitaine at Bordeaux in July, and his father died on 1
Aug. 1137: A. Luchaire, Louis VI le Gros: Annales de sa vie et de son régne (1081–1137)
(Paris, 1890), no. 589, p. 268; Actes de Louis VI, iii. 218; Suger, pp. 280–3.
[60] The plague among beasts is also referred to in the Anglo-Saxon Chronicle: ASC E, s.a. 1131.
[61] The protagonists were Urban, bishop of Llandaff, 1107–34, and Bernard, bishop of
St Davids, 1115–48. The case of Llandaff against Hereford and St Davids 'at the papal
curia had been pursued almost without intermission since the legatine council of 1127':
Councils and Synods, i (2), pp. 757–8, and references there cited; also R. R. Davies,
Conquest, Coexistence, and Change: Wales 1063–1415 (Oxford, 1987), pp. 182–4.
[62] A letter of Innocent II, and a reference in the Liber Landavensis, confirm that Urban

and a renewal of the oath from those who had.[56] In the same year Louis, king of France, who was growing old[57] and was burdened with excessive corpulence, bade his son be crowned as successor to his kingdom. When this son was killed not long afterwards through falling from his horse, he honoured the second son with the crown at the hands of the Roman pontiff [Ce the pope at Reims].[58] The son, they say, is no unworthy heir of the ancient valour of the Franks, and through his wife's marriage-contract has gained possession of Aquitaine as well,[59] which the kings of France are not known to have had under their own lordship since Louis, the son of Charlemagne.

9. In the thirty-first year of Henry's reign a destructive plague among domestic animals made its way through the whole of England. Sties full of pigs were suddenly emptied; byres of oxen, as yet untouched, were made desolate in a moment.[60] The same pestilence continued during the following years, so that no village at all in the entire kingdom was free from this calamity, and could laugh at the misfortunes of another. Then too the dispute between Bernard, bishop of St Davids, and Urban, bishop of Llandaff, for authority over the parishes that the same Urban had unlawfully appropriated, was put to its everlasting rest.[61] After being fanned for many years by so many appeals to the court of Rome, so much expenditure on journeys, so many struggles between advocates, it was at length settled, or rather broken off, by the death of Urban at Rome.[62] For the pope, after weighing the rights of the case, contented the piety and justice of the bishop of St Davids with the decision that was fitting. In the same year also William, archbishop of Canterbury, obtained in person the post of legate in England, by favour of the Roman See.[63]

died at Rome (on or before 9 Oct. 1134), although Henry of Huntingdon, and later chroniclers following him, said that he died *en route* to Rome: *Episcopal Acts and Cognate Documents Relating to Welsh Dioceses 1066–1272*, ed. J. Conway Davies, 2 vols. (Hist. Soc. of the Church in Wales; Cardiff, 1946–8), ii. 634–5, nos. L83–L87.

[63] William of Corbeil was granted legatine authority by a papal mandate of 25 Jan. 1126: *Councils and Synods*, i (2), pp. 741–3. The legation lapsed on Honorius II's death: C. R. Cheney, 'The deaths of popes and the expiry of legations in twelfth-century England', *Revue de droit canonique*, xxviii (1978), 84–96, at p. 89. The present entry would seem to refer to a renewal of the legation, possibly at Rouen in May 1131 and certainly before 7 Mar. 1132: *Councils and Synods*, i (2), p. 757 n. 1.

457 10.[a] Anno tricesimo secundo regni pridie transacto, Henricus
nonis Augusti, quo die quondam apud Westmonasterium coronae
culmen acceperat, Normanniam nauigauit.[64] Vltimus ille fatalisque
regi transitus fuit. Mira tunc prorsus prouidentia Deitatis rebus
allusit humanis, ut eo die nauem ascenderet, numquam uiuus[b]
reuersurus, quo dudum coronatus fuerat tam diu et tam feliciter
regnaturus. Erant tunc ut dixi nonae Augusti et feria quarta.
Prosecuta sunt elementa dolore suo extremum tanti principis
transitum. Nam et sol ipsa die hora sexta tetra ferrugine, ut
poetae solent dicere,[65] nitidum caput obtexit, mentes hominum
[c]eclipsi sua concutiens;[c][66] et feria sexta proxima primo mane
tantus terrae motus fuit ut penitus subsidere uideretur, horrifico
sono sub terris[d] ante audito.[67] Vidi ego et in eclipsi stellas circa
solem, et in terrae motu parietem domus in qua sedebam bifario
impetu eleuatum tertio resedisse. Fuit ergo[e] rex in Normannia
triennio continuo,[f][68] et tanto plus quantum est inter nonas
Augusti, quo die, ut[g] dictum est, mare transiuit, et kalendas
Decembris, qua nocte decessit.[h] Nec uero dubitandum, multa
eum quae non immerito scribi deberent, in Normannia gessisse;
sed consilium fuit preterire quae ad nostram notitiam non integre
peruenere. Opiniones reditus eius in Angliam multae, siue fato
quodam siue diuina uoluntate omnes frustratae.

11. Regnauit ergo annis[i] triginta quinque, et a nonis Augusti
usque ad kalendas Decembris,[69] id est, [j]mensibus quattuor, diebus
quattuor minus,[j] apud Leonas exercitio uenationis intentus,

---

[a] *Rubrics* De transitu regis Henrici et de morte eius *Ce*[1], De transitu regis Henrici et morte
sua *Ce*[2]   [b] iterum *Ce*   [c-c] defectione sua terrens *Ce*   [d] terra *Ce*
[e] *om. A*   [f] continue *A*   [g] *om. Ce*   [h] discessit *B*   [i] *om. A*
[j-j] quattuor mensibus diebus quattuor minus *AgAt* quattuor diebus minus quattuor
mensibus *Ao* mensibus quattuor minus *Ce*[1], mensibus quattuor et diebus quinque plus *Ce*[2]

[64] John of Worcester gives the day as a Wednesday, the 4 nones of August (2 Aug.),
which was the anniversary of the death of Rufus (2 Aug. 1100) and the beginning of the
rule of Henry I, after the king had ruled for 33 years: Wednesday 2 Aug. 1133 (JW iii.
208–11). William of Malmesbury, seemingly aware of these calculations, but pedantically
insisting that Henry commenced his rule on the date of his coronation, 5 Aug., produces
Wednesday 5 Aug. 1132 (where the weekday is wrong for both 1132 and 1133).

[65] Virgil, *Georg.* i. 467.

[66] This is the best-recorded eclipse of the Middle Ages, and it undoubtedly occurred on
2 Aug. 1133: R. R. Newton, *Medieval Chronicles and the Rotation of the Earth* (Baltimore,
1972), pp. 99, 160–3.

10. Having completed the thirty-second year of his reign the day before, Henry sailed to Normandy on 5 August, the day on which he had once received the supreme dignity of the crown at Westminster.[64] That was the king's last crossing and the one that brought him to his doom. God's providence jested strangely then with human affairs, that he should go on board, never to return alive, on the day when he had been crowned in the distant past to reign so long and so happily. It was then, as I have said, 5 August, and a Wednesday. The elements accompanied with their sorrow the last crossing of so great a prince. For on that very day the sun, at the sixth hour, covered its shining head with gloomy rust, as the poets are wont to say,[65] agitating men's minds by its eclipse;[66] and on the following Friday at dawn the earth quaked so terribly that it seemed to sink to the depths, and a dreadful noise was heard under the earth before this.[67] In the eclipse I myself saw stars round the sun, and in the earthquake the wall of the house in which I sat I saw lifted up by two shocks and settling down at a third. The king then was in Normandy for three years on end,[68] and as much longer as is the interval between 5 August, when, as has been said, he crossed the sea, and 1 December, on the night of which he died. Nor indeed is it to be doubted that he did many things in Normandy with just claim to be written down, but it has been my intention to pass over everything that did not fully come to my knowledge. There were many expectations of his return to England, but all, by a kind of fate or by the divine will, were disappointed.

11. He reigned then for thirty-five years and in addition, from 5 August to 1 December,[69] that is four months less four days. When occupied in hunting at Lyons-la-Forêt, he was seized by illness

---

[67] The earthquake was on Friday, 4 Aug. 1133: ibid., pp. 721–3. It is noted also in JW iii. 210–11

[68] Henry crossed to Normandy in early Aug. 1133, and died on 1 Dec. 1135. William of Malmesbury, having wrongly calculated the year of his crossing as 1132 rather than 1133, is forced here to add an additional year to his stay.

[69] This calculation is found in Bodleian Library, Auct. F. 3. 14, fo. 120ᵛ; printed in W. H. Stevenson, 'A contemporary description of the Domesday Survey', *EHR* xxii (1907), 72–84, at p. 81; identified as in the hand of William of Malmesbury by N. R. Ker, 'William of Malmesbury's handwriting', *EHR* lix (1944), 371–6, at p. 375.

ualitudine aduersa correptus decubuit. Qua in deterius crescente, euocauit[a] ad se Hugonem, quem primo ex priore de Lewis abbatem apud Radinges, mox Rotomagensem archiepiscopum, fecerat, merito sibi et heredibus suis pro tantis benefitiis obnoxium.[70] Optimates rumor[b] egritudinis celeriter contraxit. Affuit et Rotbertus filius eius, comes Gloecestriae, qui, pro integritate fidei et uirtutis eminentia, uicturam in omne seculum memoriam sui nominatim promeruit. A quibus de successore interrogatus, filiae omnem terram suam citra et ultra mare legitima et perhenni successione adiudicauit, marito eius subiratus, quod eum et minis et iniuriis aliquantis irritauerat.[71] Septimo incommodi die transacto, nocte iam intempesta naturae cessit.[72] Cuius magnanimos mores hic dicere supersedeo, quia in quinto libro regalium gestorum plenissime illos contexui.[73] Quam Christiane[c] obierit, haec subsequens epistola supradicti Rotomagensis archiepiscopi docebit.[74]

458 12.[d] 'Domino et patri suo Innocentio papae, seruus Hugo Rotomagensis sacerdos obedientiae debitum.

De domino meo rege non sine dolore memorando, pie paternitati uestre notificandum duximus, qui[e] subita preuentus egritudine, nos missis quam citissime legatis suis, egritudinis suae[f] solatiis uoluit interesse. Venimus ad ipsum, et cum ipso plenum meroribus confecimus triduum. Prout ei dicebamus ipse ore proprio sua fatebatur peccata, et manu propria pectus suum percutiebat, et malam uoluntatem dimittebat. Consilio Dei et nostro et episcoporum emendationem uitae suae obseruaturum sese promittebat. Sub ista[g] promissione, eo[h] firmiter annuente, pro nostro eum[i] offitio tertio[j] et per triduum absoluimus. Crucem

---

[a] uocauit A   [b] sue add. A   [c] autem add. Ce   [d] Rubric Epistola Rothomagensis archiepiscopi de obitu regis Henrici Ce[1]   [e] quia AB   [f] om. Ce   [g] ipsa B   [h] ista ei AB   [i] om. Ce   [j] eum add. ABCe

[70] Hugh of Amiens, archbishop of Rouen 1130–64, and previously prior of Limoges c.1115–20, prior of Lewes 1120–3, first abbot of Reading 1123–30: Heads, pp. 63, 119; Reading Abbey Cartularies, ed. B. R. Kemp, 2 vols. (Camden Soc., 4th ser. xxxi, xxxiii, 1986–7), i. 26; Peter the Venerable, ii. 99–100.
[71] Orderic says that Henry was so angry with Geoffrey that 'he would have taken his daughter away from him if God had so decreed'; both Orderic and Robert of Torigni cite

2

and took to his bed. When the illness grew worse, he summoned
Hugh, whom he had promoted from prior of Lewes to abbot of
Reading, and afterwards made archbishop of Rouen, a man with
good reason devoted to him and heirs in return for benefits so
great.[70] The report of his illness quickly brought the nobles
together. His son Robert, earl of Gloucester, also came, who, for
his steadfast loyalty and distinguished merit, has pre-eminently
deserved that the recollection of him shall live for all time. When
he was asked by them about his successor, he assigned all his lands
on both sides of the sea to his daughter in lawful and lasting
succession, being somewhat angry with her husband because he
had vexed the king by not a few threats and insults.[71] When the
seventh day of his illness had passed he died during the dead of
night.[72] I refrain from speaking of his noble character here because
I have dealt with it very fully in the fifth book of the *Deeds of the
Kings*.[73] In how Christian a fashion he died the following letter of
the aforesaid archbishop of Rouen will show.[74]

12. 'To the lord and father Pope Innocent his servant Hugh,
bishop of Rouen, offers the obedience that he owes.

Compassionate father, I thought I should give you news of my
lord the king, whom I cannot recall without sorrow; for he was
seized by sudden illness and sent representatives with all speed,
asking me to help to comfort him in that illness. I came to him,
and spent with him three days full of grief. As I bade him he
confessed his sins with his own lips, and beat his breast with his
own hand, and renounced all evil desires. By the counsel of God
and myself and the bishops he promised that he would see to the
amendment of his life. In view of that promise (earnestly made) in
virtue of my office I gave him absolution three times in the course
of the three days. He adored the crucifix; he received with

as a source of the quarrel the claim to control the Norman castles: OV vi. 444–5; RT i. 200;
and see further above, introduction, pp. xl–xlii.

[72] William of Malmesbury has just stated that Henry died on 1 Dec. The reference here
to his dying during the night explains the references in several authorities to his dying on 2
Dec., because they 'started the day at sunset': *Peter the Venerable*, ii. 104–5.

[73] On Henry's character, see esp. *GR* §411–12.

[74] This letter is found also in Oxford, Corpus Christi College MS 137, fo. 88ʳ.

Domini adorauit; corpus et sanguinem Domini deuote suscepit. Elemosinam suam disposuit ita dicendo: "Soluantur debita mea, reddantur liberationes et solidatae quibus[a] debeo. Reliqua indigentibus distribuantur." Vtinam sic fecissent qui thesauros eius tenebant et tenent! Tandem illi auctoritatem de unctione infirmorum, quam aecclesia a beato Iacobo apostolo suscepit, studiose proposuimus, et ipsius pia petitione oleo sancto eum inunximus.
459 Sic in pace quieuit. Pacem det ei Deus, quia pacem dilexit."[b] Haec prefatus Rotomagensis archiepiscopus de fide regis Henrici morientis uere contestatus est.

13. Funus regaliter curatum, proceribus[c] uicissim portantibus Rotomagum usque delatum est.[75] Illic in quodam recessu aecclesiae maioris exinteratum est, ne diuturnitate corruptum nares assidentium uel astantium exacerbaret.[76] Reliquiae interaneorum in cenobio sanctae Mariae de Pratis iuxta urbem humate; quod ipse, ut audio, a matre sua inchoatum, non paucis compendiis honorauerat.[77] Corpus Cadomi seruatum, quousque serenas auras paulo clementior hiemps inueheret, quae tum aspera inhorrebat.

460 14.[d] Interea Stephanus comes Moritonii et Bononiae, nepos regis Henrici, ut supra dixi,[78] qui post regem Scottiae primus laicorum fidem suam imperatrici obstrinxerat, in Angliam per Witsand maturauit aduentum.[79] Imperatrix certis ex causis, simul et frater eius Rotbertus comes Gloecestriae, cum omnibus pene proceribus, redire in regnum distulerunt. Quaedam tamen castella in Normannia, inter quae precipuum Danfrontum, partibus heredis se applicuere.[80] Constat sane illo die quo Stephanus

---

[a] que *AB*   [b] *Rubric* Quomodo corpus regis Henrici exinteratum est *Ce*[1]
[c] proceribusque *Ce*   [d] *Rubric* De Stephano rege in regnum promoto *Ce*

[75] William of Malmesbury had similarly described the treatment of the Conqueror's body after he died in 1087, 'regio sollemni curatum' (*GR* §283); but Orderic told a very different story (OV iv. 102–5).
[76] Other accounts of the treatment of the king's body, and the burial of its various parts, are found in OV vi. 448–51, and HH, pp. 702–5.
[77] Notre-Dame-du-Pré, in the suburbs of Rouen, a dependent priory of the abbey of Bec, patronized by Henry I, and the home of the empress in her active retirement from 1148 to 1167: M. Chibnall, 'The Empress Matilda and Bec-Hellouin', *ANS* x (1988), 35–48, esp. pp. 37–8.
[78] *HN* §3.

devotion the body and blood of the Lord. He made his arrangements for almsgiving, with these words: "Let my debts be paid, let
quittance and payment be made to my creditors; let the rest be
distributed amongst the poor." Would that they had done thus
who held and hold his treasures! At last I put it to him solicitously
that he should give me leave to perform the anointing of the sick,
which the Church has received from the blessed apostle James,
and at his own pious request I anointed him with the holy oil. So
he died in peace. God grant him peace, for peace he loved.'

This witness the aforesaid archbishop of Rouen has borne with
truth concerning King Henry's faith when he was dying.

13. The dead body was attended to as befits a king and brought to
Rouen with nobles acting as bearers in turn.[75] There it was
disembowelled in a corner of the cathedral, lest it should rot
with lapse of time and offend the nostrils of those who sat or stood
by it.[76] The innards were buried near the city in the convent of
Notre-Dame-du-Pré, which had been founded by his mother and
distinguished by himself, I hear, with no small endowments.[77] The
body was kept at Caen until winter, which was then raging
fiercely, should grow a little milder and bring gentle breezes.

14. Meanwhile Stephen, count of Mortain and Boulogne, King
Henry's nephew, as I have said,[78] he who first among the laity,
after the King of Scots, had pledged his faith to the empress,
hastened his arrival in England by way of Wissant.[79] For certain
reasons the empress, and also her brother Robert, earl of
Gloucester, together with almost all the nobles, delayed their
return to the kingdom. Yet some castles in Normandy, of which
Domfront was the chief, sided with the heiress.[80] It is certainly

[79] Stephen was 'in comitatu suo Boloniae' and crossed quickly to England on news of
Henry's death: RT i. 198; GND ii. 274–5. He made for London, being refused admission
at Dover and Canterbury: GS, pp. 4–7; Gervase of Canterbury, Historical Works, ed. W.
Stubbs, 2 vols. (RS lxxiii, 1879–80), i. 94.
[80] The capture of Domfront and Argentan are recorded by both Norman and Angevin
writers: GND ii. 274–5; RT i. 199; OV vi. 454–5; Annals of Saint-Aubin, s.a. 1135, in
Chroniques des églises d'Anjou, ed. P. Marchegay and E. Mabille (Paris, 1869), p. 34; John
de Marmoutier, in Chroniques des comtes d'Anjou, p. 225. See further Chibnall, Matilda,
pp. 66–7.

appulsus est Angliam, summo mane, contra naturam hiemis in regionibus nostris, terricrepum sonum tonitrui cum horrendo fulgure fuisse, ut paulominus mundus solui estimaretur. Ille, ubi a Lundoniensibus et Wintoniensibus in regem exceptus est, etiam Rogerium Salesberiensis episcopum et Willelmum de Ponte Arcus, custodes thesaurorum regalium, ad se transduxit.[81] Ne tamen ueritas celetur posteris, omnes eius conatus irriti fuissent, nisi Henricus frater eius Wintoniensis episcopus, qui modo[a] apostolicae sedis legatus est in Anglia, placidum ei commodasset assensum, spe scilicet captus amplissima quod Stephanus aui sui Willelmi in regni moderamine mores seruaret, precipueque in aecclesiastici uigoris disciplina.[82] Quapropter districto sacramento, quod a Stephano Willelmus Cantuariensis archiepiscopus exegit de libertate reddenda aecclesiae et conseruanda, episcopus Wintoniensis se mediatorem et uadem apposuit. Cuius sacramenti tenorem, postea scripto inditum, loco suo non pretermittam.[83]

461 15.[b] Coronatus est ergo[c] in regem [d]Angliae Stephanus[d] undecimo kalendas Ianuarii, dominica, uicesima secunda die post excessum auunculi, anno Dominicae incarnationis millesimo centesimo tricesimo quinto,[84] [e]tribus episcopis presentibus, archiepiscopo, Wintoniensi, Salesberiensi, nullis abbatibus, paucissimis optimatibus.[e] Vir quidem impiger sed imprudens,[f] [85] armis strenuus, immodici animi ad quelibet ardua inchoanda, lenis et exorabilis hostibus, affabilis omnibus: cuius cum dulcedinem in promissis suspiceres, [g]ueritatem tamen[g] dictorum et promissorum efficatiam

---

[a] om. B   [b] Rubric De coronatione Regis Stephani, et de moribus eius Ce[1]
[c] om. A   [d-d] Stephanus Anglie Ce   [e-e] tribus . . . optimatibus after dominica Ce   [f] prudens A, minus prudens Ce   [g-g] tamen ueritatem A

---

[81] William Pont de l'Arche, chamberlain of the treasury, responsible for the Winchester treasury, c.1120—c.1143: Hollister, Anglo-Norman World, pp. 209–22. On the location of the treasury, in the castle, see Winchester Studies, i. 304–5.

[82] Henry of Blois, youngest son of Stephen count of Blois and Adela daughter of the Conqueror; monk of Cluny; abbot of Glastonbury 1126–71 and (in plurality) bishop of Winchester 1129–71: L. Voss, Heinrich von Blois, Bischof von Winchester 1129–1171 (Berlin, 1932); EEA, viii; Winchester 1070–1204, ed. M. J. Franklin (Oxford, 1993), pp. xxxv–xlix, nos. 22–138, App. I, pp. 202–13.

[83] HN § 18. This passage makes clear that Stephen's Oxford 'charter of liberties' of Apr. 1136 represented promises that he had made to the Church prior to his coronation. Henry

established that on the day when Stephen landed in England, at dawn, there was, contrary to the nature of winter in our part of the world, a terrible sound of thunder accompanied by fearful lightning, so that it was almost thought to be the end of the world. On being received as king by the people of London and Winchester, he also brought over to his side Roger, bishop of Salisbury, and William Pont de l'Arche, who had charge of the royal treasury.[81] Nevertheless, so that the truth may not be concealed from posterity, all his efforts would have been in vain had not his brother Henry, bishop of Winchester—who now is legate in England of the Apostolic See—eased his path, allured indeed by a very strong hope that Stephen would continue the ways of his grandfather William in the governance of the kingdom, especially as regards strict uprightness in Church affairs.[82] Thus it was that the bishop of Winchester made himself guarantor and surety of the solemn oath that William, archbishop of Canterbury, exacted from Stephen about the restoration and maintenance of the freedom of the Church. The terms of that oath were afterwards put in writing, and I shall not fail to insert them in the proper place.[83]

15. Stephen then was crowned king of England on 22 December, a Sunday, the twenty-second day after his uncle's death, in the year of the Lord's Incarnation 1135;[84] there were present three bishops (the archbishop, Winchester, Salisbury), no abbots, and just a handful of the great men.[85] He was a man of energy but lacking in judgement, active in war, of extraordinary spirit in undertaking difficult tasks, lenient to his enemies and easily appeased, courteous to all: though you admired his kindness in promising, still you felt his words lacked truth and his promises fulfilment. And so

of Huntingdon confirms this, referring at this point to the 'pacta' made with the Church 'in die coronationis sue': HH, pp. 704–5; Davis, *Stephen*, pp. 17–18.

[84] This date is supported by *The Chronicle of Battle Abbey*, ed. E. Searle (OMT, 1980), pp. 140–1, and the revised text of JW iii. 214–15; and it has been generally accepted, as against 15 Dec. in OV vi. 454–5, and Christmas day in *ASC* E, s.a. 1135, and Richard of Hexham, in *Chronicles*, iii. 144.

[85] *Regesta*, iii, no. 270, the king's 'coronation charter' is witnessed only by William Martel. *Regesta*, iii. no. 45, dated 26 Dec. 1135, is witnessed by the three bishops named here.

desiderares. Vnde fratris consilium non multo post lapso tempore postponebat, cuius, ut dixi, auxilio munitus et aduersantes summouerat et ad regnum ascenderat.

462 16.ᵃ Anno Dominicae incarnationis millesimo centesimo tricesimo sexto,ᵇ regis Henrici corpus, lenibus flabris spirantibus, statim post Natale Domini impositum naui Angliam deuectumᶜ est; et apud Radingense cenobium, quodᵈ foris prediorum magnitudine etᵉ intus religiosorum monachorum ordine decorauerat, presente regni successore, humatum est.⁸⁶ Postea uero rex Stephanus in Northanimbriam paulo ante Quadragesimam contendit, ut Dauid regem Scottiae, qui diuersa sentire dicebatur, conueniret. Nec difficileᶠ ab eo quod uoluit impetrauit,⁸⁷ quia et ille morum lenitate et propiori iam senectute infractus, libenter in otium uel uere uel simulateᵍ pacis concessit.⁸⁸

463 17.ʰ Eodemⁱ anno post Pascha Rotbertus comes Gloecestriae ʲuenit in Angliam,⁸⁹ cuius prudentiam maxime Stephanus uerebatur.ʲ Is, dum esset in Normannia, multa cogitatione fatigarat animum quidnam sibi super hoc negotio statuendum putaret. Si enim regi Stephano subderetur, contra sacramentum quod sorori fecerat ᵏfore uidebat.ᵏ Si refrageretur, nichil sorori uel nepotibus profuturum, sibi certe immaniter nociturum intelligebat. Habebat enim, ut supra tetigi, rex immensam uim thesaurorum, quos multis annis auunculusˡ aggesserat. Estimabantur denarii, et hi exquisitissimi, fere ad centum milia libras.⁹⁰ Erant et uasa tam aurea quam

ᵃ *Rubric* De humatione regis Henrici *Ce*   ᵇ quinto *B*, postea *add. Ce*   ᶜ deuectus *ACd*   ᵈ et *add. Ce*   ᵉ *om. B*   ᶠ uero difficulter *Ce*   ᵍ simultate *ABq*   ʰ *Rubric* De aduentu Roberti comitis Gloecestre in Angliam *Ce*   ⁱ eo *B*   ʲ⁻ʲ cuius prud. rex S. max. uer. uenit in Angliam *Ce*   ᵏ⁻ᵏ uidebat fore *B*   ˡ rex Henricus auunculus suus *Ce*

⁸⁶ Reading Abbey was Henry's own foundation, intended as his mausoleum, and he was buried there on 5 Jan. 1136: *Reading Abbey Cartularies*, ed. Kemp, i. 14 n. 1. Its 'vast estates' included the property of three Anglo-Saxon monasteries, at Reading, Cholsey, and Leominster: ibid., i. 13–19. Of the 'holy monks', originally sent from Cluny, William of Malmesbury wrote warmly, and with a measure of repetition, in *GR* §413, and *GP*, p. 193.
⁸⁷ The Hexham chroniclers say that Stephen arrived at Durham 'on Ash Wednesday, 5 Feb.' [*recte* 4 Feb.]; and for fifteen days thereafter discussed terms of peace with David of Scots, who was then at Newcastle: Richard of Hexham, in *Chronicles*, iii. 145–6; John of Hexham, in SD, ii. 287. The terms of the peace agreed, which was subsequently ratified at York, are given by Richard of Hexham, in *Chronicles*, iii. 146.

after no long interval he disregarded the advice of his brother, fortified by whose aid, as I have said, he had thrust his opponents from his path and ascended the throne.

16. In the year of the Lord's Incarnation 1135, the body of King Henry was put on shipboard, when gentle winds blew, immediately after Christmas, and brought to England and buried, in the presence of his successor as king, at the monastery of Reading, which he had distinguished without by vast estates and within by an order of holy monks.[86] Then King Stephen hastened to Northumbria a little before Lent in order to meet David, king of Scots, who was said to entertain different views. He had no difficulty in obtaining from him what he wanted,[87] since David, from the mildness of his character and because he was enfeebled by the approach of old age, was glad to pass into tranquillity, whether it were of a genuine or a pretended peace.[88]

17. In the same year, after Easter, Robert, earl of Gloucester, for whose wisdom Stephen had the greatest respect, came to England.[89] He had wearied his mind with much reflection, while he was in Normandy, on what he thought he should decide to do in this matter. He could see that if he submitted to King Stephen it would be contrary to the oath he had taken to his sister. If he were to resist, it would bring no advantage to his sister or nephews, and would certainly do enormous harm to himself. For—a thing I have touched on above—the king had a vast quantity of treasure, heaped up during many years by his uncle. The coins, which were of the very finest quality, were reckoned to amount to nearly a hundred thousand pounds.[90] There were also vessels of gold and

[88] David was born c.1085, and so was around 50 years old at this date; he did not die until May 1153: Handbook of Chronology, p. 57; and see G. W. S. Barrow, David I of Scotland (1124–1153): The Balance of New and Old (Stenton Lecture for 1984: Reading, 1985), esp. pp. 4–9, and above, pp. xli–xliii.
[89] Easter Day was 22 Mar. Robert of Gloucester was not at Stephen's Easter court at Westminster, but was at Oxford before 26 Apr.: Regesta, iii, p. xl; J. W. Leedom, 'William of Malmesbury and Robert of Gloucester reconsidered', Albion, vi (1974), 251–65, at pp. 257–9.
[90] This probably refers to Henry I's resources in England. His Norman treasure was removed by Robert of Gloucester, on the king's orders according to Orderic, who estimated it at £60,000: RT i. 200–1; OV vi. 448–9.

argentea magni ponderis et inestimabilis pretii, et antiquorum regum, et Henrici potissimum, magnanimitate*a* congesta. Hanc copiam gazarum habenti auxiliatores deesse non poterant, presertim cum esset ipse in dando diffusus, et, quod minime principem decet, prodigus. Currebatur ad eum ab omnium generum militibus, et a leuis armaturae hominibus, maximeque ex Flandria et Britannia.[91] Erat genus hominum rapacissimum et uiolentissimum, qui nichil pensi haberent uel cimiteria frangere uel aecclesias expilare,*b* religiosi quinetiam ordinis uiros non solum equis proturbare, sed et in captionem abducere; nec*c* solum aduenae, sed etiam indigenae milites, qui pacem regis Henrici oderant, quod sub ea tenui uictu uitam transigebant. Hi omnes gratanter principi assenserant, quem leui negotio ad sua commoda inflectere possent, prouintialium dispendio suas fortunas urgentes. Erat preterea Stephanus, cum esset comes, facilitate morum et communione iocandi,*d* considendi, conuescendi*e* etiam cum infimis, amorem tantum demeritus quantum uix mente aliquis concipere queat. Et iam omnes proceres Angliae in eius assensum pronis mentibus transierant. Erat quidem*f* anxius prudentissimus comes ut illos delicti coargueret, et ad saniorem sententiam presenti colloquio reuocaret. Nam uiribus obuiare nulla propter prefatas causas dabatur facultas: cui nimirum nec in Angliam uenire liberum erat, nisi, quasi defectionis eorum particeps, mentis suae archanum ad tempus dissimularet. Itaque homagium regi fecit sub conditione quadam, scilicet, quamdiu ille dignitatem suam integre custodiret et sibi pacta seruaret.[92] Spectato enim iamdudum regis ingenio, instabilitatem fidei eius preuidebat.

464   18.*g* Eodem anno, non multo post aduentum comitis, iurauerunt episcopi fidelitatem regi quamdiu ille libertatem aecclesiae et uigorem disciplinae conseruaret. Ipse quoque iurauit iuxta tenorem scripti quod sic habetur in subditis.

---

a prudentia *Ce*   *b* expoliare *Ce*   *c* non *Ce*   *d* iocundi *A*
e om. *Ce*   *f* igitur *Ce*   *g* Rubric *De sacramento quod rex Stephanus fecit de seruanda iustitia et priuilegiis et legibus regni* Ce

silver of great weight and inestimable value, amassed through the enterprise of earlier kings, and most of all by Henry. As the king had this mass of treasure he could not lack helpers, particularly as he himself was a generous giver and, most inappropriately for a prince, a spendthrift. Knights of all kinds made a rush to him, men who served in light harness also, especially from Flanders and Brittany.[91] They were a class of men full of greed and violence, who cared nothing for breaking into churchyards and plundering churches; moreover, they not only rode down members of religious orders, but even dragged them off to captivity; nor was it only foreign knights that acted in this way, but also some born in England, who hated King Henry's peace because under it they had but a scanty livelihood. All these had gladly given their support to a prince whom with little trouble they could influence to their own advantage, pushing their own fortunes at the expense of the people of the country. Stephen besides, when he was a count, by his good nature and the way he would jest, sit and eat in the company even of the humblest, had earned great affection, so great that it can hardly be imagined. And already all the chief men of England had willingly gone over to his side. The most prudent earl was indeed anxious to convince them of their fault and bring them to a sounder opinion by personal conversation. For—on account of the reasons mentioned above—there was no chance of resistance by force, indeed he could not even come to England, unless he concealed his secret purpose for a time by pretending to share their breach of faith. Therefore he did homage to the king conditionally, namely for as long as the king maintained his rank unimpaired and kept the agreement.[92] Having long observed the king's disposition, he foresaw that he would be likely to break his word.

18. In the same year, not long after the earl's arrival, the bishops swore fealty to the king for as long as he should maintain the freedom of the Church and the strict observance of its discipline. He himself also swore in the terms of the document appended, to this effect:

[91] On Stephen's use of mercenaries see also Richard of Hexham, in *Chronicles*, iii. 145. Gervase of Canterbury says that Flemings were among the forces that Stephen brought to the siege of Exeter in 1136: *Historical Works*, ed. Stubbs, i. 95.

[92] See introduction, above pp. xliv–xlvi.

'Ego Stephanus, Dei gratia, assensu cleri et populi, in regem Angliae electus, et a domino Willelmo archiepiscopo Cantuariae et sanctae *aecclesiae Romanae*[a] legato consecratus, et ab Innocentio sanctae [b]sedis Romanae[b] pontifice postmodum confirmatus,[93] respectu et amore Dei sanctam aecclesiam liberam esse concedo, et debitam reuerentiam illi confirmo. Nichil me in aecclesia uel in rebus aecclesiasticis simoniace acturum uel permissurum esse promitto. Aecclesiasticarum personarum et omnium clericorum et rerum eorum iustitiam et potestatem, et distributionem bonorum aecclesiasticorum, in manu episcoporum esse perhibeo et confirmo. Dignitates aecclesiarum priuilegiis earum confirmatas, et consuetudines earum antiquo tenore habitas, inuiolate manere [c]statuo et concedo.[c] Omnes aecclesiarum possessiones et tenuras, quas die illa habuerunt qua Willelmus rex auus meus fuit uiuus et mortuus, sine omnium calumpniantium reclamatione, eis liberas et absolutas esse concedo. Si quid uero de habitis aut possessis ante mortem regis, quibus modo careat,[d] aecclesia deinceps repetierit, indulgentiae et dispensationi meae uel discutiendum uel restituendum reseruo. Quaecumque uero post mortem regis liberalitate regum, largitione principum, oblatione uel comparatione uel qualibet transmutatione fidelium collata sunt, confirmo. Pacem me et iustitiam in omnibus facturum et pro posse meo conseruaturum promitto. Forestas quas Willelmus rex auus meus et Willelmus secundus auunculus meus instituerunt et tenuerunt, michi reseruo: ceteras omnes, quas Henricus rex[e] superaddidit, aecclesiis et regno quietas reddo et concedo. Si quis autem episcopus uel[f] abbas, uel [g]alia aecclesiastica persona[g] ante mortem suam rationabiliter sua distribuerit, uel distribuenda statuerit, firmum manere concedo: si uero morte preoccupatus fuerit, pro salute animae eius aecclesiae consilio eadem fiat

---

[a-a] Romane ecclesie *A*   [b-b] Romane sedis *Ce*   [c-c] concedo et statuo *B*, statuo et confirmo *Ce*   [d] caret *A*   [e] *om. B*   [f] aut *A*   [g-g] alius ecclesiasticus *Ce*

'I Stephen, by the grace of God, with the approval of the clergy and people, elected king of England, consecrated by Lord William, archbishop of Canterbury and legate of the Holy Roman Church and afterwards confirmed by Innocent, pontiff of the Holy Roman See,[93] from regard and love for God grant that Holy Church shall be free and confirm to it the reverence that I owe. I promise that I will not do or allow anything of the nature of simony in the Church or in what appertains to it. I assert and confirm that jurisdiction and authority over churchmen and all clerks and their property and the distribution of the goods of the Church are in the hands of the bishops. I establish and concede that the prerogatives of the churches, confirmed by their privileges, and the customs which they have enjoyed from of old, shall remain inviolate. All the property of the churches and the tenures that they had on the day when my grandfather William was alive and dead I grant to them in free and absolute possession, not permitting any form of legal challenge. If a church afterwards seeks restoration of what it held or possessed before that king's death and no longer has, I reserve the investigation or restoration of this to my own indulgence and disposal. Whatever has been added after that king's death by the generosity of other kings, the bounty of princes, offerings or purchases or any kind of transfer made by the faithful, I confirm. I promise that I will bring about peace and justice in all things and maintain them so far as lies in my power. The forests that King William my grandfather and King William II my uncle established and held I reserve for myself: all the others that King Henry added I restore and grant to the churches and the kingdom in peaceful possession. If any bishop or abbot or other churchman has distributed his property before his death, or arranged for its distribution, in a reasonable fashion, I grant that this shall stand: if death seized him before he could do this, let the same distribution take place for the benefit of his soul according to

---

[93] Although this is disputed in *Actes de Louis VI*, ii, no. 396, which argues for 1137, there are strong grounds for maintaining that the bull preserved in Richard of Hexham (in *Chronicles*, iii, pp. 147–8; P. Jaffé, *Regesta Pontificum Romanorum*, ed. S. Löwenfeld *et al.* (Leipzig, 1885–8), no. 7804) is that referred to here. Richard of Hexham states this categorically, and the valuable discussion of C. Holdsworth, 'The Church', in King, *Anarchy*, pp. 207–29, at 209–10, offers further support.

distributio. Dum uero sedes propriis fuerint pastoribus uacuae, et ipsae et omnes earum possessiones in manu et custodia clericorum uel*a* proborum hominum eiusdem aecclesiae committantur, donec pastor canonice substituatur. Omnes exactiones et mescheningas et iniustitias, siue per uicecomites uel per alios quoslibet male inductas, funditus exstirpo. Bonas leges et antiquas et iustas consuetudines in murdris et placitis et aliis causis obseruabo, et obseruari precipio et constituo.*b* 94

Apud Oxeneford, anno incarnationis Domini millesimo centesimo tricesimo sexto, regni mei primo.'

465 **19.**ᶜ Nomina testium, qui multi fuerunt, apponere fastidio,⁹⁵ quia pene omnia ita perperam mutauit, quasi ad hoc tamen iurasset ut preuaricatorem sacramenti se regno toti ostenderet. Liceat enim michi, pace mansuetissimi hominis, uerum non occulere; qui, si legitime regnum ingressus fuisset, et in eo amministrando credulas aures maliuolorum susurris non exhibuisset, parum ei profecto ad regiae personae decorem defuisset. Itaque sub eo aliquarum aecclesiarum thesauri direpti, possessiones terrarum laicis datae; aecclesiae clericorum alienis uenditae; episcopi capti et*d* res suas abalienare coacti; abbatiae uel amicorum gratia uel relaxatione debitorum*e* indignis concessae. Sed haec non tam illi quam consiliariis eius ascribenda puto; qui persuadebant ei, numquam eum debere carere denariis dum monasteria essent referta thesauris.

466 **20.**ᶠ Anno Dominicae incarnationis millesimo centesimo tricesimo septimo,ᵍ rex primo tempore Quadragesimae transiit mare.⁹⁶ Comes etiam, pertemptatis illorum et cognitis animis quos datae

ᵃ et *Ce* ᵇ statuo *A* ᶜ *Rubric* Quod rex Stephanus omnia haec que iurauerat perperam mutauit *Ce*¹ ᵈ uel *B* ᵉ *om. A* ᶠ *Rubric* De transitu regis Stephani et Roberti comitis Gloecestre in Normanniam, et de insidiis habitis a rege in comitem *Ce* ᵍ sexto *Ce*

⁹⁴ William prints a full text of Stephen's 'second charter of liberties', with the exception of the witnesses, to which he draws the reader's attention, and one very significant sentence, which he does not signal at all. This is the reservation of his royal rights: 'hec uero omnia concedo et confirmo salua regia et justa dignitate mea': *Regesta*, iii, no. 271. There is a full text in Richard of Hexham (in *Chronicles*, iii. 148–50), and a more popular

the advice of the Church. While sees lack pastors of their own let them and all their property be put in the hands and guardianship of clerks and good men of the same church until a new pastor is appointed according to the canon law. I utterly abolish all exactions, miskennings and injustices, whether wrongfully introduced by sheriffs or by other persons. Good laws and ancient and just customs in what relates to murders and pleas and other cases I will observe, and I enjoin and establish that they be observed.[94]

At Oxford, in the year of the Lord's Incarnation 1136, the first of my reign.'

19. To add the names of the witnesses, who were many, would be a weary task,[95] for he changed almost everything for the worse, just as if he had sworn for no other purpose than showing the whole kingdom he could not keep an oath. It is not right that I should hide the truth, with all respect for a very kindly man; if he had acquired the kingdom in a lawful way, and in administering it had not lent trusting ears to the whispers of those who wished him ill, then undoubtedly he would have lacked little that adorns the royal character. The result was that under him the treasures of some churches were plundered, and their landed property given to laymen; churches belonging to clerks were sold to strangers; bishops were made prisoners and compelled to alienate their property; abbacies were granted to unfit persons either to oblige friends or to pay off debts. But I think these things should not be attributed to him so much as to his counsellors, who used to urge upon him that he should never lack money while the monasteries were full of treasure.

20. In the year of the Lord's Incarnation 1137, the king crossed the sea at the beginning of Lent.[96] The earl also, after thoroughly

version of what was promised—including the abolition of Danegeld—in Henry of Huntingdon (HH, pp. 704–5).
[95] The witnesses numbered in all thirty-seven magnates, including fourteen bishops and four earls, among them Robert of Gloucester: *Regesta*, iii, no. 271.
[96] Ash Wednesday in 1137 fell on 24 Feb. Orderic states that the crossing took place in the third week of March (presumably the week beginning Sunday 14 Mar.): OV vi. 480–1; cf. JW iii. 228–9 ('in March'), HH, pp. 708–9 ('in Lent').

fidei tenaciores esse nouerat, dispositoque quid deinceps agendum decerneret, ipso*a* die Pascae mare ingressus plenaque felicitate in terram euectus est.[97] Nec multo post, malignitatem aduersae fortunae paulominus expertus est. Rex enim eum, incentore quodam Willelmo de Ypra,[98] insidiis intercipere conatus est.[99] Comes autem*b* per quendam insidiarum conscium premunitus, paratos sibi euitauit dolos, et curia, quo sepe inuitabatur, aliquantis diebus abstinuit. Rex, consternatus animo quod insidiis parum profecisset, astutia agendum ratus, serenitate uultus et gratuita confessione magnitudinem culpae attenuare studuit. Iurauit tamen uerbis pro placito comitis conceptis, se numquam ulterius tanto sceleri affuturum, et ut magis in gratiam reciperetur, manu archiepiscopi Hugonis Rotomagensis in manum*c* Rotberti missa, sacramentum solidauit. Et haec quidem egit ille; sed numquam plenam ei exhibuit amicitiam, cuius semper suspectam habebat potentiam. Itaque coram*d* pulchre iocundeque comitem illum*e* appellans, retro maledicis uerbis mordebat, et quibus poterat possessionibus uellicabat. Rotbertus quoque, arte artem eludens, occultabat fronte animum; pacificeque regem in regnum redire dimittens,[100] ipse commodis suis in Normannia manens intendit. Ita Stephano multis tumultibus in Anglia impedito, et nunc super unos,*f* nunc super alios irruente,[101] ut merito illi quod de Ismaele dictum est coaptari posset, quia 'manus omnium contra illum, et illius contra omnes',[102] Rotbertus toto anno illo securum in Normannia egit otium. Rex prompte contra sibi resistentes

---

a ipse B   *b* eas add. Ce   *c* manu A   *d* comite add. AB   *e* om. Ce   *f* hos Ce

---

[97] Easter Day was on 11 Apr. If Robert of Gloucester did not cross until this day, a timing conversant with a desire once again to avoid the ceremonial of the Easter court, then the dates suggested by the editors for *Regesta*, iii, nos. 69, 594, and with them Stephen's itinerary in Normandy in 1137, must be further reconsidered: see introduction, above p. xlvii and n. 181.

[98] William of Ypres, an illegitimate son of Philip of Loo and grandson of Robert the Frisian count of Flanders, the captain of Stephen's Flemish forces, and 'un véritable *condotierre* du xii*e* siècle': Galbert of Bruges, *Histoire du meurtre de Charles le Bon, comte de Flandre (1127–1128)*, ed. H. Pirenne (Paris, 1891), p. 146 n. 3. On his career, see also K. Norgate in *Dictionary of National Biography*; Galbert of Bruges, *The Murder of Charles the Good, Count of Flanders, by Galbert of Bruges*, rev. edn., ed. J. B. Ross (New York, 1967); R. Eales, 'Local loyalties in Norman England: Kent in Stephen's reign', *ANS* viii (1986), 88–108.

testing and learning the disposition of those whom he knew to be
the more tenacious of the faith they had pledged, and after making
arrangements for the conduct of his affairs, put to sea on Easter
day itself and landed without any mishap.[97] Not long afterwards,
he almost experienced the spite of evil fortune. For the king,
instigated by a certain William of Ypres,[98] tried to catch him in an
ambush.[99] But the earl was forewarned about it by someone in the
secret and avoided the trap prepared for him, and for some days he
kept away from court, to which he was frequently invited. The
king, upset by the failure of the ambush, thought he must proceed
by subtle methods, and tried to diminish the enormity of his fault
by a genial countenance and an unsolicited confession. He swore,
however, according to a formula approved by the earl, that he
would never again take part in so great a crime. And, the better to
re-establish cordial relations, he added weight to the oath by
putting the hand of Hugh, archbishop of Rouen, into Robert's.
And yet, though he acted thus, he never showed the earl
unqualified friendship, always regarding his power with suspicion.
Accordingly, though in the earl's presence he addressed him
jovially and emphasized his rank, behind his back he criticized
him in spiteful terms, and fleeced him of what property he could.
Robert also, parrying craft by craft, let his face mask his purpose,
and—after seeing the king off with no sign of hostility on his
return to his kingdom—[100] remained in Normandy and devoted
himself to his own advantage. So, while Stephen was hampered by
many disturbances in England, attacking now some now others,[101]
so that what was said of Ishmael might justly be applied to him,
having 'every man's hand against him and his hand against every
man',[102] Robert spent all that year in Normandy in untroubled
ease. The king, it was reported, was often quick to say of his

[99] On the ambush: OV vi. 484–5; RT i. 207; John of Marmoutier, in *Chroniques des
comtes d'Anjou*, p. 225; and, for discussion, Davis, *Stephen*, p. 25 and n. 9; OV vi. 484–5
n. 4.
[100] Stephen returned to England in Dec. 1137: JW iii. 234–5; RT i. 207 ('in Advent').
[101] Stephen spent Christmas 1137 at Dunstable, and in Jan. 1138 he was engaged in the
siege of Bedford; from there he went to Northumberland, on hearing of Scottish
incursions, and thence returned to Northampton for Easter; from here he proceeded to
the West Country, first to Gloucester, and then to the siege of Hereford: JW iii. 234–43.
[102] Gen. 16: 12.

crebro,*a* ut ferebatur, dicere solebat, 'Cum me in regem elegerint,*b* cur me destituunt? Per nascentiam Dei, numquam rex deiectus appellabor.' Rotbertus, quasi positus in specula, rerum prouidebat exitum, et ne de iuramento, quod sorori fecerat, erga Deum et homines perfidiae notaretur, sedulo cogitabat.

467 **21.**^*c* Anno *d*Dominicae incarnationis*d* millesimo centesimo tricesimo octauo, intestinis discidiis Anglia quatiebatur. Multi siquidem, quos uel*e* nobilitas generis uel magnitudo animi uel potius uiridioris aetatis audacia ad illicita precipitabat, a rege hi predia, hi castella, postremo quaecumque semel collibuisset, petere non uerebantur. Quae cum ille dare differret, excusata mutilatione regni, uel quod eadem alii calumpniarentur, aut etiam possiderent, illi continuo ira commoti castella contra eum offirmabant, predas ingentes ex eius terris agebant. Nec uero ille aliquorum defectione frangebatur animo; sed modo hic, modo illic subitus aderat, semperque suo magis quam resistentium dampno rem confitiebat. Multis enim*f* et magnis laboribus suis in cassum effusis, datis uel*g* honoribus uel castellis, simulatam ad tempus pacem ab illis promerebat.*h* Denique *i*multos etiam*i* comites, qui ante non fuerant, instituit, applicitis possessionibus et redditibus quae proprio iure regi competebant.[103] Erant illi auidiores ad petendum, et is profusior ad dandum, quia fama per Angliam uolitabat, quod comes Gloecestriae Rotbertus, qui erat in Normannia, in proximo partes sororis foret adiuturus, rege tantum modo ante diffidiato.*j* Nec ueritas*k* rerum famae leuitatem destituit. Celeriter enim post Pentecosten, missis a Normannia suis regi more maiorum amicitiam et fidem interdixit, homagio etiam abdicato,[104] rationem preferens quam id iuste faceret, quia et rex illicite ad regnum aspirauerat, et omnem fidem sibi iuratam neglexerat, ne dicam

---

a crebre *AB*   *b* elegerunt *B*   *c* *Rubric* Quomodo et quibus de causis Robertus comes homagium regis abdicauit *Ce*   *d–d* incarnationis Dominice *Ce*   *e* om. *Ce*   *f* om. *B*   *g* om. *A*   *h* premerebat *A*, promerebatur *B*   *i–i* eciam multos *A*   *j* diffidato *Ce*   *k* fides *Ce*

---

[103] On Stephen's creation of earldoms, chiefly in the years 1138 to 1140, see Davis, *Stephen*, pp. 125–41; G. White, 'Continuity in government', in King, *Anarchy*, pp. 117–43, at 124–30.

opponents, 'When they have chosen me king, why do they
abandon me? By the birth of God, I will never be called a king
without a throne!' Robert, as one placed on a watch-tower, was
looking to see how things would end, and considering carefully
how he could avoid being branded before God and man as a traitor
to the oath he had taken to his sister.

21. In the year of the Lord's Incarnation 1138, England was
shaken by internal strife. There were many, impelled to wrong-
doing by high birth or lofty spirit or rather the recklessness of
youth, who did not hesitate to ask the king for estates or castles or
in fact anything that had once taken their fancy. When he put off
giving, saying that the crown estates would be maimed, or that
others laid claim to or were in actual possession of them, they were
at once moved to wrath, fortified castles against him, and carried
off immense plunder from his lands. Yet he was not broken in
spirit by any man's rebellion but appeared suddenly now here,
now there, and always settled the business with more loss to
himself than to his opponents. For after expending many great
efforts in vain, he would win a pretence of peace from them for a
time, by the gift of honours or castles. Thus he also established
many as earls who had not been earls before, with endowments of
landed estates and revenues that had belonged directly to the
king.[103] They were the more greedy in asking, and he the more
lavish in giving, because a rumour was flying over England that
Robert, earl of Gloucester, who was in Normandy, was on the
point of siding with his sister, just as soon as he had defied the
king. Nor did the insubstantial rumour lack confirmation in fact.
For immediately after Whitsuntide, the earl sent representatives
from Normandy and abandoned friendship and faith with the king
in the traditional way, also renouncing his homage,[104] giving as his
reason that he did it justly, because the king had both unlawfully
claimed the throne and disregarded, not to say belied, all the faith

[104] Robert of Torigni says that Robert reached a *concordia* with Geoffrey of Anjou
'about Easter' [3 Apr.] (RT i. 213), which would naturally have preceded the renunciation
of homage to Stephen after Whitsun [22 May] 1138. Orderic condenses the story, but does
not contradict the other chroniclers, in associating the change of allegiance with Geoffrey
of Anjou's invasion in June (OV vi. 514–17).

mentitus fuerat. Ipsemet quin etiam contra legem egisset, qui, post sacramentum quod sorori dederat, alteri cuilibet ea uiuente se manus dare non erubuisset. Animabant nimirum mentem eius multorum religiosorum responsa,[105] quos super negotio consuluerat: nullo modo eum posse sine ignominia uitam presentem transigere, uel merere beatitudinem futurae, si paternae necessitudinis sacramentum *ªirritum haberet.ª* *ᵇAdde quodᵇ* etiam apostolici decreti pre se tenorem ferebat, precipientis ut sacramento, quod presente patre fecerat, obediens esset. Cuius decreti paginam posteriori libello indicere curabo.[106] Haec uir ille, qui plena satietate litterarum scientiam combiberat, magno fructu sibi fore in posterum sciebat. Ceterum, rex egre ferens comitis magnanimitatem, omnibus eum possessionibus in Anglia *ᶜpriuauit quantum in ipso fuit,ᶜ* et quaedam eius castella complanauit.[107] Solum Bristou remansit, ut non solum hostes expelleret, sed etiam *ᵈcrebris regemᵈ* incursionibus fatigaret. Sed quia primum librum Nouellae Historiae a reditu imperatricis post mortem mariti ad patrem hucusque protraxisse suffecerit, nunc secundum ordiemur, ab eo anno quo eadem uirago in Angliam uenit, ius suum contra Stephanum assertura.

ª⁻ª haberet irritum *A*   *ᵇ⁻ᵇ* Addebant quod *A*, Ad hec *Ce*   *ᶜ⁻ᶜ* quibus poterat priuauit *Ce*   *ᵈ⁻ᵈ* regem crebris *A*

---

[105] The statement is echoed in the reference in Gilbert Foliot's letter to Brian Fitz Count to one of the earl's favourite passages in the Scriptures: text in GF, *Letters*, no. 26 (pp. 61–2); comment in A. Morey and C. N. L. Brooke, *Gilbert Foliot and his Letters* (Cambridge, 1965), pp. 115–17, and D. Crouch, 'Robert, earl of Gloucester, and the daughter of Zelophehad', *Journal of Medieval History*, xi (1985), 227–43, at pp. 232–3.

[106] The bull is not inserted later, and does not survive. David Crouch suggests that there may 'have been a general papal injunction to the English magnates (Robert included) secured by Henry I to back up the oath they had sworn': Crouch, 'Robert, earl of Gloucester', p. 242 n. 8.

he had sworn to him. The king himself had also acted contrary to law in that he, after taking the oath to his sister, had not been ashamed to give his hands to another in her lifetime. He was indeed encouraged by the answers of many ecclesiastics whom he had consulted on the matter,[105] who said that there was no way he could pass this present life without disgrace, or win blessedness in the life to come, if he neglected to keep the oath to his father's daughter. In addition to this, he took note of the terms of the papal letter, which bade him obey the oath he had taken in his father's presence. I will take care to insert a page of this letter in a later book.[106] That man, who had drunk a full draught of the knowledge of letters, knew that these things would avail him much for the future. However, the king, indignant at the earl's noble spirit, deprived him of all his English possessions in so far as he could, and levelled some of his castles.[107] Only Bristol remained, from which he could not only drive out his enemies but also harass the king with frequent raids. But because it will be enough to have extended the first book of the *Contemporary History* from the empress's return to her father, after her husband's death, up to this point, I shall now begin the second book from the year when that formidable lady came to England to vindicate her right against Stephen.

---

[107] The story is now picked up most usefully in Orderic, who refers to 'Gloucester castle and Canterbury . . . Bristol, Leeds and Dover' (OV vi. 516–19). *Leeds castle*: besieged by Gilbert de Clare (OV vi. 520–1); surrendered shortly after Christmas 1138 (HH, pp. 718–19). *Dover castle*: besieged by the queen; surrendered by Walkelin Maminot (OV vi. 520–1), on hearing of the fate of the Shrewsbury garrison (HH, pp. 712–13). *Bristol castle*: the king came to Bristol but there were divided counsels and the siege was quickly broken off (*GS*, pp. 64–7), and his troops turned their attention 'ad alia comitis castella', among which were Castle Cary and Harptree in Somerset (JW iii. 250–1). On Harptree, see further *HN* § 37.

LIBER SECUNDVS

22. Anno Dominicae incarnationis millesimo centesimo tricesimo nono, uenenum malitiae diu in animo *Stephani regis*^a nutritum tandem erupit in publicum. Serebantur in Anglia rumores iam iamque aduenturum^b e Normannia comitem Rotbertum cum sorore. Qua spe cum multi a rege non solum animo sed et facto deficerent, ipse *iniurias suas multorum dispendiis*^c sarciebat. Plures etiam pro sola suspitione diuersarum contra se partium in curia sua^d contra decus regium captos, et ad redditionem castellorum et ad quascumque uoluit conditiones adduxit. Erant tunc duo in Anglia episcopi potentissimi, Rogerius Salesberiensis et nepos eius ex fratre, Alexander Lindocoliensis.[108] Alexander ad tutamen, ut dicebat, et dignitatem episcopii castellum de Niwewerche construxerat;[109] Rogerius qui edifitiorum constructione magnanimum se uideri uellet, plura. Apud Scireburnam et apud Diuisas multum terrarum edifitiis amplexus, turritas moles erexerat.[110] Apud Malmesberiam in ipso cimiterio, ab aecclesia principali uix iactu lapidis, castellum inchoauerat.[111] Castellum Salesberiae, quod cum^e regii iuris proprium esset, ab Henrico rege impetratum, muro cinctum custodiae suae attraxerat.[112] His moti quidam potentes laici, qui se a clericis et opum congerie et municipiorum magnitudine superatum iri dolerent, cecum intra

---

^{a–a} regis Stephani *Ce*   ^b euenturum *AB*   ^{c–c} dispendia sua multorum iniuriis *Ce*   ^d om. *B*   ^e om. *AB*

---

[108] Alexander, bishop of Lincoln 1123–48: *Fasti*, ed. Greenway, iii. 1–2; *EEA*, i; *Lincoln 1067–1185*, ed. D. M. Smith (Oxford, 1980), p. xxxiv; HH, pp. liii–lvi.

[109] A series of charters shows the extent of Alexander's ambition in Newark, and suggests a date in the early 1130s for the main work of building of the castle: *Regesta*, ii, nos. 1660–1, 1770, 1772–3, 1791; H. Braun, 'Notes on Newark Castle', *Trans. Thoroton Soc.*, xxxix (1935), 53–91; *Castellarium Anglicanum*, ii. 380.

[110] On Roger's castles, see Kealey, *Roger*, pp. 86–91. The scale of his operations may still be glimpsed at Sherborne, where 'the dominating tower keep was 70ft high, and may date from around 1130': ibid., pp. 87–8; for the plan, see the Department of the Environment Guide; *Castellarium Anglicanum*, i. 128. The castle at Devizes, the finest castle in Europe according to Henry of Huntingdon (HH, pp. 720–1; cf. *GS*, pp. 78–9,

BOOK II

22. In the year of the Lord's Incarnation 1139, the poison of malice, long nurtured in King Stephen's mind, at length burst forth to be observed by all. Reports were being spread in England that Earl Robert might arrive from Normandy at any moment with his sister. And since, in expectation of this, many were deserting the king in deed as well as thought, he sought to assuage his own wrongs by inflicting loss on many. A number too, on mere suspicion of siding against him, he arrested in his own court, in a manner unbefitting a king, in addition requiring the surrender of their castles and making other such terms as he pleased. There were then in England two very powerful bishops, Roger of Salisbury and his nephew through his brother, Alexander of Lincoln.[108] Alexander had built the castle of Newark for the protection, as he said, and glorification of his bishopric;[109] Roger, who wished to be thought of as a great builder, had built several castles. At Sherborne and at Devizes, encircling a wide expanse of ground, he had made ranges of buildings surmounted by great towers.[110] At Malmesbury he had begun a castle in the churchyard itself, hardly a stone's throw from the abbey.[111] The castle at Salisbury, which properly belonged to the king, he had procured from King Henry, surrounded with a wall and brought under his own guardianship.[112] In consequence some powerful laymen, vexed that they would be surpassed by clerks in the amassing of wealth and the size of their castles, nourished within

104–5), is now destroyed: Kealey, *Roger*, pp. 89–90; *VCH Wiltshire*, x. 237–8; *Castellarium Anglicanum*, ii. 498.

[111] Roger's building at Malmesbury is not noted in the A, but appears in the B and C recensions of the *GR* (§ 408): see also *VCH Wiltshire*, iii. 216; *Eulogium*, iii. 61; *Castellarium Anglicanum*, ii. 502.

[112] It was originally of Salisbury (Old Sarum) that William wrote that Roger's buildings were so well made that each wall seemed constructed of a single block of stone: *GR* § 408. The respective rights of the king and the bishop in the borough and the castle are discussed by Sir Francis Hill in *VCH Wiltshire*, vi. 51–3, 56. On the castle, which had a quadrangle similar to that at Sherborne, see ibid., pp. 53–7; Kealey, *Roger*, pp. 86–7; *King's Works*, ii. 824–6; *Castellarium Anglicanum*, ii. 500.

pectus[a] uulnus alebant inuidiae.[113] Itaque conceptas querimonias regi effundunt. Episcopos, oblitos ordinis, in castellis edificandis insanire; nulli dubium esse debere quin haec ad pernitiem regis fierent omnia, dum illi, statim ut uenisset imperatrix, cum traditione castellorum dominae occurrerent, paternorum scilicet benefitiorum memoria inducti. Preueniendos ergo citius, et ad deditionem munitionum artandos. Alioquin regem seram penitentiam acturum, cum in potestate hostium[b] uideret quae, si saperet, sibi apponere potuisset. Haec optimates sepius.[114] Ille, quanuis eis nimio esset fauore obnoxius, aliquamdiu auribus suis blandientes dissimulauit audire, molliens dilationis amaritudinem, uel religionis in episcopis gratia, uel, quod magis opinor, suae detractionis inuidia. Denique illorum,[c] quae proceres suaserant, effectum non distulit, cum primum uolenti se occasio ingessit. Ea fuit huiusmodi.

469 23.[d] Apud Oxeneford circa octauo kalendas Iulii facto conuentu magnatum, predicti quoque pontifices aduenerunt. Inuitus ualde Salesberiensis hanc expeditionem incepit.[115] Audiui[e] eum dicentem uerba in hanc sententiam: 'Per dominam meam sanctam Mariam, nescio quo pacto, reluctatur mens mea huic itineri. Hoc scio, quod eius utilitatis ero in curia, cuius est equinus pullus in pugna.' Ita presagiebat animus mala futura. Tunc quasi fortuna [f]famulari uideretur[f] uoluntati regis, concitatus est tumultus inter homines episcoporum et Alani comitis Britanniae pro uendicandis hospitiis,[116] euentu miserabili ut homines episcopi Salesberiensis,[g] mensae assidentes, semesis epulis ad pugnam prosilirent. Primo maledictis, mox gladiis res acta. Satellites Alani fugati, nepos eius paulominus occisus.[117] Victoria non

---

[a] pectora Ce   [b] esse add. Ce   [c] illarum A   [d] Rubric De captione episcoporum Ce[1]   [e] etenim add. Ce   [f-f] uideretur fauere Ce   [g] ecclesie add. Ce

[113] Virgil, Aen. iv. 2.

[114] The Gesta Stephani refers to Waleran of Meulan and other of the king's councillors, and also says that the king prevaricated (GS, pp. 72–7); Orderic names Waleran and Robert of Leicester first, also Alan of Brittany, and 'a number of others' (OV vi. 530–3). The 'others' may be looked for in the charters associated with this council in Regesta, iii, p. xli (= nos. 452–3, 493, 621–2): these include William Martel and William d'Aubigny. The fullest treatment of 'the arrest of the bishops' is in Kealey, Roger, pp. 173–89. On the Beaumont dominance of court at this time, see Crouch, Beaumont Twins, pp. 43–5.

their hearts an unseen grudge of envy.[113] And so they poured forth
to the king the grievances that had formed in their minds. The
bishops, they said, forgetting they were churchmen, were madly
obsessed with castle-building; no one should doubt that all this was
being done for the king's ruin, against the time when, immediately
on the empress's arrival, they could meet their lady and hand over
the castles, influenced by the recollection of her father's favours.
They should therefore be anticipated with all speed, and compelled
to surrender their fortifications; otherwise the king would repent
when he saw in the power of his enemies what, if he had been wise,
he could have added to his own strength. The chief men kept on
urging this.[114] The king, though easily swayed owing to his
excessive favour towards them, pretended for some time not to
listen to their smooth words, softening the bitterness of his delay
either through regard for religion where bishops were concerned
or, as I think more probable, because he disliked exposing himself
to censure. In the end he did not postpone execution of what the
great men had advised, just as soon as an opportunity met his
wishes. It happened in this way.

23. When a council of the leading men was held at Oxford about
24 June the aforesaid bishops arrived also. The bishop of Salisbury
was most unwilling to set out.[115] I heard him speaking to this
effect: 'By my blessed lady Mary, somehow I am disinclined to
this journey, I know not why! This I do know, that I shall be as
useful at court as a colt in battle.' Thus did his mind forebode the
evil to come. Then, as if fortune were favouring the king's wishes,
a brawl arose between the bishop's men and those of Count Alan
of Brittany about claims on lodgings,[116] with the lamentable result
that the bishop of Salisbury's men, who were sitting at table, leapt
up to fight before they had finished their meal. The contest was
carried on first with abusive language, then with swords. Alan's
followers were put to flight, and his nephew almost killed.[117] Nor

[115] The bishop's reluctance is noted also in the Gloucester chronicle: JW iii. 246–7.
[116] Alan III, a count of Brittany and earl of Richmond, died 1146: *Early Yorkshire
Charters*, iv; *The Honour of Richmond, Part I*, ed. C. T. Clay (Yorks Arch. Soc., Extra Ser.
i, 1935), pp. 89–90.
[117] John of Hexham, in SD ii. 301, says that the nephew died.

incruenta episcopalibus cessit, multis sauciatis, uno etiam milite
occiso.ᵃ Rex, occasionem aucupatus, per antiquos incentores
conueniri iussit episcopos ut curiae suae satisfacerent, de hoc
quod homines eorum pacem ipsius exturbassent. Modus satisfac-
tionis foret, ut claues castellorum suorum quasi fidei uades
traderent. Illos ad satisfatiendum paratos, sed deᵇ deditione
castellorum cunctantes, ne abirent artius asseruari precepit. Ita
Rogerium episcopum absque uinculis, cancellarium, qui nepos uel
plusquam neposᶜ eiusdem episcopi esseᵈ ferebatur,¹¹⁸ compeditum, duxit ad Diuisas, ᵉscilicet castellumᵉ multis et uix numer-
abilibus sumptibus, non, ut ipse presul dictitabat,ᶠ ad ornamentum,
sed, ut se rei ueritas habet, ad aecclesiae detrimentum, edificatum.
In ipsa obsessione castella Salesberiae, Scireburniae, Malmesberiae
regi data: ipsae Diuisae post triduum redditae, cum sibi ultroneum
ieiunium episcopus indixisset,¹¹⁹ ut hac angustia sua animosita-
temᵍ episcopi Heliensis, qui eas occupauerat, flecteret. Nec
ʰepiscopus Lindocoliensis obstinatius egit, redditione castelliʰ
liberationem mercatus.¹²⁰

470   24. Hoc regis factum in diuersas sententias soluit ora multorum.
Quidam dicebant iure castellis alienatos episcopos uideri, quae
preter scita canonum edificassent. Illos euangelistas pacis esse
debere, non architectos domorum quae auctoribus ⁱforent refugium malefitii.ⁱ Haec amplioribus rationibus et sermonibus agebat
Hugo archiepiscopus Rotomagi, quantum illa facundia poterat
maximus regis propugnator.¹²¹ Alii contra, quorum partibus
assistebat Henricus Wintoniensis episcopus, sedis apostolicae in
Anglia legatus, frater regis Stephani, ut ante dixi;¹²² quem nec

ᵃ interfecto Ce   ᵇ om. A   ᶜ id est filius interl. AgAt   ᵈ esse after
nepos Ce   ᵉ⁻ᵉ si uel castellum recipere posset Ce   ᶠ dictabat B
ᵍ animum Ce   ʰ⁻ʰ Alexander ep. Lind. obst. egit, redd. castellorum Niwerh et
Eslefford Ce   ⁱ⁻ⁱ maleficii forent refugium Ce

¹¹⁸ Roger le Poer was appointed chancellor on Stephen's accession, on Roger of
Salisbury's nomination: HN §34; Regesta, iii, p. x. He may have been Roger's son by
Matilda of Ramsbury: OV vi. 533 n. 2.
¹¹⁹ Some chroniclers see this, like William, as a voluntary, others as an involuntary, fast:
see the list in Kealey, Roger, p. 184 n. 46. These represent alternative versions of a clerical
joke that had gone the rounds.
¹²⁰ Alexander of Lincoln was imprisoned at Oxford: HH, pp. 720–1. On Sleaford castle,
see Castellarium Anglicanum, i. 262.

did the bishop's men gain their victory without loss of blood, since many were wounded and one knight slain. The king, seizing the opportunity, ordered the bishops to be summoned by the old fomenters of trouble to satisfy his court for their men's disturbance of his peace. The means of satisfaction was to be the surrender of their castles as guarantees of their trustworthiness. When they were ready to give satisfaction, but hesitated about the surrender of the castles, he put them under close arrest to prevent their going away. Then he brought Bishop Roger, without chaining him, and the chancellor, who was said to be the nephew or an even closer relation of the same bishop,[118] in chains, to Devizes, which castle had been built at great, almost immeasurable expense, not, as the bishop kept on saying himself, for the adornment but, as is in fact the case, for the injury of the Church. In the course of siege-warfare the castles of Salisbury, Sherborne and Malmesbury were delivered up to the king. Devizes itself was surrendered after three days, when the bishop had imposed on himself a voluntary fast,[119] so that by undergoing this suffering he might weaken the resolve of the bishop of Ely, who had taken possession of the place. Nor did the bishop of Lincoln show any more resolution, buying his freedom with the surrender of his castle [Ce *names* Newark *and* Sleaford].[120]

24. This action of the king opened the mouths of many to express different opinions. Some were saying that they thought the bishops had rightly been deprived of castles they had built in defiance of the canon law. They should be evangelists of peace, not builders of houses that might provide a refuge for wrongdoers. This was urged, in more copious argument and language, by Hugh, archbishop of Rouen, the king's foremost champion, with all the power of his great eloquence.[121] Others took the opposite view, supported by Henry, bishop of Winchester, legate in England of the Apostolic See, King Stephen's brother, as I have said above;[122] neither brotherly affection nor fear of danger made

---

[121] Hugh came to the council of Winchester in late August, and William of Malmesbury later says that all waited in suspense to hear what he would say there: *HN* § 29.

[122] *HN* § 14.

fraterna necessitudo, nec periculi metus, a uero^a exorbitare
cogebat. Sic porro dicebat. Si episcopi tramitem iustitiae in
aliquo transgrederentur, non esse regis, sed canonum iuditium.
Sine publico et aecclesiastico concilio illos nulla possessione
priuari debuisse. Regem id non^b rectitudinis zelo, sed commodi
sui compendio fecisse; qui castella non aecclesiis, ex quarum
sumptibus et in quarum terris constructa erant, reddiderit, sed
laicis eisdemque parum religiosis contradiderit.^{123} Ista uir ille tum
priuatim, tum etiam publice coram rege affirmans, eiusdemque
aures de liberatione et restitutione pontificum appellans, omnem
consumpsit operam, in nullo auditus. Quapropter, uigorem canonum experiendum ratus, concilio, quod quarto kalendas Septembris celebraturus erat Wintoniae, fratrem incunctanter adesse
precepit.

471 **25.**^{c} Dicto die omnes fere episcopi Angliae, cum Thetbaldo
archiepiscopo Cantuariae qui Willelmo successerat,^{124} uenerunt
Wintoniam; archiepiscopus Eboracensis Turstanus^d pro ualitudine
qua grauabatur, uix enim animi uiribus corpus regebat,^{125} ceteri
uero pro guerra, litteris absentiam suam excusarunt.^{e} Lectum est
primo in concilio decretum Innocentii papae, quo iam a kalendis
Martii, si bene memini,^{f} partes sollicitudinis suae idem apostolicus
domino episcopo Wintoniensi iure^g legationis in Anglia iniun-
xerat.^{126} Exceptum id summo fauore, quod, diuturnitate temporis
temperantiam suam ostendens episcopus non se prerupta legatum
promulgasset iactantia. Processit deinceps in concilio sermo
eiusdem, latialiter ad litteratos habitus, de indignitate^h captionis

---

^{a} tunc *add. Ce* ^{b} ex *add. B* ^{c} *Rubric* De concilio habito pro captione
episcoporum *Ce*^{1} ^{d} qui *add. A* ^{e} excusabant *A* ^{f} commemini
BCe ^{g} iura *B* ^{h} indignatione *AB*

^{123} Henry of Huntingdon says that Alexander was forced to surrender Newark castle
'into the custody of strangers' (HH, pp. 720–1), who are identified elsewhere as a garrison
of Robert of Leicester: *The Registrum Antiquissimum of the Cathedral Church of Lincoln*, i,
ed. C. W. Foster (Lincoln Rec. Soc. xxvii, 1931), no. 283. Devizes came first to Hervey de
Léon (*GS*, pp. 108–9; *HN* §27), and Sherborne to William Martel (*GS*, pp. 148–9; *HN*
§51); on the subsequent history of Malmesbury see the Ce interpolation in *HN* §31.
^{124} William of Corbeil died 21 Nov. 1136. Theobald (prior 1127–36, abbot 1136–8) of
Bec was elected archbishop of Canterbury 24 Dec. 1138 and consecrated 8 Jan. 1139: *Fasti*,
ed. Greenway, ii. 4; Saltman, *Theobald*, pp. 9–13; *Councils and Synods*, i (2), pp. 768–79.

him swerve from the truth. Thus he spoke. If the bishops had in anything stepped aside from the path of justice, then it was not for the king to judge them, but for the canon law. Without a general council of churchmen they should not have been deprived of any property. The king had not acted thus through zeal for righteousness, but to serve his own advantage, seeing that he had not restored the castles to the churches at whose expense and on whose land they had been built, but handed them over to laymen and moreover men of little religion.[123] He spent all his efforts in saying these things both in private and openly in the king's presence, appealing to him to free and restore the bishops, but nothing that he said had any effect. And so, he decided he would try what force lay in the canon law, ordering his brother promptly to attend a council which he was to hold at Winchester on 29 August.

25. On the appointed day almost all the bishops of England came to Winchester, together with Theobald, archbishop of Canterbury, the successor of William;[124] Thurstan, the archbishop of York, excused his absence by letter on account of the ill-health from which he was suffering, for he could scarcely govern his body by the strength of his mind;[125] the others made the war their excuse. At the opening of the council a letter of Pope Innocent was read, whereby, as early as 1 March, if I remember rightly, the pope had given his commission to the lord bishop of Winchester with the office of legate in England.[126] It was most favourably received that the bishop had shown his restraint by delay and not hastened ostentatiously to announce himself as legate. Next he made a speech before the council, in Latin, as he was addressing educated

[125] Thurstan, nominated archbishop of York 15 Aug. 1114, died 6 Feb. 1140. He had led the northern forces to the battlefield of the Standard on 22 Aug. 1138, but had sent the dean as his deputy to the council which had elected Theobald to Canterbury the following Christmas: Richard of Hexham, in *Chronicles*, iii. 173. See D. Nicholl, *Thurstan, Archbishop of York (1114–1140)* (York, 1964); *EEA*, v; *York 1070–1154*, ed. J. E. Burton (Oxford, 1988), pp. xxvi–xxx; P. Dalton, *Conquest, Anarchy and Lordship: Yorkshire, 1066–1154* (Cambridge, 1994), pp. 148–52.

[126] This date would fit with Henry having made an arrangement with the legate Alberic of Ostia, or himself making a direct appeal to the pope, immediately following Theobald's election to Canterbury. The journey from England to Rome could take up to seven weeks: R. L. Poole, *Studies in Chronology and History* (Oxford, 1934), pp. 263–4.

episcoporum: quorum Salesberiensis in camera curiae, Lindocoliensis in diuersorio suo intercepti essent; Heliensis exemplum
simile ueritus, ueloci profugio ad Diuisas se calamitati exemisset.
Scelus miserabile, regem ab incentoribus ita fuisse seductum, ut
hominibus suis, presertim episcopis, in curiae suae pace manus inici
iussisset. Adiecta esset regio dedecori caelestis iniuria, ut, sub
obtentu culpae pontificum, aecclesiae possessionibus suis spoliar-
entur. Sibi regis contra ^alegem Dei^a excessum tanto dolori esse, ut
mallet se multo dispendio et corporis et rerum suarum affici, quam
episcopalem celsitudinem tanta indignitate deici. Quin etiam regem
de emendatione peccati multotiens commonitum; postremo tunc^b
concilii uocationem non abnuisse. Proinde archiepiscopus et ceteri
consulerent in medium quid opus esset facto. Se ad executionem
concilii nec pro regis amicitia,^c qui sibi frater erat, nec pro dampno
possessionum, nec etiam pro capitis periculo defuturum.

472 **26.** Dum^d haec ille sensim per amplificationem exponit, rex, causae
suae non diffisus, comites in concilium misit, querens cur uocatus
esset. Responsum est a legato ex compendio non debere illum, qui
se Christi fidei subiectum meminisset, indignari si a ministris
Christi ad satisfactionem uocatus esset, tanti reatus^e conscius
quantum nostra secula nusquam uidissent. Gentilium quippe
seculorum opus esset episcopos incarcerare et possessionibus
suis exuere. Dicerent ergo fratri, quod si consilio suo placidum
commodare dignaretur assensum, tale illi Deo auctore largiretur,
cui nec aecclesia Romana, nec curia regis Frantiae, nec ipse comes
Thetbaldus frater amborum,[127] sapiens profecto uir et religiosus,
ex ratione contraire posset, sed quod fauorabiliter complecti
deberent. Consulte uero impresentiarum rex faceret, si uel
rationem facti sui redderet, uel canonicum iuditium subiret. Ex

---

^{a–a} Dei legem *Ce*   ^b om. *Ce*   ^c amicitia *after* erat *Ce*   ^d Cum
AB   ^e reati *ACd*

[127] Theobald IV, count of Blois 1107–52, was the elder brother of Stephen and of
Henry of Winchester. He is found acting in concert with Louis VI, in supporting
Stephen's accession (noted in a papal bull of Feb./Mar. 1136, above n. 93); he was
involved with Louis VII during peace discussions in Nov. 1140 (*HN* § 40); and between
these dates was closely associated with the French crown: H. d'Arbois de Jubainville,
Histoire des ducs et des comtes de Champagne, 7 vols. (Paris, 1859–69), ii. 317–43.

men, on the indignity of arresting the bishops, of whom the bishop
of Salisbury had been seized in a room at court, and the bishop of
Lincoln in his lodging, while the bishop of Ely, apprehensive of a
similar fate, had escaped disaster by a speedy flight to Devizes. It
was a lamentable crime, he said, that the king had been so led
astray by those who instigated him to this as to order hands to be
laid on his men, especially when they were bishops, in the peace of
his court. To the king's disgrace had been added a wrong to
heaven, in that, under pretence of the bishops' being at fault,
churches were robbed of their property. The king's outrage upon
divine law caused him so much grief that he would sooner suffer
great damage to his person and possessions than that the dignity of
bishops should be lowered by such a humiliation. The king,
moreover, had often been urged to atone for his sin, and then
finally had not rejected a summons to the council. Therefore let
the archbishop and the others take counsel together about what
should be done. He himself would not fail to carry out the decision
of the council either out of regard for the king, who was his
brother, or for fear of loss of property or even danger to life.

26. While the legate thus expressed himself deliberately and at
length, the king, who did not lack confidence in his own case, sent
earls to the council to enquire why he had been summoned. In
summary, this was the legate's answer, that one who kept in mind
that he owed obedience to the faith of Christ should not complain
if summoned by Christ's ministers to give satisfaction, when he
knew himself guilty of an offence such as our times had nowhere
seen. It belonged to pagan times to imprison bishops and deprive
them of their property. Let them therefore tell his brother that, if
he thought fit to acquiesce calmly in his advice, he would by God's
will give him advice to which neither the Church of Rome, nor the
court of the king of France, nor even Count Theobald, the brother
of both of them,[127] certainly a wise and religious man, could
reasonably object, but which they ought to accept with favour. In
the present juncture the king would act prudently, if he either
gave an explanation of what he had done, or submitted to
judgment according to canon law. It was also his bounden duty

debito etiam oportere ut aecclesiae faueret, cuius sinu exceptus, non manu militum, in regnum promotus fuisset. Sic[a] cum dicto comites egressi nec multo post prouiso[b] responso reuersi sunt. Comitabatur eos Albericus quidam de Ver, homo causarum uarietatibus exercitatus.[128] Is responsum regis retulit, et quantum potuit causam antistitis[c] Rogerii, [d]episcopus enim Alexander abierat,[d] grauauit: modeste tamen, sine ulla uerborum[e] contumelia, quanuis quidam comitum, stantes[f] iuxta, crebro loquelam eius interrumperent, probra in episcopum iacientes.

473   27. Haec ergo fuit summa dictorum Alberici. Multis iniuriis Rogerium episcopum affecisse regem Stephanum. Rarissime ad curiam uenisse, quin homines sui, de eius potentia presumentes, seditiones mouissent. Qui cum sepe alias, tum nuper apud Oxeneford fecissent impetum in homines et in ipsum nepotem comitis Alani, in homines etiam Heruei de Liuns, qui esset tantae nobilitatis, tanti supercilii, ut numquam regi Henrico petenti animum indulserit in Angliam uenire.[129] In iniuriam ergo regis Stephani redundare, pro cuius amore uenerit, quod ei[g] tanta uis illata sit. Episcopum Lindocoliensem, ex ueteri odio in Alanum,[130] seditionis per[h] homines suos auctorem fuisse. Episcopum Salesberiensem inimicis regis clam fauere, dissimulata interim pro tempore uersutia. Id regem ex multis indubitanter comperisse; eoque potissimum, quod Rogerium de Mortemer, cum militibus regiis quos ductitabat,[i] in summo de Bristowensibus metu, nec una nocte idem episcopus Malmesberiae manere dimisisset.[131]

---

[a] om. Ce   [b] cum Ce   [c] antistis Ce   [d-d] quam manutenuit add. Ce[1], manutenuit episcopus enim A, aberat quam Ce[2]   [e] uerba A   [f] astantes Ce   [g] ea Ce   [h] super B   [i] ducebat Ce

[128] Aubrey de Vere, appointed master-chamberlain in 1133: *Regesta*, ii, p. xiii, no. 1777; iii, pp. xix, xxiii; Green, *Henry I*, p. 276. He died 15 May 1140: M. Brett, 'The annals of Bermondsey, Southwark and Merton', *Church and City, 1000–1500: Essays in Honour of Christopher Brooke*, ed. D. Abulafia *et al.* (Cambridge, 1992), pp. 279–310, at 299.

[129] Hervey *brito*, vicomte of Léon in Brittany, received from Stephen the honour of Eye *c*.1139, possibly on his marriage to one of Stephen's illegitimate daughters; was appointed earl of Wiltshire with the grant of Devizes castle in 1140; and was driven from the castle and left England in 1141: *GS*, pp. 108–9; Davis, *Stephen*, pp. 136–7; *Eye Priory Cartulary and Charters*, ed. V. Brown, 2 vols. (Suffolk Charters, xii–xiii; Woodbridge, 1992–4), ii.

to favour the Church, by whose fostering care, not by military force, he had been raised to the throne. When this had been said the earls left, and not long afterwards they returned furnished with a reply. They were accompanied by Aubrey de Vere, a man of wide experience in legal affairs.[128] He gave the king's answer and did all the harm he could to Bishop Roger's case—for Bishop Alexander was not there—yet he did it with restraint and without abusive language, though some of the earls, standing by his side, often interrupted his speech by hurling insults at the bishop.

27. This then was the sum of what Aubrey said. Bishop Roger had inflicted many wrongs on King Stephen. He had very seldom come to court without his men raising a brawl, presuming on his power. At many other times and recently at Oxford they had attacked Count Alan's men and even his nephew, as well as the men of Hervey de Léon, who was so high-born and so proud he had never deigned to come to England at King Henry's request.[129] It therefore amounted to a wrong to King Stephen, from affection for whom Hervey had come, that such violence had been offered to him. The bishop of Lincoln, owing to an old hatred for Alan,[130] had stirred up the brawl through his men. The bishop of Salisbury secretly favoured the king's enemies, though for the time being he dissembled, until circumstances should change. The king had learnt that beyond doubt by many proofs, and this especially, that the bishop had not allowed Roger de Mortimer, with the king's troops whom he was leading, to stay even one night at Malmesbury, when he was in the greatest dread of the people of Bristol.[131]

23–6. On the history of the family, see H. Guillotel, 'Les vicomtes de Léon au xi⁰ et xii⁰ siècles', *Memoires de la Société d'histoire et d'archéologie de Bretagne*, li (1971), 29–51, and for comment, see K. S. B. Keats-Rohan, 'The Bretons and Normans of England 1066–1154', *Nottingham Medieval Studies*, xxxvi (1992), 42–78.

[130] There is no patent reason for this antagonism, but Count Alan held extensive lands in Lincolnshire, and Bishop Alexander's episcopal seat at Lincoln, and his two castles of Newark and Sleaford, were situated at key points on the network of rivers and roads that led to Alan's rapidly growing and very profitable seaport of Boston. Sleaford was only 12 miles from Boston, and Alexander had the grant of a fair there: *Regesta*, iii, no. 476.

[131] No date can be suggested for the incident complained of, though it may be noted that Roger of Salisbury was staying at Malmesbury when he received the summons to the Oxford council. Roger de Mortimer is identified as son of Hugh de Mortimer (d. *c.*1148) in *CP* ix. 269–70, on evidence that is admitted to be 'purely circumstantial'.

Omnibus esse in ore, quod, statim ut imperatrix uenisset, ille se[a] ad eam cum nepotibus et castellis conferret. Rogerius itaque captus sit non ut episcopus, sed ut regis seruiens, qui et procurationes eius amministraret et solidatas acciperet. Castella non per uiolentiam rex eripuerit, sed episcopi ambo gratanter reddiderint, ut calumpniam de tumultu quem in curia concitauerant euaderent. [b]Aliquantum pecuniarum[b] rex in castellis inuenerit, quae ipsius legitime essent, quia eas[c] tempore regis Henrici, auunculi et antecessoris sui, ex fisci regii redditibus [d]Rogerius episcopus[d] collegisset. Eis tamen, sicut et castellis, idem presul pro timore commissorum in regem libens cesserit. Inde non deesse testes regi. Ipsum proinde uelle ut pacta inter se et episcopos rata permanerent.

474 **28.** Reclamatum est ab episcopo Rogerio contra sermones Alberici, quod numquam regis Stephani minister fuisset, nec ipsius solidatas[e] accepisset.[132] Minae quinetiam ab animoso uiro, et qui malis erubesceret frangi, prolatae,[f] si iustitiam de rebus sibi ablatis in illo concilio non inueniret,[g] eam in audientia maioris curiae querendam. Leniter legatus, ut cetera: 'omnia quae dicuntur contra episcopos prius in concilio aecclesiastico et accusari et an uera essent decuisset inquiri, quam in indempnes contra canonum decreta sententiam proferri. Rex itaque faciat, quod etiam in forensibus iuditiis legitimum est fieri, ut reuestiat episcopos de rebus suis. Alioquin iure gentium dissaisati[h] non placitabunt.'

475 **29.** Dictis in hunc modum utrobique multis, causa petitu regis in posterum diem dilata,[i] nec minus in crastino[j] ad aduentum archiepiscopi Rotomagensis post tridie prolongata. Is ubi uenit, omnium suspensis animis quidnam afferret, dixit se concedere ut [k]episcopi castella[k] haberent si se iure habere debere per canones

---

[a] se *after* castellis *Ce*   [b–b] Aliquantulum pecunie *A*   [c] in *add. A*
[d–d] episcopus Rogerius *A*   [e] solidates *A*   [f] prolati *ACd*   [g] inuenisset
Ce   [h] dissaisiati *CdCe*[1], dissaisiti *Ce*[2]   [i] prolata *A*   [j] crastinum
Ce   [k–k] castella episcopi *B*

Everyone was saying that as soon as the empress came he would take her side together with his nephews and his castles. Roger then had been arrested not as a bishop but as a servant of the king, who both managed his affairs and had received his pay. The king had not seized the castles by force, but both the bishops had surrendered them gladly to avoid facing a charge for the brawl they had stirred up at court. The king had found a certain amount of money in the castles, but it was money that lawfully belonged to him, because Bishop Roger had amassed it from the revenues of the royal treasury in the time of King Henry, his uncle and predecessor. Hence the said bishop, frightened of his offences against the king, had willingly yielded it up to him, just as he had his castles. The king did not lack witnesses of this. It was therefore his wish that the agreement between himself and the bishops should remain in force.

28. Bishop Roger loudly contradicted Aubrey's statements, saying that he had never been King Stephen's servant or received his pay.[132] What is more, he uttered threats, for he was a man of spirit, and one ashamed to be broken by misfortune, saying that if he did not find justice in that council for what had been taken from him he would seek it in the hearing of a higher court. The legate said, with his usual moderation: 'All the charges against the bishops should have been made, and their truth investigated in a Church council, rather than having sentence pronounced, contrary to canon law, against men who had not been proved guilty. The king should do what is proper even in other jurisdictions, and reinstate the bishops in their property. Otherwise, by natural law, if they are dispossessed they will not plead.'

29. After much had been said in this fashion on both sides, the case at the king's request was adjourned to the next day, and on the morrow was put off again till the arrival of the archbishop of Rouen two days later. When he came, with all in suspense as to what he might contribute, he said he would allow the bishops to

---

[132] Roger's importance in Stephen's administration is not in doubt, and is not being denied here. Aubrey de Vere's language, as reported, Roger would have found demeaning: he insists he was not one of the royal *ministri*, not a salaried official.

probare possent; quod quia non possent, extremae improbitatis
esse contra canones niti uelle. 'Et esto', inquit, 'iustum sit ut
habeant: certe, quia suspectum est tempus, secundum morem
aliarum gentium,[133] optimates omnes claues munitionum suarum
debent uoluntati regis contradere, qui pro omnium pace debet
militare. Ita omnis controuersia episcoporum infirmabitur.[a] Aut
enim secundum canonum scita iniustum est ut habeant castella;
aut, si hoc pro indulgentia principali toleratur, ut tradant claues
476 necessitati temporis debent cedere.' His [b]addidit predictus[b] cau-
sidicus Albericus: significatum esse regi quod mussitarent[c] inter se
pontifices, pararentque aliquos ex suis contra eum Romam mittere.
'Et hoc', ait, 'laudat uobis rex, ne quisquam uestrum presumat
facere; quia, si quis contra uoluntatem suam et regni dignitatem ab
Anglia quoquam iret,[d] difficilis ei fortassis reditus foret. Ipse
quinetiam quia se grauari uidet, ultro uos[e] ad Romam appellat.'

477 **30.** Haec postquam rex partim quasi laudando, partim minando
mandasset, intellectum est quo tenderet. Quapropter ita discessum
est, ut nec ipse censuram canonum pati uellet, nec episcopi in[f]
eum exercere[g] consultum ducerent, duplici ex causa: seu quia
principem excommunicare sine apostolica conscientia temerarium
esset; seu quoniam audirent, quidam etiam uiderent, gladios circa
se nudari. Non enim iam ludicra erant uerba, sed de uita et
sanguine pene certabatur.[134] Non omiserunt tamen legatus et
archiepiscopus quin tenorem offitii sui prosequerentur. Suppli-
citer enim pedibus regis in cubiculo affusi, orauerunt ut misereretur aecclesiae, misereretur animae et famae suae, nec pateretur
fieri discidium inter regnum et sacerdotium.[135] Ille dignanter
assurgens, quanuis a se facti eorum amoliretur inuidiam, malorum
tamen preuentus consiliis, nullam bonarum[h] promissionum exhibuit efficatiam.

[a] infirmabatur *AB*   [b-b] predictus subiecit *Ce*   [c] *Winterbottom (cf.* GR §
147.2), minitarent *A,* minaretur *B,* murmurarent *Ce*   [d] ierit *A*   [e] uos *after*
appellat *Ce*   [f] *om. AB*   [g] exerere *ACe,* execrare *Cd*   [h] bonorum *A*

[133] On the 'rendability' of castles, see introduction, p. li and n. 205.
[134] Virgil, *Aen.* xii. 764–5.
[135] So also HH, pp. 722–3 ('the king granted them nothing'), but according to the *GS,*
pp. 80–1, Stephen 'humbly accepted the penance enjoined for his fault'.

have their castles if they could prove by the canon law that they were entitled to have them; but, as they could not, it was a mark of extreme wickedness to wish to strive against the canon law. 'Even granted', he said, 'that it is right for them to have the castles, yet certainly, as it is a time of uncertainty, all the chief men, in accordance with the custom of other peoples,[133] ought to hand over the keys of their fortifications to the disposal of the king, whose duty it is to fight for the peace of all. So the bishops' whole case will fall to the ground. For either it is unjust, according to canon law, for them to have castles, or, if this is permitted by the king as an act of grace, they ought to yield to the emergencies of the time by delivering up the keys.' To this Aubrey, the advocate mentioned above, added that the king had been told that the bishops were quietly indignant, and were preparing to send some of their number to Rome against him. 'The king also admonishes you', he said, 'that no one of you should presume to do this, for if anyone went anywhere out of England, contrary to his wish and the dignity of the crown, it might be difficult for him to return. Moreover, since he sees he is being unfairly burdened, he himself for his part summons you to Rome.'

30. After this message from the king, which was a mixture of advice and threat, they understood what he was aiming at. In consequence the council broke up, for the king would not consent to bear a canonical censure, nor did the bishops think it wise to harass him, for two reasons, one, that it was rash to excommunicate a prince without the pope's cognizance, the other, that they heard, and some even saw, swords being drawn around them. For it was no longer a dialectical game, but wellnigh a struggle for men's life-blood.[134] However, the legate and the archbishop did not fail to pursue the course that their duty prescribed. For they fell as suppliants at the king's feet in his room, and begged him to take pity on the Church, pity on his soul and reputation, and not suffer a divorce to be made between the monarchy and the clergy.[135] Though he graciously stood up, and removed the stigma that their act had laid on him, yet, forestalled by the advice of wicked men, he showed no signs of carrying out his worthy promises.

478 31.^a Kalendis Septembris solutum est concilium. Pridie uero kalendarum Octobrium comes Rotbertus, tandem nexus morarum eluctatus, cum sorore imperatrice inuectus est Angliae,¹³⁶ fretus pietate Dei et fide legitimi sacramenti. Ceterum multo minore armorum apparatu quam quis alius tam periculosum bellum aggredi temptaret, non enim plusquam centum quadraginta milites tunc secum adduxit. Testimonio ueridicorum relatorum sermo meus nititur. Dicerem, nisi adulatio uideretur, non imparem fuisse^b Iulio Cesari dumtaxat animo, quem Titus Liuius commemorat quinque solum cohortes habuisse quando ciuile bellum inchoauit; cum quibus, inquiens, orbem terrarum adorsus^c est.¹³⁷ Quanuis iniqua comparatione Iulius et Rotbertus conferantur. Iulius enim, uerae fidei extorris, in fortuna sua, ut dicebat, et legionum uirtute spem reclinabat. Rotbertus, Christiana pietate insignis,^d in Sancti Spiritus et dominae sanctae Mariae patrocinio totus pendulus erat. Ille in tota Gallia, et partim in Germania et Britannia, fautores habens, omnem etiam Romanam plebem, excepto senatu, muneribus sibi deuinxerat. Iste, preter paucissimos qui fidei quondam iuratae non immemores erant, in Anglia optimates uel aduersantes uel nichil adiuuantes expertus est. Appulit ergo Arundel, ibique nouercae suae, quam, amissa matre imperatricis, ut prefatus sum,¹³⁸ ^eHenricus rex^e quondam lecto copulauerat, tuta, ut putabat, custodia sororem interim delegauit. Ipse per tam confertam barbariem, uixdum, ut^f audiui, duodecim militibus comitatus, Bristou contendit, occurrente sibi medio itineris Briano filio comitis ex Walingeford. Nec multo post cognouit sororem ex Arundel profectam. Nouerca enim feminea leuitate fidem, totiens etiam missis in Normanniam nuntiis promissam,¹³⁹ fefellerat.¹⁴⁰

^a *Rubric* De adventu imperatricis et Roberti comitis in Angliam *Ce*   ^b illum *add. Ce*   ^c adortus *Ce*   ^d insignitus *A*   ^{e-e} rex Henricus *A*   ^f om. *A*

¹³⁶ Robert of Torigni states that the landing was in August (RT i. 215); Orderic that it took place 'in autumn' (OV vi. 534–5); John of Worcester says that Robert landed 'in the month of October', while the Gloucester chronicle has 1 Aug. (JW iii. 268–9).
¹³⁷ Orosius, *Hist. adv. paganos*, vi. 15. 3, quoted from William's historical collection, Oxford, Bodleian Library, MS Arch. Seld. B 16, fo. 53ᵛ.   ¹³⁸ *HN* §2.
¹³⁹ The claims of the empress occasioned not just considerable debate but considerable correspondence. The Gloucester chronicler says that the local magnates invited the empress, 'missis nuntiis Andegauis ciuitatem', saying she could take England in five

31. The council broke up on 1 September. On 30 September Earl Robert, escaping at last from hampering delays, landed in England with his sister the empress,[136] relying on the mercy of God and his fidelity to a lawful oath. He came, however, with a far smaller military force than that with which anyone else would have ventured on so hazardous a war, for he brought with him at that time no more than 140 knights. My statement is based on the authority of trustworthy informants. Did it not seem flattery, I would say that he was not unequal, at any rate in spirit, to Julius Caesar, of whom Titus Livius tells us that he had only five cohorts when he began the civil war, with which, says Livy, he assailed the world.[137] The comparison between Julius and Robert is, however, unfair. Julius, having no part in the true faith, rested his hopes on his luck, as he said, and the valour of his legions. Robert, distinguished for his Christian piety, entirely relied on the aid of the Holy Spirit and Our Blessed Lady, Mary. Julius had supporters in the whole of Gaul and parts of Germany and Britain and had attached the entire Roman people to himself with gifts, except the Senate. Robert found that in England the nobles were either hostile or gave no help, apart from a very few who had not forgotten the faith they once swore. So he landed at Arundel, and there entrusted his sister for the time being, in what he believed to be safe guardianship, to her stepmother, whom, as I said earlier,[138] King Henry had married after the loss of the empress's mother. He himself, through such a mass of barbarians, with as yet, I have heard, hardly twelve knights to accompany him, hastened to Bristol, and Brian Fitz Count from Wallingford met him half-way on his journey. Not long after he learnt that his sister had left Arundel. For her stepmother, with a woman's fickleness, in despite of the undertakings she had given via the many messengers she had sent to Normandy,[139] broke the faith she had sworn.[140]

months (JW iii. 252–3; and Chibnall, *Matilda*, pp. 80–1); Robert of Torigni says that Adeliza's husband, William d'Aubigny, invited her (RT i. 215); William says here that Adeliza had offered support, and later (*HN* § 59) that Henry of Winchester had also done so. All may be correct, but the nature of the undertakings they gave, and the true extent of their feelings, can only be guessed at.

[140] Adeliza, on being challenged and 'fearing that she would lose the dignity that she held in England', claimed that she had simply offered hospitality to her former dependents (JW iii. 268–9); the empress and the earl had been admitted to the castle, 'quasi hospitandi gratia' (*GS*, pp. 86–7).

Dedit *porro rex*ᵃ imperatrici Wintoniensis episcopi Henrici[141] et comitis Mellentensis Waleranni conductum; quem cuilibet, quanuis*ᵇ* infestissimo inimico, negare laudabilium militum mos non est. Et Walerannus quidem ultra Calnam tendere supersedit,[142] episcopo in conductu perseuerante. Contractis ergo comes celeriter copiis ad metas a rege datas aduenit, sororemque ᶜBristou ad tutioraᶜ perduxit. Recepit illam postea in Gloecestram Milo,[143] qui castellum eiusdem urbis sub comite habebat, tempore regis Henrici dato ei homagio et fidelitatis sacramento.[144] Nam eadem ciuitas caput est sui comitatus.*ᵈ*

ᵃ⁻ᵃ ergo rex *A*, rex porro *Ce*   ᵇ quis *AB*   ᶜ⁻ᶜ ad Bristou tutior *Ce*
ᵈ *Ce adds rubric* Quomodo rex ceperat Malmesberiam, et de obsidione Trohbrigie *and text* Nonis Octobris Robertus quidam, filius Huberti, immanis ac barbarus, castellum Malmesberie, quod Rogerius episcopus infausto auspicio inchoauerat, furtim noctu ingressus, combustoque uico, quasi magno triumpho gloriatus est. Veruntamen ante quindecim dies letitia excidit, a rege fugatus. Castellum precepit rex interim asseruari, quoad pace data posset destrui. Ipse uero rex, antequam Malmesberiam uenisset, quandam munitiunculam Milonis supernominati, Cernei nomine, occupauerat, ibique milites suos posuerat. Quapropter, sicut et ibi et Malmesberie, alias sibi successurum existimans, castellum Hunfridi de Buhun, qui partibus imperatricis fauebat, uocabulo Trobrigge, inuasit, set irritus abiit.

---

[141] Henry of Winchester (concealing the fact that he had already come to an agreement with the earl of Gloucester) advised the king to let the empress go to Bristol, so that he might focus his attack there (*GS*, pp. 86–91); and so the king ordered that Henry accompany her, 'sicut cognatam suam cum honore' (JW iii. 268–9).

[142] Calne is 11 miles south of Malmesbury. It lies a little to the north of the direct route from Arundel to Bristol, which suggests that Marlborough was one of the staging points upon the way.

[143] Miles of Gloucester became sheriff and castellan of Gloucester in succession to his father Walter *c.*1126, was created earl of Hereford by the empress on 25 July 1141 (*HN* §45), and died 24 Dec. 1143: *CP* vi. 451–4; D. Walker, 'Miles of Gloucester, earl of Hereford', *Trans. of the Bristol and Gloucester Arch. Soc.*, lxxvii (1958), 66–84. Miles came first to Bristol, and thence escorted the empress to Gloucester (*Regesta*, iii, no. 391), where they arrived on 15 Oct. (JW iii. 270–1).

[144] That Miles of Gloucester was the feudal dependent of Robert of Gloucester is confirmed by John of Worcester ('ad dominum suum comitem Glaucestrensem . . . se contulit': JW iii. 270–1), and by their *conuentio* in 1142 (below, *HN* §73). This was clearly a matter which Robert of Gloucester wished to see correctly minuted.

[145] Robert Fitz Hubert was believed to be related to William of Ypres: JW iii. 286–7.

[146] John of Worcester goes from Miles's defection to the king attacking Wallingford and then investing Malmesbury; but then turns his attention to events in Worcester: JW iii. 270–7. The closest parallel to this paragraph in other chronicles is in *Gesta Stephani*, which has Stephen going from Wallingford to Trowbridge, capturing South Cerney and Malmesbury *en route*: *GS*, pp. 92–5.

Then the king gave the empress the escort of Henry, bishop of Winchester,[141] and Waleran, count of Meulan, escort which it is not the custom of honourable knights to refuse to anyone, even their bitterest enemy. Waleran for his part went no further than Calne,[142] but the bishop continued as escort. So the earl, quickly gathering his forces, arrived at the limits prescribed by the king, and brought his sister to greater safety at Bristol. She was thereafter received at Gloucester by Miles,[143] its castellan under the earl, who in the time of king Henry had done homage and sworn fealty to him.[144] For that city is the chief place of his earldom.

[Ce *adds* On 7 October a certain Robert Fitz Hubert,[145] a cruel   479 and savage man, stealthily entered by night the castle of Malmesbury, which Bishop Roger had begun under an evil star, and after burning the town boasted of it as though it were a great victory.[146] However, within fifteen days he was cast down from his rejoicing, being put to flight by the king. The king gave orders for the castle to be guarded for a time until, with the coming of peace, it could be demolished. The king himself, before arriving at Malmesbury, had seized a small fortification of the Miles mentioned above, named Cerney, and had posted a garrison there.[147] Wherefore, thinking he would be as successful elsewhere as there and at Malmesbury, he attacked a castle of Humphrey de Bohun, who sided with the empress, named Trowbridge, but went away without achieving anything.[148]]

---

[147] The *Gesta Stephani* refers to 'castellum de Cernei quod . . . Milo construxerat': *GS*, pp. 92–3; *Castellarium Anglicanum*, i. 181. South Cerney, Gloucestershire, was a demesne manor of Miles of Gloucester: D. Walker, 'The "Honours" of the earls of Hereford in the twelfth century', *Trans. of the Bristol and Gloucester Arch. Soc.*, lxxix (1960), 174–211, at pp. 198–9.

[148] Humphrey III de Bohun (d. 1165), royal steward, was a frequent attestor of the charters of Henry I, of Stephen, of the empress (to whom he transferred his allegiance after her landing), and of Henry II: *Regesta*, ii, p. xii; Green, *Henry I*, p. 236; *Regesta*, iii, pp. xviii, xxxi, no. 111; L. Delisle, *Receuil des actes de Henri II concernant les provinces françaises et les affaires de France: Introduction* (Paris, 1909), p. 385. His father, Humphrey II (d. *c.*1129), had acquired the honour of Trowbridge on his marriage to the daughter of Edward of Salisbury: I. J. Sanders, *English Baronies: A Study of their Origin and Descent, 1086–1327* (Oxford, 1960), p. 91. Humphrey III married the daughter and co-heir of Miles of Gloucester (ibid., p. 7), and he strengthened Trowbridge castle 'consilio et incitatu Milonis' (*GS*, pp. 92–3). This is the first reference to the castle: *VCH Wiltshire*, vii. 128, 131; *Castellarium Anglicanum*, ii. 502.

480 **32.**[a] Tota itaque regio circa Gloecestram usque profundas Walas, partim ui, partim beneuolentia pedetemptim residuis illius anni mensibus se dominae imperatrici applicuit. Aliquanti castellanorum, intra munitiones suas se contutantes, exitum rerum[b] speculabantur. Ciuitas Hereford sine difficultate recepta: pauci milites, in castello animis obstinatis se includentes, a foris obsessi.[149] Appropinquauit rex si forte laborantibus opem aliquam comminisci posset; sed frustratus uoto, inglorius discessit. Equitauit etiam iuxta Bristou, superiusque contendens, uillas quae [c]in circuitu Dunestore erant[c] combussit,[150] nichil omnino, in quantum ualebat, reliquum fatiens quod posset inimicis suis esui uel alicui usui esse.

481 **33.**[d] Tertio idus Decembris Rogerius episcopus Salesberiae febrem quartanam, qua iamdudum quassabatur,[e] benefitio mortis euasit. Dolore animi aiunt eum[f] contraxisse ualitudinem, utpote tantis et tam[g] crebris a rege Stephano pulsatum incommodis. Eum michi uidetur Deus exemplum diuitibus pro uolubilitate rerum exhibuisse, ne sperent in incerto diuitiarum; quas quidam, ut ait apostolus, appetentes a fide naufragauerunt.[151] Insinuatus est primo comiti Henrico, qui postmodum rex fuit, pro prudentia res domesticas amministrandi, et luxum familiae cohibendi.[152] Fuit enim Henricus ante regnum in expensis parci animi et frugi, penuria scilicet rei familiaris astrictus, fratribus Willelmo et Rotberto arroganter eum tractantibus. Cuius cognitis moribus, Rogerius ita eum tempore inopiae demeruit, ut, cum ille solium regni ascendisset, nichil ei aut parum negaret quod ipse petendum putasset. Largiri predia, aecclesias, prebendas clericorum, abbatias integras monachorum, ipsum postremo regnum fidei eius committere. Cancellarium in[h] initio regni, nec multo post episcopum

[a] *Rubric* Quomodo Hereford cessit imperatrici *Ce*   [b] rei *A*   [c-c] fuerunt in circuitu Dunestor *Ce*   [d] *Rubric* De obitu et moribus Rogerii episcopi Salesberie *Ce*   [e] a *add. Ce*   [f] *om. A*   [g] *om. B*   [h] *om. Ce*

[149] Hereford had been captured by Stephen in 1138. In Dec. 1139 the town was retaken by the Angevins, under Miles of Gloucester, and royal troops were besieged in the castle: JW iii. 242–5, 276–7; *GS*, pp. 94–7; on the castle, *King's Works*, ii. 673–7; *Castellarium Anglicanum*, i. 206.

32. So the whole district around Gloucester as far as the depth of Wales, partly under compulsion and partly from goodwill, gradually went over to the lady empress in the remaining months of that year. Some of the castellans, keeping safe within their fortifications, were watching how things would turn out. The city of Hereford was gained without difficulty: a few knights, resolutely shutting themselves up in the castle, were besieged from outside.[149] The king approached on the chance of being able to devise some help for them in their difficulties, but was disappointed of his wish, and departed ignominiously. He also led a cavalry raid near Bristol and, making his way up-country, burnt the villages round Dunster,[150] leaving nothing at all, as far as it lay in his power, that could serve his enemies for food or for any purpose.

33. On 11 December Roger, bishop of Salisbury, escaped from a quartan fever, by which he had long been afflicted, by the favour of death. They say he contracted the illness from mental suffering, having been assailed by King Stephen with injuries so many and so great. God seems to me to have displayed him to the rich as a warning of the mutability of things, lest they should trust in the uncertainty of riches, the search for which, as the Apostle says, has led some people to the shipwreck of their faith.[151] He first made his way into the confidence of Count Henry, who afterwards became king, through prudence in managing his private affairs, and checking the luxury of his household.[152] For Henry, before he began to reign, was sparing and frugal in his expenditure, being hampered by lack of means, since his brothers William and Robert treated him with disdain. Learning his character, Roger deserved so well of him in his time of need, that on ascending the throne he refused Roger little or nothing that he himself thought fit to ask. He lavished on him estates, churches, prebends of clerks, whole abbeys of monks, finally entrusting the very kingdom to him. He made him chancellor at the beginning of his reign, and not long

---

[150] William de Mohun, the lord of Dunster, had rebelled against Stephen before the empress landed (GS, pp. 80–3; OV vi. 518–19), and was created earl of Somerset by her in 1141: CP xii (1), pp. 37–9. [151] 1 Tim. 1: 19.
[152] The treatment of Roger of Salisbury here may be compared with that in GR §408, and GP, pp. 132–3.

Salesberiae, fecit.[153] Rogerius ergo agebat causas, ipse moderaba-
tur expensas, ipse seruabat gazas. Hoc quando rex erat in Anglia;
hoc sine sotio et teste quando, quod crebro et diu accidit,
morabatur Normanniae.[154] Nec solum a rege, sed et ab optimatibus, ab his etiam quos felicitatis eius inuidia clam mordebat,
maximeque a ministris et*a* debitoribus regis, ei quaecumque pene
cogitasset conferebantur. Si quid possessionibus eius contiguum
erat quod suis utilitatibus conduceret, continuo uel prece uel
pretio,[155] sin minus uiolentia, extorquebat. Ipse, singulari gloria,
quantum nostra aetas reminisci potest, in domibus edificandis,
splendida per omnes possessiones suas construxit habitacula, in
quibus solum tuendis successorum eius frustra laborabit opera.
Sedem suam mirificis ornamentis et edifitiis, citra ullam expen-
sarum parsimoniam, in immensum extulit. Erat prorsus mirum
uidere de homine illo, quanta eum in omni genere dignitatum
opum sequebatur copia, et quasi ad manum affluebat. Quantula illa
gloria, qua quid posset accidere maius, quod duos nepotes, suae
educationis opera,[156] honestae litteraturae et industriae uiros,
effecit episcopos? Nec uero exilium episcopatuum, sed Lindocoliensis et Heliensis, quibus opulentiores nescio si habet Anglia.[157]
Sentiebat ipse quantum posset,*b* et, aliquanto durius quam talem
uirum deceret, Diuinitatis abutebatur indulgentia. Denique, sicut
poeta quidam de quolibet*c* diuite dicit, 'diruit, edificat, mutat
quadrata rotundis',[158] ita Rogerius abbatias in episcopatum, res
episcopatus in abbatiam*d* alterare conatus est.*e* Malmesberiense[159]
et Abbedesberiense,[160] antiquissima cenobia, quantum in ipso fuit,

---

a tunc *add. Ce*   *b* potuit *Ag* potuit uel posset *AoAt*   *c* quodam *Ce*
d abbatias *A*   *e* om. *B*

---

[153] Roger was appointed chancellor about Easter 1101 (*Regesta*, ii, p. ix, no. 528; Kealey,
Roger, p. 12), invested as bishop of Salisbury *c.* 29 Sept. 1102, and consecrated 11 Aug.
1107 (*Fasti*, ed. Greenway, iv. 2).
[154] On Roger of Salisbury's administrative work, see Green, *Henry I*, esp. pp. 38–50.
[155] Ovid, *Fasti*, ii. 806.
[156] They were educated at the schools of Laon: Hermann of Tournai, *De miraculis S.
Mariae Laudunensis* (Migne, *PL* clvi. 982–3); F. Barlow, *The English Church 1066–1154*
(London, 1979), pp. 248–50.
[157] After Canterbury and Winchester, Lincoln and Ely were indeed two of the
wealthiest dioceses in England. Lincoln was valued at *c.* £600 in 1086 (W. J. Corbett,
'The development of Normandy and the Norman conquest of England', *Cambridge*

afterwards bishop of Salisbury.[153] So Roger pleaded the cases, controlled the expenditure himself, kept the treasure himself. All this when the king was in England; and so also—acting without colleague or witness—when the king was staying in Normandy, as he did very often and for long periods.[154] And not only from the king, but also from the nobles, even those who were gnawed in secret by envy of his prosperity, and especially from the king's servants and his debtors, he received almost anything he could think of. Anything bordering his property that suited his requirements, he extracted at once by prayer or price,[155] otherwise by force. He himself, since in building he took an especial pride unsurpassed within the recollection of our age, made magnificent dwellings on all his estates, for the mere upkeep of which his successors will spend their efforts in vain. His own see he glorified beyond measure by wondrous ornaments and buildings, without any sparing of expense. It was indeed remarkable to observe of that man, what abundance of wealth followed him in every high office he held, flowing into his hand, as it were. How little he boasted of the fact (though what greater thing could have fallen to his lot?) that he made bishops of two nephews, who thanks to the education he gave them were men of credit for learning and zeal.[156] Nor were these poor bishoprics, but those of Lincoln and Ely, as rich perhaps as any that England holds.[157] He himself was conscious of his power, and he abused God's indulgence rather more persistently than was proper for such a man. And just as a poet says of a rich man, that he 'pulls down and builds, exchanges square for round',[158] so Roger tried to turn abbeys into a bishopric, the property of a bishopric into an abbey. Two most ancient monasteries, those of Malmesbury[159] and Abbotsbury,[160] he

Medieval History, v (Cambridge, 1926), p. 511); this included Cambridgeshire, which became the diocese of Ely in 1109, and Nigel at the beginning of his episcopate (1133–69), so the monks of Ely later complained, 'had our lands and possessions in his seisin', which had been valued at c. £770 in 1086 (E. Miller, The Abbey and Bishopric of Ely (Cambridge, 1951), pp. 75–6, 287–8; Knowles, Monastic Order, p. 702).

[158] Horace, Epist. i. 1. 100.

[159] The abbacy was suspended between 1118 and 1140, and the monastery reduced to the status of a priory: see introduction, above, pp. xxvii–xxviii.

[160] The abbacy of Abbotsbury in Dorset was suspended between 1107 and 1140: Heads, p. 23.

episcopatui delegauit. Scireburnensem prioratum, qui proprius est episcopi Salesberiensis, in abbatiam mutauit,[161] abbatia de Hortuna proinde destructa et adiecta.[162]

34. Haec tempore regis Henrici, sub quo res eius, ut dixi, magnis successibus floruerunt. Sed enim sub Stephano,[a] sicut predixi,[163] retro sublapsae sunt;[164] nisi quod in initio regni eius nepotibus suis, uni cancellariam, alteri thesaurariam,[b] [165] sibi burgum Malmesberiae impetrauit,[166] subinde rege familiaribus suis ingeminante. 'Per nascentiam Dei, medietatem Angliae darem ei, si peteret, donec tempus pertranseat. Ante deficiet ipse in petendo, quam ego in dando.' Posterioribus annis fortuna, nimium [c]ante et[c] diu [d]ei blandita,[d] ad extremum scorpiacea crudeliter hominem cauda percussit. Quale fuit illud, quod ante ora sua uidit homines bene de se meritos sauciari et[e] familiarissimum militem obtruncari; postero die seipsum et,[f] ut supra fatus sum,[167] nepotes suos potentissimos episcopos, unum fugari,[g] alterum teneri, tertium, dilectissimum sibi adolescentem, compedibus uinciri; post redditionem castellorum thesauros suos diripi, et se postmodum in concilio fedissimis conuitiis proscindi; ad ultimum, cum apud Salesberiam pene anhelaret in exitum, quicquid residuum erat nummorum et uasorum,[168] quod scilicet ad perficiendam aecclesiam super altare posuerat, se inuito asportari. Extremum puto calamitatis, cuius etiam me miseret, quod, cum multis miser uideretur, paucissimis [h]erat miserabilis:[h] tantum liuoris et odii ex nimia potentia contraxerat, et immerito apud quosdam quos etiam honoribus auxerat.

---

[a] rege add. Ce   [b] thesauriam A   [c–c] ante B, et ante Ce   [d–d] blandita ei B   [e] om. Ce   [f] et after fatus sum Ce   [g] et add. A   [h–h] miserabilis erat B

---

[161] Thurstan, prior of Sherborne, was raised to the abbacy in 1122: Heads, p. 70. William wrote of the house in 1125 as 'nunc de presulatu in abbatiam mutatus': GP, p. 175.

[162] The abbey of Horton in Dorset, 'modo destructa' in 1125 (GP, p. 203), became a priory: D. Knowles and R. N. Hadcock, Medieval Religious Houses, England and Wales, 2nd edn. (London, 1971), pp. 54, 68.

[163] HN § 22 ff.

[164] Virgil, Aen. ii. 169.

[165] The chancellor was Roger le Poer, his son (HN § 23); the treasurer was Adelelm, his

attached to the bishopric as far as lay in his power. The priory of Sherborne, which belongs directly to the bishop of Salisbury, he turned into an abbey,[161] suppressing the abbey of Horton on that account and adding it to Sherborne.[162]

34. This was in the time of King Henry, under whom—as I have just said—his affairs prospered exceedingly. But under Stephen— as I have said before[163]—they suffered a decline,[164] except that at the beginning of Stephen's reign he obtained for one of his nephews the post of chancellor and for another that of treasurer,[165] and for himself the borough of Malmesbury,[166] the king repeating to his friends from time to time: 'By the birth of God! I would give him half England if he asked for it, until his time shall pass: he will grow tired of asking before I do of giving.' In later years fortune, that had favoured him excessively for so long, at last stung the man cruelly with a scorpion's tail. What grief it was that he saw before his own eyes men who had deserved well of him being wounded, a knight who was his close intimate cut down; on the next day his own arrest, whilst—as I have related above[167]—of his two nephews, bishops of great power, one was put to flight, the other arrested, while a third, a young man he dearly loved, was put in chains; after the surrender of the castles the plunder of his treasure and himself later in the council lashed with the vilest abuse; finally, when he was almost breathing his last at Salisbury, the carrying off against his will of all the money and precious vessels he had left,[168] which he had placed on the altar for the completion of the cathedral. I think it the crown of his misfortune, and I am sorry for it myself, that while to many he seemed a man of sorrows, yet very few were sorry for him. He had acquired so much envy and hatred by his excessive power, undeservedly too among some whom he had even advanced to posts of distinction.

nephew, archdeacon of Dorset, and later dean of Lincoln (*Regesta*, iii, p. xix; *Fasti*, ed. Greenway, iii. 8–9, iv. 25). On them see Kealey, *Roger*, pp. 272–4.

[166] *Regesta*, iii, no. 784.

[167] *HN* §23.

[168] John of Worcester says he does not know how much the treasure was worth, but, according to the Gloucester chronicle, 'there are some who say' that the coins alone came to more than 40,000 marks: JW iii. 276–7. The author of the *Gesta Stephani* claimed that the canons of Salisbury offered the treasure to the king: *GS*, pp. 96–9.

482 **35.**[a] Anno incarnati Verbi millesimo centesimo quadragesimo, monachi abbatiarum quas Rogerius episcopus contra fas tenuerat, rege adito, antiqua priuilegia et abbates habere meruerunt.[169] Electus est in abbatem Malmesberiae a monachis, secundum tenorem priuilegii quod beatus Aldelmus a Sergio papa iam ante quadringentos et sexaginta sex annos impetrauerat,[170] et a regibus Westsaxonum Ina, Mertiorum Ethelredo, roborari fecerat,[171] eiusdem loci monachus Iohannes,[b] uir benignitate morum et animi liberalitate apprime insignis. Probauit legatus causam, improbauit personam. Nullo enim modo menti eius persuaderi poterat regem preter dationem pecuniae electioni consensisse. Et quidem aliquantum nummorum promissum fuerat, causa libertatis aecclesiae, non electionis personae. Itaque Iohannes, quanuis immatura morte anno eodem prereptus fuerit,[172] aeternam tamen et laudabilem sui memoriam cunctis post se seculis dereliquit. Nullus enim, uere fateor, eius loci monachus tantae magnanimitatis facto assisteret, nisi Iohannes inchoasset. Itaque habeant successores eius laudem si libertatem aecclesiae tutati fuerint; ipse proculdubio eam a seruitute uendicauit.

483 **36.**[c] Totus annus ille asperitate guerrae inhorruit.[173] Castella erant crebra[d] per totam Angliam, quaeque suas partes defendentia, immo ut uerius dicam, depopulantia. Milites castellorum abduce-bant ab agris et pecora et pecudes, nec aecclesiis nec cimiteriis parcentes.[e] Domibus miserorum ruricolarum usque ad stratum[f] expilatis, ipsos uinctos incarcerabant; nec, nisi omnibus quaecum-que habebant,[g] et[h] quocumque modo adquirere poterant, in

---

[a] *Rubric* De restitutione abbatiarum *Ce*   [b] Iohannes *after* fecerat *A*
[c] *Rubric* De confusione guerre per Angliam *Ce*   [d] om. *A*   [e] Vauassores, rusticos, quicumque pecuniosi putabantur, intercipientes, suppliciorum magnitudine ad quoduis promittendum cogebant *add. Ce*   [f] stramen *Ce*   [g] et quecumque *add. AB*   [h] om. *A*

---

[169] Stephen kept Christmas 1139 at Salisbury and moved early in Jan. 1140 to Reading to keep the anniversary of Henry I's burial; there he appointed John as abbot of Malmesbury and Geoffrey as abbot of Abbotsbury: JW iii. 278–81; *GS*, pp. 98–9; *Heads*, pp. 23, 55.

[170] The bull of Pope Sergius is given in *GP*, pp. 367–70; this is William of Malmesbury's own translation of the Anglo-Saxon version found in BL Cotton MS Otho C. i, fos. 68–9: see N. Berry, 'St Aldhelm, William of Malmesbury, and the liberty of

35. In the year of the Incarnate Word 1140, the monks of the abbeys that Bishop Roger had unlawfully held approached the king, and obtained the restoration of their ancient privileges and their abbots.[169] In accordance with the terms of the privilege that the blessed Aldhelm had gained from Pope Sergius 466 years before,[170] and had ratified by Ine king of Wessex and Æthelred king of Mercia,[171] the monks elected as abbot of Malmesbury a monk of that place named John, a man especially distinguished by his kindly nature and noble mind. The legate approved their claim to elect but disapproved of the person elected, for in no way could he be convinced that the king had agreed to the election without a bribe. And it is a fact that a certain amount of money had been promised, but it was to secure the freedom of the Church, not the election of a person. So John, though carried off that same year by an untimely death,[172] yet left a lasting and honourable recollection of himself to all succeeding ages. For no monk of that place, I frankly confess, would have taken part in so spirited an act had not John given a lead. So let his successors be praised if they maintain the freedom of the Church, but it was he beyond doubt who rescued it from slavery.

36. That whole year was troubled by the brutalities of war.[173] There were many castles all over England, each defending its own district or, to be more truthful, plundering it. The knights from the castles carried off both herds and flocks, sparing neither churches nor graveyards. [**Ce** *adds* Under-tenants, peasants, any who were thought wealthy, they kidnapped and compelled to promise anything by the severity of their tortures.] After plundering the dwellings of the wretched countrymen to their very foundations, they bound the owners and imprisoned them, and did not let them go until they had spent for their ransom all they

Malmesbury Abbey', *Reading Medieval Studies*, xvi (1990), 15–38, reproducing the passage on election as no. [5] on pp. 32–3.

[171] *GP*, p. 374.

[172] Abbot John died on 19 Aug. 1140: JW iii. 280–1; and see further introduction, above pp. xxx–xxxi.

[173] There are echoes here of the main themes of the classic description of the anarchy in *ASC*, s.a. 1137, and the treatment in other chronicles, which draw ultimately on the provisions for the Peace of God: for a recent survey see *The Peace of God: Social Violence and Religious Response in France around the Year 1000*, ed. T. Head and R. Landes (Ithaca, NY, 1992); and see further introduction, pp. xcv–xcvi.

redemptionem consumptis, dimittebant. Plures in ipsis tormentis quibus ad se redimendum constringebantur dulces efflabant animas,[174] quod solum poterant, Deo miserias suas applorantes. Et quidem, ex uoluntate comitis, legatus cum episcopis omnes effractores cimiteriorum et uiolatores aecclesiarum, et qui sacri uel religiosi ordinis hominibus uel eorum famulis manus iniecissent, multotiens excommunicauit; sed nichil propemodum hac profecit industria. Erat ergo uidere calamitatem, Angliam, preclarissimam quondam pacis[a] nutriculam, speciale domicilium quietis, ad hoc miseriae deuolutam esse, ut nec etiam episcopi nec monachi de uilla in uillam tuto possent progredi. Sub Henrico rege multi alienigenae, qui genialis humi inquietationibus[b] exagitabantur, Angliam annauigabant, et sub [c]eius alis[c] quietum otium agebant. Sub Stephano plures ex Flandria et Britannia, rapto uiuere assueti,[175] spe magnarum predarum Angliam inuolabant.

37. Comes[d] interea modeste [e]se agere,[e] nichil magis cauere quam ne uel paruo detrimento suorum[f] uinceret. Magnates Anglorum, quos ad religionem iurisiurandi seruandam flectere non posset, satis habebat in offitio continere, ut qui nichil adiuuare uellent minus nocerent, uolens[g] secundum comicum quod posset, dum non posset quod uellet.[176] Vbicumque tamen commode fieri posse uidebat, et militis et ducis probe offitium exequebatur. Denique munitiones, quae potissimum partibus susceptis nocebant, strenue debellabat;[h] fratrem etiam suum Rainaldum in tanta difficultate

[a] om. B   [b] turbelis B   [c-c] alis eius A   [d] Gloecestre Robertus add. Ce   [e-e] agere se AB   [f] om. B   [g] uolens after comicum Ce   [h] debellauit Ce adding scilicet Harpetreu, quam rex Stephanus a quibusdam militibus comitis, antequam in Angliam uenisset, ceperat; et alias multas, Sudleie, Cernei, quam rex, ut dixi, militibus suis impleuerat; et castellum quod idem rex contra Valengeford offirmauerat, solo complanauit

[174] Virgil, *Aen.* iii. 140.   [175] Virgil, *Aen.* ix. 613.
[176] Terence, *Andria*, ii. 5–6; the same passage is used again, below §66.
[177] For Stephen's investment and capture of Harptree (*Castellarium Anglicanum*, ii. 443), see JW iii. 250–1, and *GS*, pp. 66–9, which identifies the earl of Gloucester's tenant as William Fitz John.
[178] Sudeley, the 'south place' of Winchcombe, lies in Gloucestershire adjacent to the county boundary with Wiltshire: *Castellarium Anglicanum*, i. 183. It was in the hands of John Fitz Harold, a grandson of Ralph earl of Hereford (d. 1057): see D. Bates, 'Lord Sudeley's ancestors; the family of the counts of Amiens, Valois and the Vexin in France and England during the 11th century', *The Sudeleys—Lords of Toddington* (Manorial

possessed, or could in any way obtain. Many breathed forth their dear lives[174] during the very tortures by which they were being forced to ransom themselves, lamenting their sufferings to God, which was all they could do. And indeed, by the earl's wish, the legate, with the bishops, many times excommunicated all who broke into graveyards and outraged churches, and who laid hands on men of a holy or religious order or their servants, but he accomplished hardly anything by these efforts. So a dreadful thing could be seen, that England, once the noblest nurse of peace, the peculiar habitation of tranquillity, had sunk to such wretchedness, that even bishops or monks could not safely pass from village to village. Under King Henry many foreigners, displaced by troubles in their native land, sailed to England and lived in undisturbed peace under his wings. Under Stephen many from Flanders and Brittany, who were wont to live by plunder,[175] flew to England in the hope of great booty.

37. Meanwhile the earl behaved with restraint, and avoided nothing more carefully than even a slight loss of men to gain a battle. The great ones of England whom he could not influence to keep their solemn oath he was content to maintain in their positions, so that those who would give no help might do less harm, in the words of the comic poet, wishing to do what he could as he could not what he would.[176] Still, wherever he saw that it could conveniently be done, he nobly fulfilled the duty of a knight and a leader. For instance he reduced with vigour the fortifications that did most harm to the cause he had adopted; [Ce *adds* for example Harptree, which the king had taken from some of the earl's knights before he came to England,[177] and many others, Sudeley,[178] Cerney, which the king, as I said,[179] garrisoned; and he levelled to the ground the castle the king had fortified against Wallingford[180]] and, in view of the great difficulties of the time, he

Society of Great Britain, 1987), pp. 34–48, at 35. John of Worcester says that Waleran of Meulan raided the area early in Dec. 1139, on hearing that John Fitz Harold had deserted to the empress (JW iii. 274–7), and that almost two months later, early in Feb. 1140, Miles of Gloucester attacked and burnt Winchcombe, then moved against Sudeley, but was driven back by the king's knights (JW iii. 282–3).　　　　　　　　　　[179] *HN* §31.
[180] Wallingford in Berkshire was the *caput* of the honour of Brian Fitz Count. Stephen moved against Wallingford immediately after the empress landed in 1139, but abandoned

temporis comitem Cornubiae creauit.[181] Nec uero minor erat regi
animus ad*a* adeunda quae sibi competebant munia, qui nullam
occasionem pretermittebat quo minus sepe et aduersarios propul-
saret et sua defenderet. Sed frustrabatur successibus uergebantque
in peius omnia, pro iustitiae penuria. Iamque caritas annonae
paulatim crescebat, et pro falsitate difficultas *b* monetae tanta erat,
ut interdum ex decem et eo amplius solidis uix duodecim denarii
reciperentur. Ferebatur ipse rex pondus denariorum, quod fuerat
tempore regis Henrici, alleuiari iussisse;[182] quia, exhausto pre-
decessoris sui immenso illo thesauro, tot militum expensis
nequiret sufficere. Erant igitur Angliae cuncta uenalia;[183] et iam
non clam, sed palam, aecclesiae et abbatiae uenum distrahebantur.

484   38.*c* Eo anno in Quadragesima, tertiodecimo kalendas Aprilis hora
nona feria quarta, fuit eclipsis, per totam Angliam ut accepi.[184]
Apud nos certe, et apud omnes uicinos nostros, ita notabiliter solis
deliquium fuit, ut homines, quod tunc fere ubique accidit,*d* mensis
assidentes, primum*e* antiquum chaos timerent;[185] mox, re cognita,
progredientes, stellas circa solem cernerent. Cogitatum et dictum
est a multis, non falso, regem non perannaturum in regno.*f*

485   39.*g* Sequenti ebdomada, ipso tempore Passionis, septimo kalendas
Aprilis, *h*Rotbertus quidam filius Huberti immanis et barbarus et *h*
ad furta belli peridoneus, castellum de Diuisis clanculo intercepit.
Homo cunctorum quos nostri seculi memoria complectitur imma-
nissimus, in Deum etiam blasphemus. Vltro quippe gloriari
solebat se interfuisse ubi quater uiginti monachi pariter cum
aecclesia concremati fuerint: idem se in Anglia factitaturum et

    a om. Ce   *b* enim add. Ce   *c* Rubric De eclipsi solis Ce   *d* erat enim
quadragesima add. Ce   *e* om. Ce   *f* sine dispendio add. Ce   *g* Rubric
De captione Roberti filii Huberti Ce[1]   *h-h* prefatus barbarus Robertus filius Huberti
Ce

the siege and set up two siege-castles: GS, pp. 90–3; John of Worcester also refers to
antecastellis, JW, iii. 272–3; and see further Castellarium Anglicanum, i. 12–13, ii, App.,
pp. 566–7.

[181] GS, pp. 100–3, states that William Fitz Richard gave Reginald his daughter in
marriage, admitted him to one of the royal castles, and thus transferred to him the
comitatus of Cornwall; and see further Davis, Stephen, p. 136. Reginald was an illegitimate

made his brother Reginald earl of Cornwall.[181] Nor yet did the king show less spirit in dealing with the tasks that fell to his lot. He never missed a chance, and they were many, of driving back his opponents and defending his own. But he had no success, and things went from bad to worse, for the lack of justice. The price of grain rose steadily; and because of counterfeiting there were such problems with the coinage, that on occasion hardly 12 pennies could be accepted out of 10 shillings or more. It was said that the king himself had ordered the weight of pennies to be reduced from what it had been in King Henry's time,[182] because, after exhausting his predecessor's huge treasure, he could not meet the expenses of so many knights. So everything in England was for sale,[183] and now churches and abbeys were split up and sold not secretly but openly.

38. That year in Lent, on 20 March, at the ninth hour on a Wednesday, there was an eclipse, all over England, I have heard.[184] With us certainly and all our neighbours the sun was so notably absent that at first men sitting at table, as they mostly were at the time, feared the primeval chaos;[185] then, hearing what it was, they went out and saw the stars round the sun. It was thought and said by many, nor were they wrong, that the king would not survive the year in office [**Ce** *adds* without loss].

39. In the following week, just at the time of the Passion, on 26 March, a certain Robert Fitz Hubert, a cruel and savage man, well suited to the stratagems of war, took by stealth the castle of Devizes. He was the cruellest of all men within the recollection of our age, and also a blasphemer against God. He used to boast gratuitously that he had been present when eighty monks were burnt together with their church, and said he would do the same

son of Henry I by Sibyl Corbet: *CP* xi, App. D, pp. 107–8; he remained earl of Cornwall until his death on 1 July 1175.

[182] M. Blackburn, 'Coinage and currency', in King, *Anarchy*, pp. 145–205, at 169–73, shows that there is evidence of weight reduction in coins from some mints, including Wilton, at the end of Type I.   [183] Sallust, *Bell. Iug.* viii. 1.

[184] On the eclipse of 20 Mar. 1140, see Newton, *Medieval Chronicles and the Rotation of the Earth*, pp. 99–100, 163–6. Other contemporary recordings are found in John of Worcester (JW iii. 284–5), and the *Anglo-Saxon Chronicle* (*ASC* E, s.a. 1140).

[185] Ovid, *Met.* ii. 299.

Deum contristaturum depredatione Wiltoniensis aecclesiae et*a*
subuersione Malmesberiensis, cum monachorum illius loci
omnium cede. Id se muneris eis repensurum, quod regem ad
nocumentum sui admississent; hoc enim illis*b* imponebat, sed falso.
Hisce auribus audiui, quod si quando captiuos, quod quidem
rarissime fuit, immunes absque tortionibus dimittebat, et gratiae
ipsi de Dei parte agebantur, audiui, inquam, eum respondisse,
'Numquam michi Deus grates sciat.' Captiuos melle litos flagran-
tissimo sole nudos sub diuo*c* exponebat, muscas et id generis
animalia ad eos compungendum irritans. Iam uero nactus Diuisas,
iactare*d* non dubitauit se totam regionem a Wintonia usque
Lundoniam per id castellum occupaturum, et ad tuitionem sui
pro militibus Flandriam missurum. Haec facere meditantem ultio
caelestis impediuit per Iohannem quendam,*e* magnae uersutiae
uirum, qui apud Merleberge castellum habebat.[186] Ab eo siquidem*f* uinculis innodatus, quia Diuisas dominae suae imperatrici
reddere detrectabat,*g* *h*more latronum suspensus*h* est. Miro circa
sacrilegum Dei iuditio concitato, ut non a rege cui aduersabatur,
sed ab illis quibus fauere uidebatur, exitium tam turpe meruerit.
Mortis illius auctores digno *i*attollendi preconio,*i* qui tanta peste
patriam liberarent ac intestinum hostem tam iuste dampnarent.

486   40.*j* Eodem anno in Pentecoste resedit rex Lundoniae in Turri,
episcopo tantummodo Sagiensi presente.[187] Ceteri uel fastidierunt
uel timuerunt uenire. Aliquanto post, mediante legato, colloquium
indictum est inter imperatricem et regem, si forte Deo inspirante
pax reformari posset. Conuentum iuxta Bathoniam,[188] misso ex

a etiam *Ce*   *b* om. B   *c* aere *Ce*   *d* iactitare *Ce*   *e* filium
Gildeberti *Ce*   *f* quidem *A*   *g* detractabat *BCe*   *h–h* patibulo appensus
et exanimatus *Ce*   *i–i* preconio attollendi *A*   *j* Rubric De conuentu legati et
archiepiscopi et regine, et Roberti comitis Gloecestre, pro federe pacis agendo inter regem
et imperatricem *Ce*

---

[186] John Fitz Gilbert, alias John the Marshal, in which capacity he served Henry I,
Stephen, the empress, and Duke Henry: *Regesta*, ii, p. xvii; Green, *Henry I*, pp. 248–9;
Regesta, iii, pp. xx–xxi, xxxii, xxxviii. On this episode, see further *GS*, pp. 104–9; JW iii.
284–91; D. Crouch, *William Marshal: Court, Career and Chivalry in the Angevin Empire
1147–1219* (London, 1990), pp. 11–13.
[187] John, bishop of Sées 1124–44. He held the bishopric of Rochester for a part at least
of the vacancy of 1137–42, and this is one reason, argues C. Flight, why 'John II, bishop of
Rochester, did not exist', *EHR* cvi (1991), 921–31.

thing again and again in England, and vex God by plundering the church at Wilton and destroying the one at Malmesbury, slaughtering all the monks of that house. This would be his revenge, he said, for their having admitted the king to do him harm; for he made this false accusation against them. I have heard with my own ears, if ever he let prisoners go (and it was a very uncommon thing) without a ransom and without torturing them, and they thanked him in God's name, I have heard him answer, I say, 'May God never be grateful to me!' He used to smear prisoners with honey, and expose them naked in the open air in the full blaze of the sun, stirring up flies and similar insects to sting them. Now, having acquired Devizes, he did not hesitate to boast that by means of that castle he would gain possession of the whole district from Winchester to London, and send to Flanders for knights to act as his bodyguard. As he was preparing to do these things the vengeance of heaven prevented him by the agency of one John [Ce John Fitz Gilbert], a man of great cunning who was castellan of Marlborough.[186] As he objected to handing over Devizes to his lady the empress, John chained him and hanged him like a common thief. Wondrously was God's judgment exercised upon a sacrilegious man, in that he earned so shameful an end not from the king, to whom he was an enemy, but from those whom he seemed to favour. Those who brought about his death must be given the praise they deserve, for ridding the country of such a plague, and so justly punishing an enemy in their midst.

40. In the same year, at Whitsuntide, the king stayed at London in the Tower, with no bishop in his company except him of Sées.[187] The others either disdained to come or feared to do so. Some time afterwards, by the mediation of the legate, a parley was appointed between the empress and the king, on the chance that peace might be restored by the inspiration of God. The meeting was near Bath:[188] on the empress's side her brother

---

[188] The chronicle of John of Worcester concludes shortly before Robert Fitz Hubert's death: JW iii. 288–9. The Gloucester continuation notes the earl of Gloucester moving his forces to Bath after 15 Aug. 1140, and skirmishing thereafter between his forces and the king's: JW iii. 290–1. If the peace discussions here described followed after this, then Henry of Winchester's diplomatic mission to France must have followed immediately.

parte imperatricis Rotberto fratre et ceteris suis, ex parte regis legato et archiepiscopo, simul et regina. Sed inaniter, inaniter inquam, triuerunt et*a* uerba et tempora, infectaque pace discessum. Nec fuit ambarum partium aequum discidium, dum imperatrix, ad bonum pronior, aecclesiasticum non se uereri iuditium mandasset, et *b*rex illud quam maxime caueret, consiliis illorum*c* male credulus, qui nichil minus quam pacem uellent, dum ei *b* dominari ad utilitates suas ualerent. Postremo*d* Septembri legatus, qui nosset offitii sui potissimum interesse ut pax conueniret, pro ea restituenda laborem itineris transmarini aggressus, in Galliam nauigare maturauit. Ibi a rege Francorum et comite Thetbaldo, multisque religiosi ordinis personis, magno et sollicito tractatu de pace Angliae habito, reuersus est in fine pene Nouembris, salubria patriae mandata referens, si esset qui uerba factis apponeret. Et plane imperatrix et comes confestim assensere; rex uero de die in diem producere, postremo in summa frustrari. Tum demum legatus se intra se continuit, rerum exitum, ut ceteri, speculaturus. Quid enim attinet contra torrentem brachia tendere,*e* [189] cum laboribus non nisi odium querere extremae sit, ut quidam ait, dementiae? [190]

a om. B   *b–b* regii illud quod maxime nollent dum Ce   *c* eorum A
d Proximo Ce   *e* et add. AB

[189] Juvenal, iv. 89–90.   [190] Sallust, *Bell. Iug.* iii. 3.

Robert was sent and the rest of her advisers, on the king's, the legate and the archbishop, together with the queen. But vainly, vainly, I say, they wasted both words and time and parted without making peace. Yet the two sides did not separate for the same reasons, the empress, more inclined to good, having sent a message that she did not fear the decision of the Church; but the king was most concerned to guard against this, foolishly lending his ear to the counsels of those who desired nothing less than peace, while they were able to manipulate him to their own advantage. Then in September the legate, knowing it was the special concern of his office that peace should be agreed on, undertook the hardships of a sea-crossing for its restoration and hastened to sail to France. After having long and anxious discussions there on peace in England, with the king of France, Count Theobald, and many churchmen, he came back near the end of November, bringing instructions that would have benefited the country had there been anyone to combine words and deeds. And indeed the empress and the earl agreed at once; the king put off a decision from day to day, and finally made the whole plan of no avail. Then at last the legate withdrew within himself, watching, like the others, to see how things would turn out. For what is the use of contending against a racing stream,[189] and is not the height of folly, as someone says, to seek nothing but hatred by one's efforts?[190]

LIBER TERTIVS

⟨*PROLOGUS*⟩

Anno incarnationis Dominicae millesimo centesimo quadragesimo secundo, inextricabilem laberinthum rerum et negotiorum quae acciderunt in Anglia aggredior euoluere; ea causa, ne per nostram incuriam lateat posteros, cum sit opere pretium cognoscere uolubilitatem fortunae statusque humani*ᵃ* mutabilitatem, Deo dumtaxat permittente uel iubente. Itaque quia moderni non mediocriter et merito reprehendunt predecessores nostros, qui nec sui nec suorum post Bedam ullam reliquerunt memoriam, ego, qui a nobis hanc proposui summouere infamiam,¹⁹¹ debeo apud lectores bonam, si recte iudicabunt, pacisci gratiam.*ᵇ*

487 **41.**ᶜ Rex Stephanus ante Natale a Lindocolina prouintia pacifice abscesserat, comitemque Cestrensem et eius fratrem honoribus auxerat.¹⁹² Is comes filiam comitis Gloecestriae iamdudum a tempore regis Henrici duxerat.¹⁹³ Ciues*ᵈ* interim Lindocolinae ciuitatis, qui uellent apud regem grandem locare amicitiam, eum Lundoniae manentem per nuntios certiorem faciunt ambos fratres in castello eiusdem urbis securos resedisse.¹⁹⁴ Eos, nichil minus quam regis aduentum opinantes, leui negotio posse circumueniri.

ᵃ *om. AB*   ᵇ gloriam *Ce*   ᶜ *Rubrics* Quomodo rex uenerit ad obsidionem Lindcolnie *Ce*¹ Quomodo rex uenerit ad obsidionem Lundonie *Ce*²   ᵈ Burgenses *Ce*

---

¹⁹¹ Cf. *GR*, i, prologue, and §62.

¹⁹² Ranulf II 'de Gernons', earl of Chester 1129–53, was son of 'the Countess' Lucy by her third husband, Ranulf I 'Meschin', earl of Chester; 'his brother' is William de Roumare (subsequently earl of Lincoln, d. *c.*1160), Lucy's son by her second husband, Roger Fitz Gerold: *CP* vii, App. J, pp. 743–6. The phrase 'honoribus auxerat' suggests a grant to them by the king of land and/or office. In *Regesta*, iii, no. 178, Stephen granted the earl of Chester 'castellum Lincolnie et ciuitatem'. The charter is there dated 1146, but this may represent the updating of an earlier grant, to which *HN* here refers: see the valuable discussion of P. Dalton, '*In neutro latere*: The armed neutrality of Ranulf II earl of Chester in King Stephen's reign', *ANS* xiv (1992), 39–59, at pp. 45–7. The *Gesta Stephani* also speaks of the king having made an agreement with the earl of Chester, though it says that the earl had broken it by his exploitation of the city and the surrounding countryside:

BOOK III

⟨PROLOGUE⟩

In the year of the Lord's Incarnation 1142, I am undertaking to unravel the trackless maze of events and occurrences that befell in England, with the aim that posterity should not be ignorant of these matters through our lack of care, it being worth while to learn the changefulness of fortune and the mutability of the human lot, by God's permission or bidding. Therefore, as we men of the present day severely and rightly blame our predecessors, who since Bede have left no record of themselves and their doings, I, who have set myself to remove this disgrace from us,[191] may fairly claim the kindly favour of my readers if they judge aright.

41. King Stephen had gone away in peace from Lincolnshire before Christmas [1140], and had added to the honours of the earl of Chester and his brother.[192] That earl had married the earl of Gloucester's daughter long since in King Henry's time.[193] Meanwhile the citizens [Ce burgesses] of Lincoln, wishing to lay the king under a great obligation, informed him by messengers when he was staying at London that the two brothers had settled unsuspiciously in the city's castle.[194] As they expected nothing less than the king's arrival, they could easily be surrounded. They

GS, pp. 110–11; the passage that would have provided the context is regrettably missing in the surviving manuscripts.

[193] Matilda, here identified as married in or before 1135 (not 'about 1141', as in CP iii. 167), died 29 July 1189; and see further The Charters of the Anglo-Norman Earls of Chester, c. 1071–1237, ed. G. Barraclough (Rec. Soc. of Lancashire and Cheshire, cxxvi, 1988), pp. 71–2.

[194] The Gesta Stephani also suggests a peaceful residence: 'commorans castello', GS, pp. 110–11). The other chroniclers, most notably Henry of Huntingdon and those who followed him, either assert or insinuate a more violent occupation: 'fraudulenter inuaserunt' (OV vi. 538–9); 'fraudulenter ceperat' (HH, pp. 724–5); 'ingenio ceperat' (RT i. 220); 'dolo intrauerat' (William of Newburgh, The History of English Affairs, Book I, ed. P. G. Walsh and M. J. Kennedy (Warminster, 1988), pp. 60–1); 'occupauit' (John of Hexham, in SD ii. 306). On the castle, King's Works, ii. 704–5; Castellarium Anglicanum, i. 261–2.

Se daturos operam ut quam occultissime rex castello potiatur. Ille, qui nullam occasionem ampliandae potestatis omittere uellet, laetus eo contendit. Ita fratres circumuenti et obsessi sunt in ipsis Natalis Dominici feriis. Iniquum id uisum multis, quia, sicut dixi, nulla suspitione rancoris ab eis ante festum abscesserat, nec modo more maiorum amicitiam suam eis interdixerat, quod diffidiare dicunt. Porro comes Cestrensis, quanuis ancipiti periculo inuolutus, probe tamen castelli angustias euasit. Non diffinio qua uersutia, siue consensu aliquorum obsidentium, siue quia uirtus deprehensa[195] solet multis modis querere et plerumque inuenire consilium. Itaque non contentus sua solum liberatione, de salute fratris et uxoris, quos[a] in castello reliquerat, sollicitus, animum partes uersabat in omnes.[196] Sanior sententia uisa flagitare a socero auxilium, quanuis animos eius iamdudum nonnullis ex causis offendisset, maxime quia in neutro latere fidus uideretur esse. Misit ergo perpetuam per nuntios pactus fidelitatem imperatrici, si, respectu pietatis magis quam ullius sui meriti, periclitantes, qui in ipsis captionis faucibus tenebantur, eximeret iniuriae.

488   42.[b] Non habuit comes Gloecestriae difficiles aures, indignitatem rei non ferens. Simul etiam pertesus more, quia preclarissima patria causa duorum hominum intestinis rapinis et cedibus uexabatur, maluit, si Deus permisisset, rem in extremos deducere casus. Sperabat etiam diuinum in incepto fauorem, quia rex generum suum nullis eius culpis iniuriauerat, filiam obsidebat, aecclesiam beatae Dei genitricis de Lindocolino incastellauerat. Haec quanti apud mentem principis esse debebant! Nonne prestaret mori et gloriose occumbere, quam tam insignem contumeliam pati? Vlciscendi ergo causa Deum et sororem, simulque necessitudines suas liberandi, dedit se discrimini. Comitati sunt eum impigre suae fautores partis, quorum erat maior

---

[a] quas *Ce*   [b] *Rubric* Quomodo comes Gloecestre Robertus ierit ad succurrendum obsessis *Ce*

---

[195] Lucan, iv. 469–70.
[196] Virgil, *Aen.* iv. 630.

themselves would see to it that the king got possession of the castle with the greatest secrecy. He, unwilling to miss any chance of increasing his power, hastened thither joyfully. And so the brothers were surrounded and besieged during the Christmas festival itself. This seemed unfair to many because, as I have said, he had left them before the festival without any suspicion of ill-will, and had not, in the traditional way, renounced his friend-ship with them, which is termed defiance. But the earl of Chester, though involved in critical danger, yet made good his escape from the close siege of the castle. By what device I do not determine, whether by the collusion of some of the besiegers, or because valour, when caught in a snare,[195] will cast around for and commonly find a remedy. Then, not satisfied solely with his freedom, but being anxious also about the freedom of his brother and wife, whom he had left in the castle, he turned his mind in every direction.[196] It seemed the wisest policy to beg aid from his father-in-law, though he had long since offended him for various reasons, chiefly because he seemed ambivalent in his loyalty. So he sent to him promising by the messengers a lasting fidelity to the empress if, from motives of pity rather than any deserts of his own, he would rescue from wrong those who were in danger and on the very brink of captivity.

42. The earl of Gloucester was not hard to persuade, for he could not bear the shame of the situation. At the same time, loathing delay because his noble country, for the sake of two persons, was being tormented by the plunder and slaughter of civil war, he preferred, if God should allow it, to hazard a final decision. He also hoped for the divine approval in his enterprise, because the king had wronged his son-in-law who was in no way at fault, was besieging his daughter, and had turned into a castle the church of the Blessed Mother of God at Lincoln. How greatly these things must have influenced the prince's mind! Would it not be better to die and fall with glory, rather than bear so signal an affront? So, for the sake of avenging God and his sister, and to free his relatives, he took the risk. The adherents of his party, most of them disinherited men inflamed to war by grief for what they had

exheredatorum numerus, quos in martem accendebat rerum amissarum dolor et conscia uirtus,[197] quanuis toto itinere, quod protenditur a Gloecestria in Lindocolinum, ipse callide intentionem dissimularet, quibusdam ambagibus totum exercitum preter paucissimos suspendens.

489 43.[a] Ventum ad suppremum ipso die Purificationis beatissimae Mariae, ad flumen quod inter duos exercitus preterfluebat, Trenta nomine, quod et ortu suo et pluuiarum profluuio tam magnum fuerat ut nullatenus uado transitum preberet.[198] Tum demum et genero, qui cum manu ualida occurrerat, et ceteris quos ductauerat, detegens animum, hoc sibi propositum iam dudum esse adiecit, quod nulla umquam necessitate terga uerteret; uel moriendum uel capiendum esse, si non uicisset. Cunctis igitur bona spe ipsum implentibus, mirabile auditu, ilico belli discrimen initurus, predicti rapacitatem fluminis cum omnibus suis nando transgressus est. Tantus erat comiti ardor finem malis[b] imponere, ut mallet ultima experiri quam regni calamitatem ulterius protendi. Nam et rex cum comitibus quamplurimis,[c] et non inerti militum copia, bello se animose, intermissa obsidione, optulerat.[199] Temptauere primo regii proludium pugnae facere, quod iustam uocant,[200] quia tali periti erant arte. At ubi uiderunt quod consulares,[201] ut ita dictum sit, non lanceis eminus, sed gladiis comminus rem gererent, et infestis uiribus uexillisque aciem regalem perrumperent, fuga sibi omnes ad unum comites consuluere.[202] Pauci[d] barones predicandae fidei et fortitudinis, qui

[a] Rubric De pugna comitis Gloecestre et captione regis *Ce*   [b] om. *Ce*
[c] quampluribus *B*   [d] Sex enim cum rege comites bellum inierant. Plures *Ce*

---

[197] Virgil, *Aen.* v. 455.

[198] The river Trent at Newark, its probable crossing-place, lies 16 miles from Lincoln. On arrival outside Lincoln the army would face a further water obstacle at the Fossdyke, which probably is the *flumen* referred to here. Henry of Huntingdon refers to the crossing of 'an almost impassable marsh' (HH, pp. 724–5); the *Gesta Stephani* to a well defended ford (*GS*, pp. 112–13). J. Beeler, *Warfare in England 1066–1189* (Ithaca, NY, 1966), pp. 111–12 provides a good discussion.

[199] Henry of Huntingdon, archdeacon in the Lincoln diocese (*Fasti*, ed. Greenway, iii. 27; HH, pp. xl-lii), and the *Gesta Stephani* are the main sources for the battle of Lincoln: HH, pp. 724–39; *GS*, pp. 112–15. There are good modern discussions in Beeler, *Warfare in England*, pp. 112–19, and Davis, *Stephen*, pp. 49–51.

[200] This passage suggests that, while both sides had mustered substantial forces, the king's party had not expected battle: M. Strickland, 'Against the Lord's anointed: Aspects

lost and conscious valour,[197] followed him eagerly, though he cunningly concealed his purpose all the way from Gloucester to Lincoln, keeping the whole army in uncertainty, except for a very few, by taking an indirect route.

43. The time of decision came on the very day of the Purification of the most blessed Mary [2 Feb. 1141], beside the river that flowed between the two armies, named Trent, which was then so much swollen by a heavy fall of rain as well as water from its source that there was no possibility of fording it.[198] Only then did the earl disclose his intention to his son-in-law, who had met him with a strong body of troops, and the rest of his followers, adding that he had long since made up his mind that nothing should ever compel him to retreat; he would die or be captured if he did not win the victory. All filled him with good hope, and so—wonderful to hear—he resolved to risk a battle at once, and swam across the racing current of the river mentioned above with all his men. So eager was the earl to make an end of the troubles, that he would sooner face the final danger than have the kingdom's misfortune prolonged. For the king on his side had broken off the siege and offered battle with spirit, accompanied by very many earls and an active body of knights.[199] The royalists first attempted that prelude to the fight which is called jousting,[200] for in this they were accomplished. But when they saw that the 'earlists',[201] if the expression may be allowed, were fighting not with lances at a distance but with swords at close quarters and, charging with their banners in the van, were breaking through the king's line, then all the earls to a man sought safety in flight.[202] [**Ce** *adds* There were six earls who had entered the battle on the king's side.[203]] A few

of warfare and baronial rebellion in England and Normandy, 1075–1265', *Law and Government*, pp. 56–79, at 66.

[201] The term *consulares* is a play on the title *consul* which Robert of Gloucester used in preference to *comes* in his charters, and presumably preferred to have used in his presence also: *Gloucester Charters*, pp. 22–3; D. Crouch, *The Image of Aristocracy in Britain, 1000–1300* (London, 1992), pp. 43–4, 97. William used *consul* in the prologue to the *HN*, as a form of address, as did Geoffrey of Monmouth: *Historia regum Britannie*, i, ed. N. Wright, §4.

[202] 'The chroniclers are unanimous in their condemnation of the royalist earls': Beeler, *Warfare in England*, p. 115.

[203] The six earls are named as Alan of Brittany, Waleran of Meulan, William de Warenne, Hugh Bigod, Simon de Senlis, and William of Aumale, in HH, pp. 736–7, from which this interpolation derives.

regem nec in hac necessitate deserendum ducerent, capti.[a] [204] Rex
ipse, quanuis ad se defensandum non ei defuisset animus, tandem
a militibus comitis Gloecestriae circumquaque aggressus, ictu
lapidis cuiusdam terrae procubuit. A quo autem id factum
fuerit, ignoratur.[205] Ita omnibus circa se uel captis uel fugatis,
cedendum pro tempore, et teneri sustinuit. Predicandus itaque
comes Gloecestriae precepit regem uiuum et illesum asseruari,[b]
non passus etiam ullo exprobrationis conuitio illum proscindi.[c] Et
quem iratus modo impugnabat regno fastigatum, placidus ecce
protegit triumphatum, ut, compositis irae et letitiae motibus, et
consanguinitati impenderet humanitatem, et in captiuo diadematis
respiceret dignitatem. Vulgus uero ciuium[d] Lindocolinum multa
parte obtruncatum est, iusta ira illorum qui uicissent, nullo dolore
illorum qui uicti essent, quod ipsi principium et fomes istius mali
fuissent.[206]

490 **44.**[e] Rex iuxta[f] morem illius generis hominum quos captiuos
nominant, imperatrici a fratre presentatus Gloecestriae; post
etiam ad Bristou ductus, et ibi honorifice preter progrediendi
facultatem seruatus est primo.[207] Succedenti uero[g] tempore,
propter insolentiam quorundam palam et probrose dictitantium
non expedire comiti ut regem secus ac ipsi uellent seruaret, simul
et quia ipse ferebatur plusquam semel, uel elusis uel delinitis
custodibus, extra statutam custodiam noctu presertim inuentus,
anulis ferreis innodatus est.

491 **45.**[h] Interim et imperatrix et comes apud legatum fratrem eius
nuntiis egerunt, ut ipsam, tanquam regis Henrici filiam, et cui

---

[a] sunt *add. A*   [b] reseruari *A*, conseruari *Ce*   [c] irretiri *Ce*   [d] burgensium *Ce*   [e] *Rubric* Quomodo rex imperatrici presentatur *Ce*   [f] uero *A*,
uero iuxta *Ce*   [g] enim *Ce*   [h] *Rubric* Quomodo imperatrix, industria comitis
Gloecestre, a legato et quibusdam episcopis et primatibus Wintonie recepta sit *Ce*

---

[204] A list of those taken prisoner, many of them northerners and 'all men of respected
baronial families', is given in Davis, *Stephen*, p. 50, citing John of Hexham, in SD ii. 307–
8, HH, pp. 736–9, and OV vi. 542–5.

[205] He is named by Henry of Huntingdon as William de Cahaignes, a member of a
family which held, *inter alia*, the bishopric of Lincoln: HH, pp. 738–9 and n. 109; L. F.
Salzman, 'Sussex Domesday tenants, iii, William de Cahagnes and the family of Keynes',
Sussex Archaeological Collections, lxiii (1922), 180–202.

[Ce Many] barons, of notable loyalty and courage, thinking they should not abandon the king even at this desperate moment, were taken prisoners.[204] The king himself, though he did not lack spirit in self-defence, was at length attacked on all sides by the earl of Gloucester's knights and fell to the ground on being struck by a stone. It is not known who dealt the blow.[205] So, as all around him were captured or put to flight, he brought himself to yield for a time and be held a prisoner. Therefore the worthy earl of Gloucester gave orders that the king should be kept alive and unharmed, not suffering even that he should be the victim of any insulting language. Behold, he mildly protected in humiliation him whom he had just been furiously assailing when exalted in majesty, so that, controlling emotions of anger and joy, he both showed kindness to a relative and had regard, even in the person of a captive, to the splendour of the crown. But the mass of the citizens [Ce burgesses] of Lincoln was in great part cut down, through the just anger of the victors and without causing any grief to the vanquished, since it was they who by their instigation had given rise to this calamity.[206]

44. The king, as is customary for those who bear the name of captive, was brought before the empress at Gloucester by her brother, then taken to Bristol and kept there at first in a manner that was honourable, except that he was not allowed to leave his quarters.[207] Later on, because of the insolence of some who said openly and continually, in an offensive way, that it was not to the earl's advantage to keep the king in a different fashion from what they themselves desired, and also because he himself was said to have been found more than once, especially at night, outside his appointed place of custody, after deceiving or winning over his guards, he was confined in iron rings.

45. Meanwhile both the empress and the earl sent messengers urging his brother the legate, that she should be received without

---

[206] Orderic has a vivid description of the sack of the city, and the citizens drowning in their rush to escape: OV vi. 544–7; also HH, pp. 738–9, *GS*, pp. 112–13.

[207] The Gloucester chronicle confirms Stephen's itinerary in captivity, and says that he was in Gloucester on 9 Feb.: JW iii. 292–3.

omnis Anglia et Normannia iurata esset, incunctanter in aecclesiam et regnum reciperet. Quarto decimo kalendas Martii eo anno prima dominica Quadragesimae fuit. Ita, mediantibus utrobique nuntiis, ad hoc res expedita, ut ad colloquium in patenti planitie camporum citra Wintoniam conueniretur. Ventum ergo dominica tertia Quadragesimae,[208] pluuioso et nebuloso die, quasi mestam cause uicissitudinem fata portenderent. Iurauit et affidauit imperatrix episcopo, quod omnia maiora negotia in Anglia, precipueque donationes episcopatuum et abbatiarum, eius nutum spectarent, si eam ipse cum[a] sancta aecclesia in dominam reciperet, et perpetuam ei fidelitatem teneret. Idem iurauerunt cum ea, et affidauerunt pro ea, Rotbertus frater eius comes Gloecestriae, et Brianus filius comitis marchio de Walingeford,[209] et Milo de Gloecestria, postea comes de Hereford,[210] et nonnulli alii. Nec dubitauit episcopus imperatricem in dominam Angliae recipere, et ei cum quibusdam suis affidare, quod, quamdiu ipsa pactum non infringeret, ipse quoque fidem ei custodiret. Crastino, quod fuit quinto nonas Martii, honorifica facta processione recepta est in aecclesia episcopatus Wintoniae, episcopo, eodemque legato, eam ducente in dextro latere, Bernardo uero de sancto Dauid episcopo in sinistro.[211] Affuerunt preterea episcopi Alexander de Lindocolino, Rotbertus de Hereford,[212] Nigellus de Heli, Rotbertus de Bathonia,[213] abbates etiam Ingulfus de Abbendonia,[214] Edwardus de Radinges,[215] Petrus de Malmesberia,[216] Gilebertus de Gloecestria,[217] Rogerius de Theokesberia,[218] et nonnulli alii. Paucis post diebus Thetbaldus Cantuariae archiepiscopus uenit

---

[a] in Ce

[208] The Gloucester chronicle says that the empress left Gloucester on 17 Feb., accompanied by Bernard, bishop of St Davids, Nigel, bishop of Ely, and Gilbert [Foliot], abbot of Gloucester: JW iii. 292–5. These are three of the first four witnesses to *Regesta*, iii, no. 343, which refers to this meeting and confirms the date (reading for this 'dominica tercia Quadragesime' for 'dominica intrantis' or 'dominica incarnacionis', the variants of the MSS).

[209] The title marquis ('comitis marchio') is not used by Brian Fitz Count in his charters or correspondence, but may have been current in Angevin circles; on its implications, see Crouch, *The Image of Aristocracy*, pp. 98–100.

[210] The grant of the earldom is *Regesta*, iii, no. 393, dated at Oxford 25 July 1141.

[211] Bernard, consecrated 19 Sept. 1115 (*Handbook of Chronology*, p. 297), was after the legate the senior of the bishops present.

hesitation by church and state, since she was King Henry's daughter and the whole of England and Normandy was sworn to her. In that year the first Sunday of Lent was on 16 February. So it was settled, after envoys had been sent from each side, that they should meet for conference on an open plain on the approach to Winchester. They came then on the third Sunday of Lent [2 March],[208] a rainy and cloudy day, as though the fates presaged a turn of ill-fortune for their cause. The empress swore and gave assurance to the bishop that all important business in England, especially gifts of bishoprics and abbacies, should be subject to his control, if he and Holy Church received her as lady, and he kept his faith to her unbroken. The same oath was taken with her, and assurance given for her, by her brother Robert, earl of Gloucester, Brian Fitz Count, marquis of Wallingford,[209] Miles of Gloucester, afterwards earl of Hereford,[210] and a number of others. Nor did the bishop hesitate to receive her as lady of England and give her assurance, together with some of his followers, that as long as she did not break the agreement he would keep faith with her himself. The next day, which was 3 March, she was received in Winchester cathedral in ceremonial procession, with the bishop, who was also legate, escorting her on the right side and Bernard, bishop of St Davids, on the left.[211] There were also present, of the bishops, Alexander of Lincoln, Robert of Hereford,[212] Nigel of Ely and Robert of Bath,[213] and of the abbots Ingulf of Abingdon,[214] Edward of Reading,[215] Peter of Malmesbury,[216] Gilbert of Glou-cester,[217] Roger of Tewkesbury,[218] and a number of others. A few days later Theobald, archbishop of Canterbury, came to the

---

[212] Robert de Béthune, bishop of Hereford 1131–48: *EEA*, vii; *Hereford 1079–1234*, ed. J. Barrow (Oxford, 1993), pp. xxxvii–xl.

[213] Robert of Lewes, bishop of Bath 1136–66; for details of his career, and argument for his authorship, see *GS*, pp. xviii–xl.

[214] Ingulf, abbot of Abingdon 1130–59: *Heads*, p. 25.

[215] Edward, abbot of Reading 1136–*c*.1154: *Heads*, p. 63.

[216] Peter Moraunt, monk of Cluny, abbot of Malmesbury 1140–*c*.1158/9: *Heads*, p. 55; JW iii. 292–3, stating he was previouly prior of La Charité, a point questioned by G. Constable in *Peter the Venerable*, ii. 298.

[217] Gilbert Foliot, abbot of Gloucester 1139–48, bishop of Hereford 1148–63, bishop of London 1163–87. See Morey and Brooke, *Gilbert Foliot and his Letters*; GF, *Letters*.

[218] Roger, abbot of Tewkesbury 1137–61: *Heads*, p. 73. Tewkesbury was one of the main centres of the honour of Gloucester, and the abbey's goods had suffered severely from Waleran of Meulan's attack on it in 1140: JW iii. 282–5.

ad imperatricem apud Wiltunam,*a* inuitatus a legato.[219] Distulit
sane fidelitatem dominae facere, inconsulto rege alias diuertere
famae personaeque*b* suae indignum arbitratus. Itaque et ipse et
plerique presules, cum aliquantis laicis, permissi ad regem ire et
colloqui, dignanterque impetrata uenia ut in necessitatem temporis transirent, in sententiam legati cessere. Pascha, quod tunc
fuit tertio kalendas Aprilis, imperatrix apud Oxeneford egit;[220] a
ceteris in sua discessum.

492 **46.**\ *c* Feria secunda post octauas Paschae, concilium archiepiscopi
Cantuariae Thetbaldi et omnium episcoporum Angliae multor-
umque abbatum, legato presidente, Wintoniae ingenti apparatu
inceptum.[221] Si qui defuerunt, legatis et litteris causas cur non
uenissent dederunt. Cuius concilii actioni quia interfui, integram
rerum ueritatem posteris non negabo; egregie quippe memini. Ipsa
die, post recitata scripta excusatoria quibus absentiam suam
quidam tutati sunt, seuocauit in partem legatus episcopos, habuit-
que cum eis archanum consilii sui. *d*Mox abbates, postremo
archidiaconi conuocati. Ex consilio nichil processit in publicum;
uolutabatur tamen per omnium mentes et ora quid foret agendum.

493 **47.**\ *e* Feria tertia hoc fere sensu legati cucurrit oratio. Dignatione
papae se uices eius in Anglia tenere. Ideoque per eius auctoritatem
clerum Angliae ad hoc concilium congregatum, ut de pace patriae,
quae grandi periculo naufragabatur, consuleretur in medium.
Tempore regis Henrici auunculi sui singulare domicilium pacis
in Anglia fuisse, ita ut per uiuacitatem, animositatem, industriam
eiusdem precellentissimi uiri non solum indigenae, cuiuscumque
potentiae uel dignitatis essent, nichil turbare auderent, sed etiam
eius exemplo finitimi quicumque reges et principes in otium et*f*
ipsi concederent, et subiectos uel inuitarent uel impellerent.*g* Qui

a Wintoniam *A*   *b* et persone *A*   *c* *Rubric* Quomodo solempni concilio
imperatricem in dominam Anglie confirmauerint *Ce*   *d* Post *add.* *Ce*[1]
e *Rubric* Quomodo legatus debitam et legitimam successionem imperatricis in regnum
commendauerit *Ce*[1]   *f* om. *B*   *g* compellerent *Ce*[1]

[219] 'ad salutandum eam': JW iii. 294–5.
[220] The Gloucester chronicle says that the empress spent the Easter festival at Wilton,
and only went to Oxford after she had been at Reading at Rogationtide (early May): JW iii.

empress at Wilton on the legate's invitation.[219] He, it must be said, put off swearing fealty to her as his lady, as he thought it unbefitting his reputation and position to transfer his allegiance without consulting the king. Therefore both he and most of the bishops, together with a number of laymen, were allowed to go to the king and confer with him, and, on obtaining a courteous permission to change over as the times required, they adopted the legate's opinion. Easter, which then fell on 30 March, the empress spent at Oxford;[220] the others went away to their own homes.

46. On the Monday after Easter week a council of Theobald, archbishop of Canterbury, and all the bishops of England and many abbots, under the presidency of the legate, was begun at Winchester in great state.[221] Any who failed to attend gave reasons for not coming by representatives and letters. As I took part in the proceedings of the council, I will not deny posterity the whole truth of what occurred, for my memory is very clear. That same day, after the reading of the letters of excuse by which some defended their absence, the legate called the bishops aside and conferred with them in secret. Next the abbots were summoned, and finally the archdeacons. No part of their deliberations was made public, but the minds and lips of all were busy with what had to be done.

47. On the Tuesday the legate's speech was much to this effect. By appointment of the pope he took his place in England. And so it was on his authority that the clergy of England were gathered at this council to discuss the peace of their country, which was suffering from a very perilous shipwreck. In the time of King Henry, his uncle, England had been the peculiar habitation of peace, so that through the activity, spirit and vigour of that pre-eminent man not only did the natives, whatever their power or position, not venture to create any disturbance, but similarly all the neighbouring kings and princes, following his example, both

294–5; and see H. W. C. Davis, 'Some documents of the anarchy', *Essays in History Presented to R. Lane Poole*, ed. H. W. C. Davis (Oxford, 1927), pp. 168–89, at 181–2.
[221] *Councils and Synods*, i (2), no. 142, pp. 788–92. The council sat from Monday 7 to Thursday 10 Apr. 1141. The account which follows gives details of each day's business.

uidelicet rex, nonnullis ante obitum annis, filiae suae quondam imperatrici, quae sola sibi proles ex desponsata quondam coniuge supererat, omne regnum Angliae, simul et ducatum Normanniae, iurari ab omnibus episcopis simulque baronibus fecerit, si successore masculo ex illa, quam ex Lotharingia duxerat, uxore careret. 'Et inuidit', inquit,*a* 'atrox fortuna precellentissimo auunculo meo, ut sine masculo herede in Normannia decederet. Itaque quia longum uidebatur dominam expectare, quae moras ad ueniendum in Angliam nectebat, in Normannia quippe residebat, prouisum est paci patriae, et regnare permissus frater meus. Enimuero, quanuis ego uadem me apposuerim inter *b*eum et Deum*b* quod sanctam aecclesiam honoraret et exaltaret, et bonas leges manuteneret, malas uero abrogaret, piget meminisse, pudet narrare, qualem se in regno exhibuerit: quomodo in presumptores nulla iustitia exercitata, quomodo pax omnis statim ipso pene anno abolita; episcopi capti, et ad redditionem possessionum suarum coacti; abbatiae uenditae, aecclesiae thesauris depilatae; consilia prauorum audita, bonorum uel suspensa uel omnino contempta. Scitis quotiens eum cum per me tum per episcopos conuenerim, concilio presertim anno preterito*c* ad hoc indicto, et nichil nisi odium acquisierim. Nec illud quemquam, qui recte pensare uelit, latet, debere me*d* fratrem meum mortalem diligere, sed causam*e* Patris immortalis multo pluris facere. Itaque quia Deus iuditium suum de fratre meo exercuit, ut eum, me nesciente, in potestatem potentium incidere permitteret: ne regnum uacillet, si regnante careat, omnes uos pro iure legationis meae huc conuenire inuitaui. Ventilata est hesterno die causa secreto coram maiori parte cleri Angliae, ad cuius ius*f* potissimum spectat principem eligere, simulque ordinare. Inuocata itaque primo, ut par est, in auxilium Diuinitate, filiam pacifici regis, gloriosi regis, diuitis regis, boni regis, et nostro tempore incomparabilis, in Angliae Normanniaeque dominam eligimus, et ei fidem et manutenementum promittimus.'

---

a om. B　　　*b–b* Deum et eum B　　　*c* predicto Ce¹　　　*d* me om. A
e causa A　　　*f* om. Ce¹

inclined to peace themselves and urged or forced their subjects to it. That king, some years before his death, had had the whole kingdom of England, and also the duchy of Normandy, confirmed on oath by all the bishops and barons to his daughter, formerly empress, his only surviving offspring by his first wife, if he failed of a male successor by his wife from Lorraine. 'And cruel fortune,' he said, 'showed a grudge against my pre-eminent uncle, so that he died in Normandy without a male heir. Therefore, because it seemed tedious to wait for the lady, who made delays in coming to England since her residence was in Normandy, provision was made for the peace of the country and my brother allowed to reign. But, though I made myself guarantor between him and God that he would honour and exalt Holy Church, maintain good laws and repeal bad ones, I am vexed to remember and ashamed to tell what manner of man he showed himself as king: how no justice was enforced upon transgressors, and how peace was at once brought entirely to an end, almost in that very year; bishops were arrested and compelled to surrender their property; abbacies were sold and churches despoiled of their treasure; the advice of the wicked was hearkened to, that of the good either not put into effect or altogether disregarded. You know how often I made application to him, sometimes personally and sometimes through the bishops, especially when, the year before last, I called a council for this purpose, and gained nothing but hatred. And, if anyone will consider the matter aright, he cannot be unaware that, while I should love my mortal brother, I should esteem more highly the cause of my immortal Father. Therefore, since God has executed his judgment on my brother in allowing him to fall into the power of the strong without my knowledge, so that the kingdom may not totter without a ruler, I have invited you all to meet here in virtue of my position as legate. The case was discussed in secret yesterday before the chief part of the clergy of England, whose special prerogative it is to choose and consecrate a prince. Therefore, first, as is fitting, calling God to our aid, we choose as lady of England and Normandy the daughter of a king who was a peacemaker, a glorious king, a wealthy king, a good king, without peer in our time, and we promise her faith and support.'

494 48.^{a} Cumque omnes presentes uel modeste acclamassent sententiae, uel silentes non contradixissent, subiecit:^{b} 'Lundonienses, qui
sunt quasi optimates pro magnitudine ciuitatis in Anglia, nuntiis
nostris conuenimus, et conductum ut tuto ueniant misimus.^{222} Eos
quia confido non ultra hunc diem moraturos, bona uenia usque
cras sustineamus.'

495 49. Feria quarta uenerunt Lundonienses, et, in concilium intro-
ducti, causam suam eatenus egerunt ut dicerent, missos se a
communione quam uocant Lundoniarum, non certamina sed
preces afferre,^{c} ut dominus suus rex de captione liberaretur. Hoc
omnes barones, qui in eorum communionem iamdudum recepti
fuerant, summopere flagitare a domino legato et ab archiepiscopo,
simulque^d omni clero qui presens erat. Responsum est eis a legato
ubertim et splendide; et, quo minus fieret quod rogabant, eadem
oratio quae pridie habita. Adiectum quinetiam,^{e} non decere ut
Lundonienses, qui precipui habebantur in Anglia sicut proceres,
illorum partes fouerent^f qui dominum suum in bello reliquerant,
quorum consilio idem sanctam aecclesiam exhonorauerat, qui
postremo non ob aliud ipsis Lundoniensibus fauere uidebantur
nisi ut eos pecuniis emungerent.

496 50.^{g} Interea surrexit quidam, cuius nomen, si bene memini,
Christianus, reginae ut audiui clericus,^{223} porrexitque cartam
legato. Qua ille sub silentio lecta, uoce quantum potuit exaltata
dixit non esse legitimam, nec quae deberet in tanto, presertimque
sullimium et religiosarum personarum, conuentu recitari. Preter
cetera enim quae reprehensibilia et notabilia erant scripta, testem
appositum qui preterito anno, in eodem quo tunc sedebant
capitulo, uenerabiles episcopos maxima uerborum affecerit^h
contumelia.^{224} Ita illo tricante, clericus legationi suae non defuit,

---

^{a} *Rubric* Quomodo Londonienses in concilio *Ce*^{1} ^{b} legatus *add. Ce*^{1}
^{c} offerre *Ce*^{1} ^{d} ab *add. Ce*^{1} ^{e} etiam *A* ^{f} fauerent *B* ^{g} *Rubric*
De clerico regine *Ce*^{1} ^{h} effecerit *A*

---

^{222} The late summoning of the Londoners meant that a church assembly was
broadened, on the legate's initiative, to include all those recognized as having an interest
in the succession to the kingdom. On the Londoners' claims, see M. McKisack, 'London

48. When all present had either discreetly applauded his speech or acquiesced in it by their silence he added: 'The Londoners who are in effect magnates because of the greatness of their city in England, we have summoned by messengers, and sent them safe conduct.[222] As I am sure they will not be later than today, with your kind permission let us wait until tomorrow.'

49. The Londoners came on the Wednesday and, on being introduced into the council, pleaded their cause to the extent of saying they had been sent by what they call the commune of London, and brought not contentiousness but a request that their lord the king should be released from captivity. All the barons who had earlier been received into their commune were urgent in demanding this from the lord legate, the archbishop, and all the clergy who were present. The legate answered them at length and with eloquence, saying exactly what he had said the day before, in opposition to what they asked. Moreover, he added, it was not fitting that the Londoners, who ranked among the leading men of England, should give comfort to those who had abandoned their lord in war, by whose advice he had dishonoured Holy Church, and who finally seemed to favour the Londoners with no other object than squeezing money out of them.

50. Meanwhile a certain man, named Christian if I remember rightly, a clerk of the queen as I have heard,[223] stood up and held out a document to the legate. He read it in silence, and said at the top of his voice that it was not valid and ought not to be read out in so great an assembly, especially one of persons of rank and religion. For, he said, apart from the other things written in it that were worthy of reproof and censure, the name of a witness had been added who the year before, in the same chapter-house in which they were sitting, had used the most insulting language to reverend bishops.[224] While he was havering in this fashion, the

and the succession to the crown during the middle ages', *Studies in Medieval History presented to F. M. Powicke*, ed. R. W. Hunt *et al.* (Oxford, 1948), pp. 76–89; on the commune see introduction, pp. lviii–lix.

[223] He is not one of the queen's clerks named in the *Regesta*, iii, p. xiii.

[224] This may be William Martel, who was about to be excommunicated.

sed preclara fidutia litteras legit in audientia, quarum haec erat summa. Rogabat regina obnixe omnem clerum congregatum, et nuncupatim[a] episcopum Wintoniensem fratrem domini sui, ut eundem dominum regno restituerent, quem iniqui uiri, qui etiam homines sui essent, in uincula coniecissent. Huic suggestioni retulit legatus uerba in eandem sententiam qua et Lundoniensibus. Illi, communicato consilio, dixerunt se decretum concilii conuicaneis suis relaturos, et fauorem suum quantum possent prestituros.

51. Feria quinta solutum est concilium, excommunicatis ante multis qui regiarum erant partium: nominatim Willelmo Martello, qui quondam pincerna regis Henrici, tunc dapifer Stephani.[225] Iste immaniter exulcerauerat legati animum, multis rebus eius interceptis et subreptis.[226]

497 **52.**[b] Itaque multae fuit molis Lundoniensium animos permulcere posse, ut, cum haec statim post Pascha, ut dixi, fuerint actitata, uix paucis ante Natiuitatem beati Iohannis diebus imperatricem reciperent.[c] [227] Pleraque tunc pars Angliae dignanter[d] dominatum eius suspitiebat.[228] Frater eius Rotbertus assiduus circa eam omnibus [e]quibus decebat modis[e] eius gloriam exaltare, proceres benigne appellando, multa pollicendo, diuersas partes uel terrendo uel etiam per internuntios ad pacem sollicitando, iam iamque in omnibus partibus imperatrici fauentibus iustitiam et patrias leges et pacem reformando. Satisque constat quod, si eius moderationi et sapientiae a suis esset creditum, non tam sinistrum postea sensissent aleae casum. Aderat et dominus legatus sedula, ut

---

[a] nuncupatum B   [b] *Rubric* Quomodo imperatrix a Londoniensibus recepta sit Ce[1]   [c] receperunt A   [d] om. Ce[1]   [e-e] modis degebat B, modis ut decebat Cd

[225] William Martel attests royal charters after 1128 (*Regesta*, ii, but not there as butler); he was a royal steward at the beginning of Stephen's reign, and in constant attendance on him: *Regesta*, iii, pp. xvii–xviii; on his importance, see Green, 'Financing', pp. 112–13.

[226] Henry of Winchester and William Martel were two powerful men, whose paths had crossed on numerous occasions. Among the possible sources of the legate's exasperation were the following: (*1*) Henry was dean of St Martin le Grand in London. *Regesta*, iii, no. 524 is an order for the restitution of property in Cripplegate, blaming a *minister* of William Martel; several other charters relate to the same area, though the offenders are not named: ibid., iii, no. 532; *EEA*, viii; *Winchester 1070–1204*, ed. M. J. Franklin, nos. 71–2. (2) In 1141 Henry of Winchester was administering the diocese of Salisbury, and William Martel

clerk did not fail to perform his commission, but with a splendid boldness read the letter before that audience, the substance being as follows: 'The queen earnestly begs all the assembled clergy, and especially the bishop of Winchester, her lord's brother, to restore to the throne that same lord, whom cruel men, who are at the same time his own men, have cast into chains.' The legate's answer to this proposal was to the same effect as to the Londoners. They, after discussing the matter, said they would take back the decision of the council to their colleagues, and give it all the support they could.

51. The council broke up on the Thursday, having excommunicated many of the king's adherents, notably William Martel, who had formerly been King Henry's butler and was then King Stephen's steward.[225] He had mightily exasperated the legate by seizing and stealing much of his property.[226]

52. So difficult was it to reduce the Londoners to acquiescence that, though these proceedings took place, as I have said, immediately after Easter, it was not until a few days before the Nativity of St John that they received the empress.[227] At that time the greater part of England had graciously accepted her lordship.[228] Her brother Robert, constantly with her, increased her prestige in every fitting way, by speaking affably to the chief men, making many promises, either intimidating the opposition or urging it to peace by his envoys, and beginning the restoration of justice and of the ancestral laws and peace in every region that supported the empress. It is well established that, if the other members of his party had trusted his restraint and wisdom, they would not afterwards have endured such a turn of ill-fortune. The lord legate also was at hand to serve the

was castellan of Sherborne: *GS*, pp. 148–9; Davis, *Stephen*, pp. 53–4. (3) William Martel may have been sheriff of Surrey, which was in the Winchester diocese: Green, 'Financing', p. 112 and n. 162.

[227] The council broke up on 10 Apr. 1141; the feast of the Nativity of St John was on 24 June.

[228] She was 'received as lady by all the English nation except for the men of Kent': HH, pp. 738–9; 'the greater part of the kingdom at once submitted to the countess and her adherents': *GS*, pp. 116–17.

uidebatur, fide imperatricis commodis presto. Sed ecce, dum ipsa putaretur omni Anglia statim posse potiri, mutata omnia. Lundonienses, semper suspecti et intra se frementes, tunĉ in aperti odii uocem eruperunt; insidiis etiam, ut fertur, dominam eiusque comites appetiuerunt.[229] Quibus illi precognitis et uitatis, sensim sine tumultu quadam militari disciplina urbe cesserunt.[230] Comitati sunt imperatricem legatus, et rex Scottiae Dauid auunculus eiusdem uiraginis, et frater eius Rotbertus, in omnibus ut semper, sic et tunc, fortunarum sororis sotius, et, ut de compendio dicam, partium eius omnes ad unum incolumes. Lundonienses, cognito eorum abscessu, in hospitia inuolant, quicquid rerum pro festinatione relictum erat abradentes.[231]

498   53.[a] Nec multis post diebus surrexit simultas inter legatum et imperatricem, quem casum[b] uere possum dicere fomitem omnium malorum rursum in Anglia fuisse. Quod qualiter acciderit, expediam.[232] Habebat rex Stephanus filium[c] Eustachium nomine ex filia Eustachii comitis Bononiensis susceptum.[233] Rex enim Henricus, pater imperatricis, ut altius repetam, ne ueritas gestorum lateat posteros, sororem uxoris suae, matris istius dominae, Mariam nomine, nuptum dedit[d] predicto comiti, quod esset is et amplis maioribus ortus, simulque prudentia et fortitudine iuxta insignis.[234] Ex Maria Eustachius nichil liberorum tulit preter filiam Mathildem uocabulo. Hanc patre defuncto nubilem idem magnificentissimus rex Stephano nepoti legitimo matrimonio copulauit, et pariter Bononiensem comitatum industrie adquisiuit.[235] Nam antea Moritoliensem in Normannia

---

[a] *Rubric* De discordia imperatricis et legati *Ce*[1]   [b] casu *B*   [c] filium *after* susceptum *Ce*[1]   [d] dederat *Ce*[1]

[229] William of Malmesbury gives a highly condensed account of events in the crucial days when the empress was in London and Westminster. The text here is discussed with reference to the other sources in the introduction, pp. lvi–lxii.

[230] This is termed a 'disorderly flight' in *GS*, pp. 124–5; they fled 'ignominiously', JW iii. 296–7.

[231] For the plunder of the lodgings, *GS*, pp. 124–5.

[232] William of Malmesbury does not say, as does the author of the *Gesta Stephani* (ibid.), that Henry of Blois was a party to the plot. He puts a distance between his criticism of Matilda's lack of wisdom and this discussion of her treatment of Eustace's inheritance; but this, a continuing discussion now focused on the problems caused by Stephen's imprisonment, may have come to a head but can hardly have been inaugurated *after* the

empress with what seemed to be a zealous loyalty. But, behold, when it was thought that she was about to gain possession of the whole of England, everything was changed. The Londoners, who had always been under suspicion and in a state of secret indignation, then gave vent to expressions of unconcealed hatred; they even laid a plot, it is said, against their lady and her companions.[229] The latter, forewarned of it and avoiding it, left the city gradually and calmly and with some kind of military discipline.[230] The empress was accompanied by the legate, David, king of Scots, uncle of that formidable lady, by her brother Robert, then as always sharing his sister's fortune in everything, and, in brief, by all her adherents, unharmed to a man. The Londoners, learning of their departure, dashed into their lodgings, and carried off whatever had been left behind in their haste.[231]

53. Not many days later a quarrel arose between the legate and the empress, a mischance that I may truly call the origin of all the evils that followed in England. I will explain how it happened.[232] King Stephen had a son named Eustace by the daughter of Eustace, count of Boulogne.[233] To go back further, so that posterity may not be unaware of the truth about these events, King Henry, the empress's father, had given Mary, the sister of his wife the empress's mother, in marriage to the aforesaid count, because he was both of distinguished birth and eminent alike for prudence and valour.[234] Eustace had no children by Mary except a daughter named Matilda. As she was of marriageable age on her father's death, that most splendid of kings united her in lawful wedlock with his nephew Stephen, and at the same time took trouble to gain for him the county of Boulogne.[235] He had already given him

retreat from London. The Gloucester chronicle places the discussion before the flight from London: JW iii. 296–7.

[233] Eustace, eldest son of Stephen and Matilda of Boulogne, born *c.*1129, died *c.*17 Aug. 1153: *Handbook of Chronology*, p. 35.

[234] On Matilda, wife of Henry I, see *HN* § 2; her sister Mary married Eustace III, count of Boulogne, in 1102: JW iii. 102–3. The marriages of the two sisters are noted in *GR* § 228; on the distinguished ancestry of the counts of Boulogne, see *GR* § 123 (King Alfred), 373 (Charlemagne). Stephen's parentage is noted also in OV vi. 42–3; *GND* ii. 262–3.

[235] The recent marriage is referred to in a charter of Eustace III 'late count of Boulogne', dated 1125, in favour of the monks of Cluny: *Receuil des chartes de l'abbaye de Cluny*, ed. A. Bernard and A. Bruel, 6 vols. (Paris, 1876–1903), v. 340–1 (no. 3984).

ex suo dederat.[236] Hos comitatus nepoti suo quem nominaui, Eustachio, legatus iure dandos[a] destinauerat dum pater in captione teneretur; imperatrice prorsus abnuente, incertum an aliis etiam promittente. Qua ille offensus iniuria, multis diebus ab eius abstinuit curia, et, quanuis sepe reuocaretur, negare perseuerauit. Interea familiare apud Geldeford cum regina, [b]fratris uxore,[b] colloquium habuit, eiusque[c] lacrimis et satisfactione infractus ad liberationem germani animum intendit; omnes etiam illius partis quos in concilio excommunicauerat inconsultis episcopis absoluit. Ferebantur et per Angliam eius [d]in imperatricem querelae:[d] quod eum capere uoluerit; quod quicquid ei iurauerat pro nichilo haberet; omnes barones Angliae fidem suam circa eam implesse, sed ipsam temerasse, quae adquisitis uti modeste nesciret.

499 54.[e] Ad hos motus, si posset, componendos comes Gloecestriae non adeo denso comitatu Wintoniam contendit; sed re infecta ad Oxeneford rediit, ubi soror statiua mansione iamdudum se continuerat.[f] Ipsa itaque, ex his quae continue audiebat et a fratre tunc cognouit, [g]legatum nichil[g] molle ad suas partes cogitare intelligens, Wintoniam cum quanto potuit apparatu uenit.[237] Illic intra castellum regium sine cunctatione recepta, bona [h]forsitan mente[h] per nuntios episcopum conuenit, ut, quia ipsa presens erat, non pigritaretur ad eam uenire. Ille, non integrum sibi fore arbitratus si ueniret, ambiguo responso nuntios elusit hoc tantum[i] uerbo: 'Ego parabo me', statimque [j]propter omnes misit[j] quos regi fauturos[k] sciebat.[238] Venerunt ergo fere omnes comites Angliae. Erant enim iuuenes et leues, et qui mallent equitationum discursus quam pacem. Preterea plures illorum, confusi quia regem bellantem, ut

---

[a] dandas B   [b-b] uxore fratris A   [c] et eius A   [d-d] querele in imperatricem A   [e] Rubric Quomodo comes Gloecestre legatum conuenerit cum imperatrice et coadiutoribus suis Ce¹   [f] continuauerat Ce¹   [g-g] nichil legatum Ce¹   [h-h] mente forsitan A   [i] tamen ACe¹   [j-j] misit propter omnes A   [k] fautoris A

[236] The county of Mortain was forfeit by Count William after the Battle of Tinchebrai, and subsequently given to Stephen by Henry I: OV vi. 42–3 (amplifying the material on the family ibid., iii. 116–17). The grant may be dated to between Sept. 1110 (*Actes de Louis VI*, i, no. 46) and Feb. 1113 (OV vi. 174–7).

[237] According to the Gloucester chronicle, after the flight from London the empress went first to Oxford and then to Gloucester, and from there went to Winchester (without

that of Mortain in Normandy from his own possessions.[236] These
counties the legate had intended to give to his nephew Eustace,
whom I have mentioned, as being his lawful property while his
father was held prisoner, but the empress categorically refused
and, it may be, even promised them to others. The legate, enraged
by this affront, kept away from her court for many days and,
though often summoned back, persisted in refusal. Meanwhile he
had a family conference at Guildford with the queen, his brother's
wife, and influenced by her tears and offers of amends he resolved
to free his brother; he also gave absolution, without consulting the
bishops, to all the members of his brother's party whom he had
excommunicated in the council. His complaints against the
empress were borne throughout England: that she had wished to
arrest him; that she had disregarded everything she had sworn to
him; that all the barons of England had kept their faith with her
but she had broken hers, being unable to show restraint in the
enjoyment of what she had gained.

54. The earl of Gloucester, with no very large retinue, hastened to
Winchester to settle these disturbances if he could, but having
accomplished nothing went back to Oxford, where his sister had
long been in permanent quarters. Then she, perceiving from what
she had always been hearing and then learnt from her brother, that
the legate had no kindly intentions towards her party, came to
Winchester with as large a force as she could.[237] There she was at
once received within the royal castle and summoned the legate by
messengers, perhaps meaning him no harm, not to delay coming to
her as she herself had arrived. He, thinking he would lose his
freedom of action if he did come, fobbed off the messengers by an
ambiguous answer, saying merely, 'I will get ready', and sent
immediately for all those who he knew would favour the king.[238]
So almost all the earls in England came, for they were young and
frivolous, men who preferred cavalry-raids to peace. Most of

Robert of Gloucester's knowledge); she arrived on 31 July: JW iii. 298–9; for the date, see
below, p. 107 n. 254.
[238] As the empress came in through one gate the bishop rode out through another, 'and
made off to his castles at full speed': GS, pp. 126–7; so also JW iii. 298–9.

superius dictum est,[239] deseruerant, conuentu illo fugae suae obprobium lenire conabantur. Pauci uero cum imperatrice uenerant:[a] rex Scottiae Dauid,[240] Rotbertus comes Gloecestriae, Milo de Hereford, et barones pauci. Rannulfus[b] comes Cestriae tarde et inutiliter aduenit.[c][241]

55. Vt ergo magnam seriem rerum breui uerborum compendio explicem: a regina, et comitibus qui uenerant, undique foras muros Wintoniae obseruatae sunt uiae, ne uictualia [d]imperatricis fidelibus[d] inferrentur. Andeuera etiam uicus incensus.[242] Ab occidente itaque[e] raro et anguste importabantur necessaria, uiatoribus nonnullis interceptis, et[f] uel occisis uel parte membrorum mutilatis. Ab oriente uero toto tramite uersus Lundoniam constipabantur semitae multitudine commeatuum, episcopo et suis importandorum;[g] et Lundoniensibus maxime annitentibus, nichilque[h] omnino quod possent pretermittentibus quo imperatricem contristarent. Wintonienses porro uel tacito ei fauebant iuditio, memores fidei quam ei pacti fuerant cum inuiti propemodum ab episcopo ad hoc adacti essent. Interea ex turre pontificis iaculatum incendium in domos burgensium,[244] qui, ut dixi, proniores erant [i]imperatricis felicitati[i] quam episcopi, comprehendit et combussit abbatiam totam sanctimonialium intra urbem, simulque cenobium monachorum[j] quod dicitur Ad Hidam extra.[245] Erat ibi imago

[a] conuenerant B   [b] enim add. B   [c] uenit B   [d-d] fidelibus imperatricis A   [e] om. A   [f] om. Ce¹   [g] Gaufrido de Mandeuilla, qui iam iterum auxilio eorum cesserat, antea enim post captionem regis imperatrici fidelitatem iurauerat add. Ce¹   [h] nichil A   [i] felicitati imperatricis A   [j] om. Ce¹

[239] HN § 43.

[240] David, king of Scots, was with the empress at Westminster, Oxford, and Winchester in summer 1141: GS, pp. 120–1; A. O. Anderson, Scottish Annals from English Chroniclers, A.D. 500 to 1286 (London, 1908), pp. 217–21; Regesta, iii, nos. 328, 377, 393, 429, 629, 899.

[241] The Gesta Stephani gives a much longer list of the empress's supporters at Winchester (including each of those named here), and emphasizes their strength: GS, pp. 128–9.

[242] Andover lies 12 miles NNW of Winchester.

[243] Geoffrey de Mandeville was created earl of Essex by Stephen c. Dec. 1140 and died Sept. 1144: CP v. 113–16. This interpolated passage, which has him fighting alongside the Londoners on behalf of Stephen, comes almost immediately after the probable date of Regesta, iii, no. 275 (the empress's second charter (M2) for Geoffrey de Mandeville; see introduction, p. lxii and n. 252), in which the Londoners are described as his 'mortal enemies', and at the same time as the Tower of London was under attack by them: Brett, 'The annals of Bermondsey, Southwark and Merton', p. 300.

them, moreover, ashamed of having abandoned the king in battle, as has been said above,[239] were trying to palliate the disgrace of their flight by assembling then. Only a few had come with the empress: David, king of Scots,[240] Robert, earl of Gloucester, Miles, earl of Hereford and a few barons. Ranulf earl of Chester's arrival was late and ineffective.[241]

55. So, to unfold a long succession of events in a brief account, everywhere outside the walls of Winchester the roads were being watched by the queen and the earls who had come, to prevent provisions being brought in to the empress's adherents. Also the township of Andover was burnt.[242] So from the west necessities were being brought in seldom and on a limited scale, and of those who conveyed them a number were captured or killed or mutilated in some part of their limbs. In the east, all the way to London, the tracks were crowded with masses of provisions being taken to the bishop and his men; [**Ce** *adds* Geoffrey de Mandeville,[243] who had again gone over to aid them, for formerly, after the king's capture, he had sworn allegiance to the empress] and the Londoners were making the greatest efforts, and not letting slip a single thing that lay in their power whereby they might distress the empress. But the people of Winchester gave her their unspoken loyalty, remembering the faith they had pledged to her when they were induced to do it, almost against their will, by the bishop. Meanwhile firebrands, flung from the bishop's tower upon the houses of the citizens,[244] who, as I have said, were more ready to promote the empress's happiness than the bishop's, caught and burned an entire nunnery within the city and the monastery called Hyde without.[245] There was in it a likeness of the crucified Lord with a

[244] The *Gesta Stephani* refers to the bishop's castle, which he had build in an elegant style 'in ciuitatis medio', and notes that firebrands were thrown from this castle whilst it was besieged: *GS*, pp. 126–7, 130–1. The references in the *GS* and the *HN* are to a fortification at the royal palace (in the centre of the city), not to the royal castle (in the south-west, occupied by the empress: *GS*, pp. 118–19; JW iii. 298–9), or the bishop's palace at Wolvesey (in the south-east): see the magisterial discussion by M. Biddle, in *Winchester Studies*, i. 297–8 (royal palace), 324–6 (Wolvesey).

[245] The 'nunnery' was St Mary's Abbey, or Nunnaminster: *Winchester Studies*, i. 321–3. The 'monastery called Hyde' was Hyde Abbey: originally New Minster, in the centre of the city, it moved in the reign of Henry I to a less constricted and more salubrious site at Hyde in the northern suburbs: ibid., i. 318–21; *The Liber Vitae of the New Minster and*

crucifixi Domini magna mole auri et argenti simulque gemmarum, dono^a Cnutonis quondam regis operosa deuotione fabrefacta.[246] Haec, igne tunc comprehensa et solo prostrata, post etiam ^{b}iubente legato^b excrustata est.[247] Inuentae plusquam quingentae argenti marcae,^{c} auri triginta, donatiuo militum profecere.[248] Combusta est etiam abbatia sanctimonialium de Warewella a quodam Willelmo de Ypra, homine nefando, qui nec Deo nec hominibus reuerentiam obseruaret, quod in ea quidam imperatricis fautores se contutati essent.[249]

500 **56.**^{d} Comes^e interea, quanuis cotidiano regiorum prelio cum suis afflictaretur, minusque quam cogitaret^f res ex sententia cederet, semper tamen ab incendio aecclesiarum temperandum putauit, quanuis in uicino^g sancti Swithuni hospitatus esset.[250] Veruntamen indignitatem rei ultra non ferens, se suosque pene obsideri et fortunam in alteros declinare, cedendum tempori ratus, compositis ordinibus discessionem parauit. Itaque in primo agmine ut libere abiret sororem premittens cum reliquis, ipse, cum paucis qui auderent animis multos non timere, lente progrediebatur.^{h} Quapropter comitibus^{i} ^{j}confestim insecutis, dum et ipse fugere pudori et citra dignitatem suam estimat, et^j solus ab omnibus precipue

^{a} dano A ex dono Cd $^{b-b}$ legato iubente B ^{c} et add. A ^{d} Rubric De discessu comitis Gloecestre a Wintonia et captione sua Ce^1 ^{e} Gloecestre add. Ce^1 ^{f} cogitarat AB ^{g} uicinio Ce^1 ^{h} progreditur B ^{i} regiis add. Ce^1 $^{j-j}$ om. B

Hyde Abbey Winchester, ed. S. Keynes (Early English Manuscripts in Facsimile, xxvi; Copenhagen, 1996), pp. 16–48. The burning of the two houses is noted also in *GS*, pp. 130–1; JW iii. 298–9; *Liber Vitae: Register and Martyrology of New Minster and Hyde Abbey, Winchester*, ed. W. de G. Birch (Hampshire Rec. Soc., 1892), p. 2.

[246] The cross is shown in the frontispiece to the Winchester *Liber Vitae*, discussed in *Liber Vitae of New Minster and Hyde Abbey*, ed. S. Keynes, pp. 35–7 and plate V; reproduced also in J. Campbell, E. John, and P. Wormald, *The Anglo-Saxons* (Oxford, 1982), p. 208, plate 182.

[247] Henry of Winchester held the monastery of Hyde in his own hands from the beginning of Stephen's reign until 1142: W. Dugdale, *Monasticon Anglicanum*, rev. J. Caley et al., 6 vols. in 8 (1817–30), ii. 437. The monks' complaints about the bishop's behaviour underlie a memorandum they made about the house's history, which mentions this episode (ibid., ii. 435–7), and they inform the fuller description in *HN* and in the Gloucester chronicle (JW iii. 298–301): see the discussion in *Liber Vitae of New Minster and Hyde Abbey*, ed. S. Keynes, pp. 35–6.

[248] The Gloucester chronicle gives the figure of 500 pounds of silver and 30 marks of

great mass of gold and silver, also precious stones, wrought with laborious devotion as a gift from Cnut, a king in former times.[246] This was caught by the fire and fell to the ground, and was afterwards stripped by the legate's order.[247] More than 500 marks of silver were found and 30 of gold, and they helped to provide largesse for the knights.[248] Also the nunnery of Wherwell was burnt by a certain William of Ypres, a wicked man who respected neither God nor men, on the grounds that some of the empress's adherents had taken refuge in it.[249]

56. Meanwhile the earl of Gloucester, though he was hard-pressed by daily battles between the king's men and his own, and his success was not proportionate to his expectations, still always thought he must refrain from burning churches, though he was lodged in the neighbourhood of St Swithun's.[250] But since he could no longer bear the shame of the situation, in that he and his men were practically besieged and fortune was turning to favour the other side, he thought he must bow to the exigencies of the time, and prepared an orderly withdrawal. And so he sent his sister and all the others on ahead in the vanguard, to allow her to escape unharmed, while he himself advanced slowly, with a few who had the courage not to fear being outnumbered. Wherefore, as the earls [**Ce** *adds* of the king's party] pursued at speed, and he himself thought it unbecoming and beneath his dignity to flee, and was alone the special object of everyone's attack, he was taken

gold, and has further details of the cross (JW iii. 302–3); the bishop's hiring of mercenaries, at great expense, is referred to in the *Gesta Stephani* (*GS*, pp. 128–9).

[249] The *Gesta Stephani* says that the empress's party intended to build a castle at the abbey, to control the road: *GS*, pp. 130–3. The Gloucester chronicle says that John the Marshal was pursued into the nunnery, and blames Henry of Winchester's knights for its burning, not William of Ypres: JW iii. 302–3. The Marshal family tradition concerning this episode is found in *L'Histoire de Guillaume le Maréchal*, ed. P. Meyer, 3 vols. (1891–1901), i. 8–11 (French abstract, iii. 4–7), and discussed by Crouch, *William Marshal*, pp. 13–14.

[250] St Swithun's was the dedication of the cathedral priory at Winchester: Winchester Studies, i. 306–13. Robert of Gloucester had a number of properties in Winchester: ibid., i. 82 and n. 2, 103, 388–9. The location of the 'hospitia' described here is discussed in D. Keene, *Survey of Medieval Winchester*, 2 vols. (Winchester Studies, ii; Oxford, 1985), ii, no. 234, where it is suggested that 'there are good reasons for believing that it lay somewhere near the entry to Minster Street at the NW corner of the site of the royal palace'. The present passage, not cited by Keene, provides evidence in support of his hypothesis.

impetitur, captus est.[251] Ceteri ceptum iter proceres presertim continuare, summaque[a] cum festinatione Diuisas peruenerunt.[252] Sic a Wintonia die sanctae Crucis Exaltationis, que tunc habebatur in dominica,[253] discessum, cum illuc paucis ante Assumptionem beatae Dei genetricis diebus uentum fuisset.[254] Nonnullisque miraculi exemplum et multorum materia sermonum fuit in Anglia, quod sicut rex dominica in dominae nostrae Purificatione, [b:]ita comes dominica in uiuificae Crucis Exaltatione,[b] unam eandemque sortem experti sunt. Illud uero percelebre magnificumque fuit, quod pro isto euentu nemo comitem Gloecestriae uel infractum mente, uel etiam tristem uultu, uidit.[c] Ita conscientiam altae nobilitatis spirabat, ne se fortunae ludibrio subiceret. Quanuis enim primo blanditiis inuitatus, post etiam minis lacesseretur, numquam tamen inflexus est ut de liberatione sua preter conscientiam[d] sororis tractaretur. Ad ultimum eo modo res uentilata, ut aequis conditionibus et rex et ipse absoluerentur, nullo pacto alio interueniente, nisi ut quisque[e] partes suas pro posse, sicut [f]et prius,[f] tutaretur.

57. Haec ab Exaltatione sanctae Crucis usque ad festum[g] Omnium Sanctorum plurimo[h] uerborum agmine sepe uersata, tunc demum debito fine conclusa.[255] Ea enim die rex eluctatus captionem, in eadem apud Bristou reginam suam et filium cum duobus magnatibus reliquit, uades liberandi comitis, continuo cum festinato itinere rex Wintoniam uenisset. Ibi enim asseruabatur comes, reductus a Rofacestra, quo prius abductus fuerat. Tertio die, mox ut rex Wintoniam uenit, comes abscessit, dimisso ibi, quousque regina absolueretur, in eodem[i] obsidatu filio suo

---

[a] et summa *A*   [b-b] om. *Ce[1]*   [c] uiderit *Ce[1]*   [d] consensum *Ce[1]*
[e] quisquis *A*   [f-f] prius *A*, et superius *B*   [g] festiuitatem *A*
[h] plurimorum *A*   [i] die add. *B*

---

[251] Robert of Gloucester was captured at Stockbridge ford by the Earl Warenne and a party of Flemings, taken before the queen, given by her into the custody of William of Ypres, and thence taken to Rochester: JW iii. 302–3; R. Hill, 'The Battle of Stockbridge, 1141', *Studies in Medieval History Presented to R. Allen Brown*, ed. C. Harper-Bill *et al.* (Woodbridge, 1989), pp. 173–7.

[252] For the empress's route, see ibid., p. 176: according to the Gloucester chronicle she spent a night at Ludgershall before reaching Devizes, and thence was sent in a litter 'quasi cadauer' to Gloucester: JW iii. 300–1.

prisoner.[251] The others, particularly those of high rank, went on with the journey they had begun and reached Devizes in the greatest haste.[252] Such was the departure from Winchester on the day of the Exaltation of the Holy Cross, which then fell on a Sunday [14 Sept.],[253] the arrival having been a few days before the Assumption of the Blessed Mother of God [15 Aug.].[254] It was a matter of some wonder and much talk in England, that the king and the earl met one and the same fate, the former on a Sunday, the Purification of Our Lady, the latter on a Sunday, the Exaltation of the life-giving Cross. It was widely reported, and brought him much honour, that no one saw the earl of Gloucester broken in spirit or even gloomy of countenance because of that mischance. Such consciousness of his lofty rank did he breathe, that he could not be humbled by the outrage of fortune. For though he was first lured by flatteries, and afterwards even assailed by threats, he could not be induced to allow negotiations for his release to proceed behind his sister's back. The discussions ended in an agreement that the king and he should be released on the same terms, no other condition being involved except each should guard his own region to the best of his ability, as before.

57. These matters were argued at very great length from the Exaltation of the Holy Cross to the feast of All Saints [1 Nov.], and only then reached a suitable conclusion.[255] For that was the day the king emerged from captivity, on the same day leaving his queen and son with two men of high rank at Bristol, there to serve as sureties for the earl's release immediately the king by travelling at speed could reach Winchester. That was where the earl was kept, having been brought there from Rochester, where he was taken at first. On the third day, as soon as the king came to Winchester, the earl departed, leaving his son William there as a hostage in the same manner until the queen's release. So he

---

[253] This date is given also in the Gloucester chronicle: ibid.

[254] The empress in fact arrived several days before this, for the Winchester *Liber Vitae* has Thursday 31 July [1140, correct for 1141], and the Gloucester chronicle 'before the feast of St Peter in Chains' [1 Aug.]: *Liber Vitae of New Minster and Hyde Abbey, Winchester*, ed. W. de G. Birch, p. 2; JW iii. 298–9.

[255] More details of the negotiations are given below, *HN* §63–9.

Willelmo. Celeriter igitur permensa uia Bristou ueniens, reginam absoluit. Cuius reditu Willelmus filius comitis ab obsidatu liberatur.[256] Satis autem constat, toto tempore captionis, *et sequentibus* mensibus usque ad Natale, multis et magnis pollicitationibus sollicitatum ut a sorore desciscerent,[257] pluris semper pietatem germanitatis quam quaslibet promissiones fecisse. Nam et relictis rebus castellisque*b* suis, quibus commode frui posset, circa germanam sedulo apud Oxeneford mansitabat; quo loco, ut prefatus sum, illa *sedem sibi* constituens curiam fecerat.[258]

501   **58.***d* Interea legatus, immodici animi pontifex, qui quod semel proposuisset non ineffectum relinquere uellet, concilium pro iure legationis suae apud Westmonasterium die octauarum sancti Andreae coegit.[259] Eius concilii actionem non ita exacta fide pronuntio ut superioris, quia non interfui. Auditum est lectas in eo litteras domini apostolici, quibus modeste legatum argueret quod liberare fratrem suum dissimulasset. Delicti tamen superioris gratiam facere; et magnopere cohortari, ut quocumque modo, uel aecclesiastico uel seculari, posset, ad germani liberationem accingeretur. Regem ipsum in concilium introisse, et apud sanctum conuentum querimoniam deposuisse, quod homines sui et eum ceperint, et afflictione contumeliarum paulominus exstinxerint, qui iustitiam eis numquam negasset. Ipsum legatum magnis eloquentiae uiribus factorum suorum inuidiam temptasse alleuiare, quod scilicet imperatricem non uoluntate sed necessitate recepisset, quippe cum recenti adhuc fratris sui clade, omnibus comitibus uel fugatis, uel euentum rei suspecta mente prestolantibus, ipsa cum suis muros Wintoniae circumsonasset. Ipsam quaecumque pepigerat ad aecclesiarum ius pertinentia obstinate fregisse; quin etiam certis auctoribus ad se delatum eam et suos

---

a–a sequenti *B*, sequentibus *Cd*, sequentibusque *Ce*[1]   *b* et castellis *A*
c–c sibi sedem *A*   *d* *Rubric* De concilio quo legatus temptauit lenire causam receptionis imperatricis in dominam *Ce*[1]

---

[256] William succeeded to the earldom on his father's death in 1147 and died 23 Nov. 1183: *CP* v. 687–9; *Gloucester Charters*, pp. 3–5.
[257] *HN* §64, 69.
[258] Referring back to *HN* §54, 'statiua mansione iamdudum se continuerat'. The

travelled rapidly, came to Bristol, and released the queen. On her return the earl's son William was released from custody as a hostage.[256] It is well established that all through the time of his imprisonment and in the following months up to Christmas the earl was incited to abandon his sister by many great promises,[257] yet always set more store by his fraternal duty than by any promises whatsoever. For forsaking his property and his castles, which he might have enjoyed at his ease, he constantly remained with his sister at Oxford, in which place, as I have already said, she had settled and made her court.[258]

58. Meanwhile the legate, a prelate of haughty spirit and unwilling to leave undone what he had once set himself to do, in his official capacity summoned a council at Westminster on the octave of St Andrew [7 Dec.].[259] I cannot relate the proceedings of that council with as much confidence as those of the earlier one, because I was not present. I heard that a letter from the pope was read in it in which he mildly rebuked the legate for evading the task of his brother's release. He none the less forgave him his previous fault; and he strongly urged him to gird himself to procure his brother's freedom by any means, ecclesiastical or secular. The king himself entered the council and laid a complaint before that holy assembly, saying that his men had both captured him and had almost killed, by the grievous burden of their insults, one who had never refused them justice. The legate himself tried to diminish by his great eloquence his unpopularity for what he had done, saying that he had received the empress not of his own will but under compulsion, because, when his brother had just suffered disaster, and all the earls had either been put to flight or were waiting in a doubtful frame of mind to see how things would turn out, she and her men had surrounded Winchester with noise of arms. She herself had persistently broken all her pledges relating to the freedom of the

empress's residence at Oxford seems not to have predated the battle of Lincoln, and may have been as late as the early summer of 1141: *Regesta*, iii, p. xliv (itinerary); and above, p. lxii.

[259] William of Malmesbury has the only record of this meeting: *Councils and Synods*, i (2), pp. 792–4.

non solum dignitati suae, sed et uitae, struxisse insidias. Ceterum Deum pro sua clementia secus quam ipsa sperasset uertisse negotia, ut et ipse pernitiem uitaret, et fratrem suum uinculis eximeret. Itaque iubere se de parte Dei et apostolici, ut regem, uoluntate populi et assensu sedis apostolicae inunctum, quantis possent uiribus enixe iuuarent; turbatores uero*a* pacis, qui comitissae Andegauensi fauerent, ad excommunicationem uocandos, preter eam quae Andegauorum domina esset.[260]

502   **59.***b* Haec eius uerba non dico quod omnes clerici*c* gratis animis exceperint, certe nullus expugnauit. Omnes*d* uel metu uel reuerentia frenarunt ora. Vnus fuit laicus, imperatricis nuntius, qui palam legato interdixit, ne per fidem quam ei pactus fuerat quicquam in illo concilio statueret quod eius honori aduersum foret. Fidem ab eo hanc*e* *f*imperatrici factam,*f* ne fratrem suum ullo auxilio iuuaret,*g* nisi forte *h*ei uiginti*h* milites nec plures mitteret.[261] Quod in Angliam ipsa uenisset, frequentibus epistolis eius factum: quod regem cepisset, quod in captione*i* tenuisset, ipso potissimum coniuente actum. Dixit nuntius*j* haec et alia pleraque magna uerborum austeritate, nichil omnino legato blanditus. Nec uero ullo sermonum pondere ille moueri potuit ut iram proderet, semel incepti, ut prius dixi, sui non segnis executor.*k* Fuit ergo*l* hic annus, cuius tragedias compendio digessi, fatalis et pene pernitiosus Angliae; in quo cum aliquo modo sibi ad libertatem respirandum putasset, rursum in erumnam recidit, et, nisi Dei misericordia mature occurrat, diu herebit.

---

   a om. A   *b* *Rubric* Quomodo quidam fautor imperatricis locutus fuerit pro imperatrice *Ce*¹   *c* om. *Ce*¹   *d* clerici *add. Ce*¹   *e* om. *Ce*¹   *f-f* factam imperatrici A   *g* adiuuaret B   *h-h* uiginti ei *BkBqCd*, uiginti *Ce*¹   *i* captionem A   *j* om. *Ce*¹   *k* insecutor *Ce*¹   *l* om. B

---

[260] The title 'countess of Anjou', which the empress herself never used, was the common usage among Stephen's party (as the *Gesta Stephani* makes clear), and its ascription here to Henry of Winchester neatly signals his change of loyalty.

[261] In 1101 the count of Flanders in his agreement with Henry I promised if summoned by the French king into England to bring with him only 'tam paruam fortitudinem hominum quam minorem poterit, ita tamen ne inde feodum suum . . . forisfaciat', and twenty knights are later specified as such a token force: *English Diplomatic Documents*, i; *1101–1272*, ed. P. Chaplais (London, 1964), no. 1, pp. 1–4 (cf. the agreements of 1110 and

churches. Moreover, he said, he had been informed on reliable authority that she and her men had plotted not only against his position, but against his life. However, God in His mercy had given affairs a different course from what she had hoped, so that he might avoid destruction himself and rescue his brother from bondage. Therefore, in the name of God and the pope, he bade them aid zealously to the utmost of their power a king anointed with the goodwill of the people and the approval of the Apostolic See; those disturbers of the peace who supported the countess of Anjou must be sentenced to excommunication, all except the lady of the Angevins herself.[260]

59. I do not say that these words of the legate were gladly received by all the clergy, but certainly no one refuted them. All kept silent from fear or out of respect. There was one layman, an envoy from the empress, who publicly forbade the legate, by the pledge he had given to the empress, to make any decision in that council to the prejudice of her position. He had given her this pledge, that he would not aid his brother in any way, unless perchance he sent him twenty knights, but no more.[261] Her own coming to England had been caused by frequent letters from him: the king's capture and imprisonment were mainly due to his connivance. The envoy said this and a great deal more in very harsh terms, making no attempt to appease the legate. Yet he could not be induced by any severity of language to betray anger, being, as I said before, a man not slow to carry out what he had once taken in hand. So all this year, whose tragedies I have briefly related, was ill-omened and almost mortal to England, which, after thinking that it might now in some sort draw a breath of freedom, fell back again into misery, and thus, unless God's mercy sends a remedy soon, it will long remain.

1163, ibid., nos. 2–3, pp. 5–12). The same figure of twenty knights is found in a similar context in the agreement later in the reign between the earls of Chester and Leicester: Sir Frank Stenton, *The First Century of English Feudalism 1066–1166*, 2nd edn. (Oxford, 1961), pp. 286–8. And see now M. Strickland, *War and Chivalry: The Conduct and Perception of War in England and Normandy, 1066–1217* (Cambridge, 1996), pp. 236–8.

503 **60.**[a] Principia gestorum huius anni, qui est incarnationis Dominicae millesimus centesimus quadragesimus tertius, ex reliquis superioris anni successit animo resarcire;[262] simulque summam rerum quae de Rotberto filio regis Henrici comite Gloecestriae sparsim dictae sunt, quasi in fasciculum collectam, lectoris estimationi per recapitulationem proponere. Ipse quippe sicut primus ad partes sororis suae iuste defendendas initium suscepit, ita semper inuicto animo in incepto gratis perseuerauit. Gratis dico, quia nonnulli fautorum eius uel fortunam sequentes cum eius uolubilitate mutantur, uel, multa iam emolumenta consecuti, spe ampliorum premiorum pro iustitia pugnant. Solus uel pene solus Rotbertus in neutram partem pronior, nec spe compendii nec dispendii timore umquam flexus est, sicut ex sequentibus[b] liquebit. Non ergo alicui, si haec integre scribo, adulationis subrepat suspitio. Nichil enim a me dabitur gratiae, sed sola ueritas historiae sine ullo fuco mendatii posterorum producetur notitiae.

504 **61.** Dictum est de comite quo modo primus omnium primatum[c] post Dauid regem Scottiae, presente patre Henrico, fidelitatem sorori suae imperatrici de regno Angliae et ducatu Normanniae sacramento firmauit, nonnulla, ut dixi, contentione inter eum et Stephanum tunc Bononiae comitem, postmodum Angliae regem, quisnam prior sacramentum faceret: Rotberto excellentiam filii, 505 Stephano dignitatem nepotis defendentibus.[263] Dictum est etiam[d] quam rationabiles [e]eum cause[e] a Decembri, quo pater defunctus est, usque post sequens Pascha in Normannia continuerint, ne statim in Angliam ueniens sororis iniurias uindicaret; postremo ueniens, quam prudenti consilio et qua exceptione ad hominium regis se inclinauerit,[264] et quam iuste idem sequenti anno et 506 deinceps abiecerit.[265] Nec est pretermissus secundus eius post

---

[a] *Rubric* Recapitulatio de comite Gloecestre *Ce*¹   [b] consequentibus *Ce*¹
[c] *om. Ce*¹   [d] autem *A*, enim *Cd*   [e-e] cause eum *A*

---

[262] William of Malmesbury is here writing in 1143, but 'this year' in his text is 1142, and 'what is left over from the year before' refers to the later months of 1141: see the introduction, p. xxxii.
[263] *HN* §3.   [264] *HN* §17.

60. It has occurred to me to join up the early events of this year, which is the year of the Lord's Incarnation 1143, with what is left over from the year before;[262] and at the same time to make into a parcel, as it were, the main points scattered through my text bearing on the conduct of Robert, earl of Gloucester, King Henry's son, and to present them in a recapitulation for the reader to evaluate. As he took the lead in the just defence of his sister's cause, so he has always persisted in the undertaking with unconquerable spirit and without self-interest. I say 'without self-interest' because a number of her adherents are either followers of fortune and change as it changes or, having already made great gains, fight for justice in the hope of yet richer rewards. Robert alone, or almost alone, inclining neither way, has never been influenced by hope of gain or fear of loss, as will be clear from what follows. So, if I write these things honestly, let no suspicion of flattery creep into anyone's mind. For I shall make no concession to favour, but rather the truth of history alone, without any colouring of falsehood, will be set forth for the knowledge of posterity.

61. It has been said about the earl how as first of all the great men after David, king of Scots, in the presence of his father Henry, he confirmed by oath his allegiance to his sister the empress with regard to the kingdom of England and duchy of Normandy, after some dispute, as I have said, between him and Stephen, then count of Boulogne, afterwards king of England, as to which should take the oath first, Robert maintaining the pre-eminence of a son, Stephen the rank of a nephew.[263] It has also been said what valid reasons kept him in Normandy from December, when his father died, until after the following Easter, and prevented his coming to England at once and avenging his sister's wrongs; and thereafter, when he came, by what prudent judgement and with what reservation he submitted to pay the king homage,[264] and how justly he abjured that homage in the following year and thereafter.[265] Nor have I overlooked his second arrival in England from

---

[265] Robert of Gloucester renounced his homage in 1138 (*HN* §21), two years after he had performed it.

mortem patris a Normannia in Angliam cum sorore aduentus; in
quam se sicut in quandam siluam frementium beluarum immersit,
Dei quidem gratia et animi confidentia fretus, sed uix centum
quadraginta militibus stipatus. Sed nec illud tacitum, quod in
tanto motu bellorum, cum sollicitae ubique pretenderentur excu-
biae, cum solis duodecim militibus impigre ad Bristou uenit,
sorore interim apud Arundel fida, ut putabat, custodia com-
missa.²⁶⁶ Qua prudentia et tunc sororem suam e mediis hostibus
ad se receperit, et postmodum in omnibus pro posse prouexerit;²⁶⁷
semper circa eam conuersatus, ipsius commoda procurans, sua
postponens, cum quidam abutentes eius absentia terras ipsius
undique uellicarent. Ad postremum, qua necessitate adductus,
ut generum suum, quem rex incluserat, periculo eximeret, bello
ᵃgraui seᵃ dederit regemqueᵇ ceperit.²⁶⁸

62. Sed tam felicem euentum captioᶜ apud Wintoniam, ut in
superioris anni gestis perstrinxi,ᵈ paulominus decolorauit,ᵉ quam-
quam ea captione non tam miserandum quam laudandum se ipse
per Dei gratiam exhibuerit. Cum enim uideret regios comites ita
obstinatos ad persequendumᶠ ut sine suorum detrimento res
transigi nequiret, omnes quibus timebat nominatimqueᵍ imperatricem premisit. Quibus pregressis,ʰ ut iam tuto possent euadere,
ipse sensim equitans, ne similis fugae profectio putaretur, admisit
in se persequentium manus, amicorum liberationem impedimento
suo mercatus. Iam uero in ipsa captione nemo eum, ut ante dixi,²⁶⁹
uel sensit deiectum animo, uel audiuit humilem in uerbo: adeo
supra fortunam eminere uidebatur, ut persecutores suos, nolo
enimⁱ dicere hostes, ad reuerentiam sui excitaret. Itaque regina,
quae licet meminisset uirum suum eius iussu fuisse compeditum,
nichil ei umquam uinculorum inferri permisit, nec quicquam
inhonestum de sua maiestate presumpsit. Denique apud
Rofacestram, illuc quippe ductus fuit, libere ad aecclesias infra

ᵃ⁻ᵃ se graui *A*   ᵇ et regem *A*   ᶜ eius *add. Ce*¹   ᵈ perstrinximus *A*
ᵉ declinauit *Ce*¹   ᶠ sequendum *B*   ᵍ et nominatim *A*   ʰ pretergressis
*Ce*¹   ⁱ *om. Ce*¹

²⁶⁶ *HN* §31.   ²⁶⁷ *HN* §37.   ²⁶⁸ *HN* §42-3.   ²⁶⁹ *HN* §56.

Normandy with his sister after his father's death; he plunged into a country that was like a forest full of raging wild beasts, trusting indeed in God's grace and his own resolute spirit, but with scarce so many as 140 knights in his pay. Neither have I failed to mention that amid such stirrings of war, when pickets were on the alert for him everywhere, he boldly came to Bristol with only twelve knights, meanwhile leaving his sister at Arundel in what he thought to be faithful guardianship.[266] I have said with what judgement he then rescued his sister from the midst of her enemies, and afterwards advanced her cause in all things to the utmost of his power,[267] always in her company, attending to her interest and neglecting his own, though certain persons, taking advantage of his absence, were everywhere snatching away his lands. Finally I have said how, compelled to save from danger his son-in-law, whom the king had besieged, he faced a grievous conflict and captured the king.[268]

62. But, a matter I have touched on among the events of the year before, the lustre of this triumph was almost tarnished by his capture at Winchester; though in that capture, by God's grace, he made himself an object less of pity than of praise. For, when he saw the earls of the king's party so determined in pursuit that the action could not end without loss to his own side, he sent on all for whom he feared, especially the empress. And when they had gone ahead, so that they could now escape in safety, he himself rode slowly, to prevent his journey being thought like a flight, and so let himself fall into the hands of the pursuers, buying his friends' freedom with the loss of his own. Moreover in the actual capture no one, as I said before,[269] either noticed that he was downcast in mind, or heard anything abject in his language: so much did he seem to rise above ill-fortune that he aroused the respect of his pursuers (I will not call them his enemies). Therefore the queen, though she remembered her husband had been fettered by his orders, never allowed any chains to be put on him or ventured anything that would have dishonoured his rank. Finally at Rochester, for he was taken there, he was free to go to the churches beneath the castle when he liked, and to talk with

castellum quo libebat ibat, et quibus libebat loquebatur, ipsa dumtaxat regina presente. Nam post profectionem eius in turrim sub libera custodia ductus est,²⁷⁰ adeo presenti et securo animo ut ab hominibus suis de Cantia accepta pecunia equos non parui pretii compararet, qui ei post aliquanto tempore et usui et commodo fuere.

507   **63.**ᵃ Temptauere primo comites, et hi quorum intererat de talibus loqui, si forte regem et se sineret aequis conditionibus liberari. Hoc quanuis Mabilia comitissa pre desiderio uiri suiᵇ statim amplexa nuntiis acceptis esset, in eius liberationem coniugali caritate propensior, ille profundiori consilio contradixit, regem et comitem non aequalis ponderis esse asseuerans. Ceterum, si permitterent omnes qui uel secum uel sui causa capti essent liberari, id se posse pati. Sed noluerunt assentireᶜ comites, et alii qui regalium partium erant, regem quidem liberari cupientes, sed citra suas in pecuniae amissione iacturas. Nam etᵈ Gillebertus comes²⁷¹ Willelmum de Salesberia,²⁷² etᵉ Willelmus de Ypra Hunfridum de Buhun,ᶠet nonnulliᶠ alii quos potuerant, Wintoniae ceperant, ᵍmultis in eorum redemptione marcis inhiantes.ᵍ ²⁷³

508   **64.**ʰ Itaque alia uia comitem adorsi, promissis ingentibus, si forte possent, illicere cupiebant. Concederet, sorore dimissa, in partes regis, habiturus proinde totius terrae dominatum, et ad ipsius arbitrium penderent omnia, essetque in sola corona rege inferior, ceteris omnibus pro uelle principaturus. Repulit comes immensas promissiones memorabili responso, quod posteritas audiat et miretur uolo. 'Non sum', ⁱinquit, 'meusⁱ sed alieni iuris. Cum

---

  ᵃ *Rubric* De liberatione regis *Ce*¹   ᵇ dilecti *add. Ce*¹   ᶜ assentiri *A*
ᵈ *om. A*   ᵉ *om. Ce*¹   ᶠ⁻ᶠ nonnullique *B*, nonnulli *Ce*¹   ᵍ multis marcis inhiantis in eorum redemptione *A*   ʰ *Rubric* Quomodo temptatum est comitem Gloecestre posse inflecti in partes regis *Ce*¹   ⁱ⁻ⁱ meus inquit *A*

²⁷⁰ Rochester castle was granted in 1127 to William of Corbeil, archbishop of Canterbury (*Regesta*, ii, no. 1475), and it was he who built the great keep: *King's Works*, ii. 806–7; *Castellarium Anglicanum*, i. 232–3; C. L. H. Coulson, 'Rochester Castle', in E. King, *Medieval England* (Oxford, 1988), pp. 110–11.

²⁷¹ Gilbert Fitz Richard de Clare, earl of Hertford: *CP* vi. 498–9; Davis, *Stephen*, p. 133.

²⁷² William of Salisbury, son of Walter of Salisbury, and elder brother of Patrick, later earl of Salisbury: *CP* xi. 375.

whom he liked, at least as long as the queen was there. For after she had gone away he was brought into the keep under open arrest,[270] so unruffled and calm in mind that on receiving money from his men in Kent he bought some expensive horses, and these afterwards were of service and advantage to him for a considerable time.

63. At first the earls, and those whose concern it was to speak of such things, tried if the earl would allow the king and himself to be released on equal terms. Though the Countess Mabel, on account of her longing for her [Ce adds beloved] husband, at once accepted this proposal when she received the messengers, being from a wife's affection the more eager for his release, he with deeper judgement refused, saying that a king and an earl were not of equal importance. However, he could consent to it if they would allow the release of all who had been taken with him or on his account. But the earls, and others on the king's side, would not agree, desiring indeed the king's release, but not if it meant any loss of money to themselves. For at Winchester Earl Gilbert[271] had taken William of Salisbury,[272] William of Ypres had taken Humphrey de Bohun, and numerous others had their captives, and they were eager for many marks as their ransom.[273]

64. Therefore, approaching the earl in another way, they desired to win him over by vast promises, if only they could. Let him abandon his sister and come over to the king's side; thereby he would have the lordship over the whole land, so that everything would be dependent on his will and he would be lower than the king only as regards the crown, controlling all other matters as he would. The earl rejected their huge promises with a memorable answer, which I want posterity to hear and admire: 'I am not under my own control,' he said, 'but in the power of others; my

[273] It is later stated that the king's party refused a general exchange of prisoners (HN §67), but both William of Salisbury and Humphrey de Bohun were released, if not at the same time as Robert of Gloucester then shortly thereafter. William of Salisbury was in charge of Salisbury for the empress, took part in an attack on Wilton nunnery on 1 July 1143, and died thereafter: GS, pp. 146–9. Humphrey de Bohun may have been with the empress at Oxford in 1142, and was certainly with her by the following year: Regesta, iii, nos. 190, 370–1.

meae potestatis me uidero, quicquid ratio de re quam*ᵃ* allegatis dictauerit, facturum me respondeo.'

₅₀₉ **65.** Tum illi concitatiores et nonnichil moti, cum blanditiis nichil promouerent, minas intentare ceperunt, quod eum ultra mare in Bononiam mitterent, perpetuis uinculis usque ad mortem innodandum. Enimuero ille, minas sereno uultu dissoluens, nichil minus se timere protestatus est. Constanter et uere. Confidebat enim in magnanimitate comitissae, uxoris suae,*ᵇ* et animositate suorum, qui statim regem in Hiberniam mitterent, si quid perperam in comitem factum audissent.

₅₁₀ **66.** Transiit in his mensis.²⁷⁴ Tantae molis erat *ᶜliberari posseᶜ* principes quos fortuna sua innexuisset catena.²⁷⁵ Tandem porro communicato consilio, quicumque imperatrici fauebant crebris legationibus comitem conueniunt, ut quia non posset quod uellet, secundem comici dictum, uellet quod posset.²⁷⁶ Pateretur ergo*ᵈ* regem et se liberari mutuis conditionibus. 'Alioquin timemus', aiebant, 'ne comites facti sui maximi et preclarissimi, quo te ceperunt, erecti conscientia unos et unos ex nobis inuadant, castella expugnent,*ᵉ* ipsam sororem tuam oppugnent.'*ᶠ*

₅₁₁ **67.** Tum*ᵍ* demum Rotbertus mollitus legato et archiepiscopo assensit, ita tamen, ne quicquam castellorum uel terrarum redderetur quod post regis captionem in ius imperatricis uel quorumque*ʰ* fidelium eius transierat.*ⁱ* Illud sane nullo potuit obtinere modo quatinus sui secum liberarentur; offensis uidelicet aliis, quod tantas eorum promissiones de principatu totius regni, quodam quasi*ʲ* fastu fastidiens, repudiauerat. Et quia maxime annitebantur ut propter regiam dignitatem primo rex liberaretur, deinde*ᵏ* comes, cum id ille dubitaret concedere, firmauerunt iureiurando legatus et archiepiscopus, quod, si rex post

---

ᵃ qua me *A*   *ᵇ* scilicet *add. Ce¹*   *ᶜ⁻ᶜ* posse liberari *B*   *ᵈ om. A*
ᵉ oppugnent *ACe¹*   *ᶠ* obsideant *Ce¹*   *ᵍ* Tunc *A*   *ʰ* quorumcumque
BkCe¹   *ⁱ* transierant *A*   *ʲ om. A*   *ᵏ* deinceps *Ce¹*

---

²⁷⁴ From late Sept. to late Oct. 1141.
²⁷⁵ Virgil, *Aen.* i. 33.   ²⁷⁶ Terence, *Andria*, ii. 5–6.

answer is that when I see myself my own master I will do whatever reason dictates with regard to your proposal.'

65. Then they, becoming more excited and considerably disturbed, as they had achieved nothing by their flattery, began to threaten that they would send him overseas to Boulogne to be kept in bondage for life. But he, making light of their threats with a calm countenance, asserted that he feared nothing less. A true and resolute response. For he had confidence in the high spirit of his wife the countess, and the determination of his men, who would send the king to Ireland at once if they heard of any wrong done to the earl.

66. A month passed in these negotiations.[274] So hard was it to release princes whom fortune had put in her chains.[275] But at last, after taking counsel, the empress's adherents, repeatedly sending envoys, urged the earl to do what he could, in the comic poet's words, since he could not do what he would.[276] Let him allow the king and himself to be released on terms of equal exchange. 'Otherwise,' they said, 'we are afraid that the earls, encouraged by the knowledge of their very great deed in taking you, may attack us one by one, storm our castles, and besiege your sister herself.'

67. Then at last Robert was softened and made an agreement with the legate and the archbishop, on condition, however, that no castles or lands should be restored that had passed into the hands of the empress or any of her adherents after the king's capture. The point he could by no means gain was that his men should be released with him, the reason being that others had taken offence at his rejecting, with a kind of proud indifference, their great promises to make him the chief man of the whole kingdom. And as they were especially insistent that the king should be released first, on account of his royal rank, and then the earl; when the earl hesitated to grant this the legate and the archbishop gave an assurance on oath that if the king, after his own release, held back

liberationem suam detractaret comitem liberare, ipsi se in captionem comitis incunctanter inicerent, quocumque ipsi libuisset abducendi.

512 **68.** Nec adhuc quieuit, sed preter *a* haec quo sibi preuideret *b* sagax animus inuenit. Posset nempe fieri, ut rex, malorum quod sepe fit preuentus consilio, captionem fratris sui et archiepiscopi parui duceret, dummodo ipse liber in pluma iaceret. Exegit ergo ab utroque singillatim breuia et sigilla sua ad apostolicum in hunc sensum. Sciret dominus apostolicus eos ob *c* regis liberationem et regni pacem hoc se pacto comiti astrinxisse, quod, si eum rex post suam ipsius liberationem liberare dissimularet, ipsi ultro se in captionem ipsius immitterent. Quapropter, si ad hoc infortunium peruentum foret, obnixe rogare, quod apostolicae *d* humanitatis esset sponte facere, ut et eos qui suffraganei ipsius erant, et comitem pariter, ab indebitis nexibus exueret. Et quaedam talia.

513 **69.** Haec scripta Rotbertus ab utrisque pontificibus recepta tuto loco deposuit, et Wintoniam cum eisdem simulque *e* magna baronum copia uenit. Rex quoque, ut in preteritis dictum est, non multo post eodem ueniens, familiare colloquium cum comite communicauit.[277] Sed quanuis et ipse rex, et cuncti principes qui aderant, magno annisu satagerent comitem in sua uota traducere, ille, 'uelut pelagi rupes immota resistens',[278] omnes eorum conatus uel irritos fecit uel rationabiliter compescuit, non esse rationis, dicens, sed nec humanitatis, ut sororem suam desereret, cuius partes iuste defendendas suscepisset. Nullius commodi causa, nec tam regis odio quam sacramenti sui respectu, quod uiolare nefas esse ipsi quoque deberent attendere, presertim cum ab apostolico sibi mandatum meminisset ut sacramento quod sorori presente patre fecerat obedientiam exhiberet. Ita infecta pace ab utrisque discessum.

a propter *A*   *b* prouideret *Ce¹*   *c* om. *A*   *d* apostolici *B*   *e* et simul *A*

[277] During the exchange of hostages (*HN* §57), where it is stated that the earl of Gloucester left Winchester immediately the king arrived there.

from releasing the earl they would immediately make themselves
the earl's prisoners, to be taken off wherever he chose.

68. Even then he was not satisfied, since his shrewd mind foresaw
other difficulties. It might come to pass that the king, overborne
by evil counsellors, as often happens, would care little for the
imprisonment of his brother and the archbishop, provided that he
himself was a free man living in comfort. He therefore extracted
from each individually a sealed letter to the pope to this effect. Let
the Apostolic Lord know that for the release of the king and peace
of the kingdom they had bound themselves to the earl by this
condition, that if the king after his own release made any difficulty
in releasing the earl, they would voluntarily make themselves the
earl's prisoners. Therefore, they earnestly requested, something
that would come naturally to someone of the pope's refinement,
that if this misfortune should come to pass, he would rescue from
undeserved bondage those who were his own suffragans, and in
like manner the earl. And more of the same sort.

69. Having got these letters from the two prelates Robert put them
in a safe place, and came to Winchester with the prelates and a
great number of barons. The king, as was said earlier, also came
there not long afterwards and had a friendly conversation with the
earl.[277] But though the king himself and all the nobles present
made great efforts to bring the earl over to their wishes he,
'resisting like an immovable rock in the ocean',[278] either baffled
all their attempts or checked them by reasoned arguments, saying
that it would neither be reasonable nor even show decent feeling to
abandon his sister, the just defence of whose cause he had
undertaken. He would not do it on any account, not so much
from hatred of the king as regard for his oath, which they
themselves ought to perceive it was a crime to break, especially
as he remembered an injunction from the pope to obey the oath he
had taken to his sister in his father's presence. So the two sides
parted without making peace.

[278] Virgil, *Aen.* vii. 586.

514 **70.** Haec ideo[a] in superioris anni gestis non apposui, quia clam conscientia mea erant. Semper quippe horrori habui aliquid ad posteros transmittendum stilo committere, quod nescirem solida ueritate subsistere. Ea porro, quae de presenti anno dicenda sunt, hoc habebunt principium.

515 **71.**[b] Vtraeque partes, imperatricis et regis, se cum quietis modestia egerunt a Natale[c] usque ad Quadragesimam, magis sua custodire quam aliena incursare studentes. Rex in superiores regiones abscessit, nescio quae compositurus.[279] Superueniens Quadragesima [d]omnibus uacationem[d] bellorum indixit. Qua mediante, imperatrix cum suis ad Diuisas uenit, illic misterium consilii sui[e] habitura.[f] Quod tamen eatenus exiit in uulgus, ut sciretur omnibus fautoribus eius complacitum quatinus pro comite Andegauensi mitteretur, qui coniugis et filiorum hereditatem in Anglia iure defensitare deberet. Missi sunt ergo spectabiles uiri, et qui merito tantae rei curam exequerentur.

516 **72.**[g] Non multo post, in ipsis pene[h] Paschalibus feriis, regem quaedam, ut aiunt, dura meditantem grauis incommodum morbi apud Northamtonam detinuit, adeo ut in tota propemodum Anglia sicut mortuus conclamaretur. Durauit inprospera ualitudo usque post Pentecosten. Tunc enim sensim refusus salutis uigor eum in pedes erexit.[280]

517 **73.** Interim nuntii ex Andegauis redeuntes, iterato apud Diuisas in ipsis octauis Pentecostes coacto concilio, imperatrici et principibus audita reportant. Comitem Andegauensem legationibus procerum nonnulla ex parte fauere. Ceterum, solum ex omnibus comitem Gloecestrensem cognoscere,[i] eiusque prudentiam et fidem, magnanimitatem et industriam, probatam iam olim habuisse. Is si ad se transito mari adueniat,[j] uoluntati eius se pro posse non defuturum. Alioquin ceteros in eundo et redeundo frustra laborem

---

[a] sic *add. Ce*[1]   [b] *Rubric* Tractatus ut pro comite Andegauense mitteretur *Ce*[1]   [c] Natiuitate *A*   [d-d] uacaturam uel cessationem *Ce*[1]   [e] cum suis *Ce*[1]   [f] habitum *A*   [g] *Rubric* De infirmitate regis *Ce*[1]   [h] *om. Ce*[1]   [i] recognoscere *B*   [j] ueniat *Ce*[1]

---

[279] John of Hexham says that Stephen came to York after Easter, his immediate business being to stop a tournament between William, earl of York, and Alan, earl of

70. I did not include these things among the events of the previous year, because I was ignorant of them at the time. For I have always dreaded putting in writing, for transmission to posterity, anything that I did not know to be established fact. What is to be said about the present year [1142] will begin at this point.

71. Both sides, the empress's and the king's, behaved with calm restraint from Christmas to Lent, seeking rather to keep their own than to assail what belonged to others. The king went to distant parts, I know not on what business.[279] The arrival of Lent enjoined upon all a truce from war. Taking advantage of this the empress came to Devizes with her counsellors to hold a secret conference there. The purport of this was, however, so far made public that it was known all her adherents approved sending for the count of Anjou, it being his duty to maintain the inheritance of his wife and sons in England. So men of reputation were sent, qualified to undertake so great a charge.

72. Not long afterwards, just before Easter week itself, the king, while preparing some harsh measures, it is said, was kept at Northampton by an illness so dangerous that in nearly the whole of England he was proclaimed as dead. His ill-health lasted until after Whitsuntide. Then the vigour of health gradually came back and put him on his feet again.[280]

73. Meanwhile the envoys returned from Anjou and, when a council had again been summoned at Devizes a week after Whit Sunday [14 June], announced to the empress and the chief men what they had been told. The count of Anjou in some respects approved what the nobles proposed. But he knew none of them except the earl of Gloucester, and had long been assured of his prudence and loyalty, noble spirit and energy. If the earl would cross the sea and come to him, he would meet his wishes as far as

Richmond, and his general concern being to restore the integrity of the kingdom: SD ii. 312.

[280] John of Hexham also refers to the king's illness, saying that it forced him to disband the considerable forces he had mustered: SD ii. 312.

518 consumpturos. *Ita omnium audientium spebus erectis, ad comitem preces uerse, ut hunc laborem pro sororis et nepotum hereditate dignaretur. Dissimulauit ille primo, difficilem rem pretendens, suspectum per confertissimos hostes iter citra et ultra mare, periculosum sorori, quam in absentia eius alii egre tuerentur, qui eam in captione sua pene reliquerant, rebus *ipsi suis* diffisi. Fauens tandem omnium unanimi uoluntati, obsides poposcit singillatim ab his qui optimates uidebantur, secum in Normanniam ducendos, uadesque* futuros tam comiti Andegauensi quam* imperatrici, quod omnes iunctis umbonibus ab ea, dum ipse abesset, iniurias propulsarent, uicibus suis apud Oxeneford manentes.²⁸¹ Acclamatum est sententiae, datique obsides Normanniam ducendi.

519 74.* Rotbertus ergo ualefatiens sorori, ductis secum obsidibus,²⁸² cum expeditis militibus per tuta hospitia ad Warham profectus est, quem uicum cum castello iamdudum commiserat filio suo primogenito Willelmo.²⁸³ Ibi aliquanto post festum sancti Iohannis alto se per Dei gratiam committens, naues quas tunc habebat soluit. Que fere in medium mare delatae, omnes preter duas tempestate coorta in diuersa iactatae; quaedamque* retro uersae, quaedam ultra destinatum propulsae sunt. Duae solummodo, in quarum una comes cum fidissimis erat, rectum cursum tenentes, in idoneam stationem appulerunt. Veniens itaque Cadomum, comitem Andegauensem per nuntios accersiuit. Venit ille non aspernanter, sed auditae legationi sua impedimenta et ea multa obiecit: inter quae, quod rebellione multorum castellorum in Normannia

ᵃ *Rubric* Quomodo comes Gloecestre ad comitem Andegauensem ierit *Ce¹* ᵇ⁻ᵇ suis ipsi *A*   ᶜ et uades *A*   ᵈ etiam *add. B*   ᵉ *Rubric* Quomodo comes Andegauense auxilio comitis Gloecestre decem castella in Normannia ceperit *Ce¹*   ᶠ et quedam *A*

²⁸¹ An agreement between Robert of Gloucester and Miles earl of Hereford is usually dated to this occasion. In it Mahel, son of the earl of Hereford (for whom any other healthy son may be substituted), serves as hostage 'donec guerra inter imperatricem et regem Stephanum et Henricum filium imperatricis finiatur': *Gloucester Charters*, no. 95; R. H. C. Davis, *From Alfred the Great to Stephen* (London, 1991), pp. 255–63.
²⁸² 'ducens secum obsides, filios scilicet comitum et magnatum Anglie qui imperatrici fauebat': RT i. 225–6.
²⁸³ Baldwin de Redvers had landed at Wareham in the summer of 1139, its castellan, Robert Fitz Alured of Lincoln, having declared for the empress in the previous year (*GS*,

he could. If not, it would merely be a waste of time for anyone else to come and go. So the hopes of all the hearers were raised, and they turned to entreat the earl to accept this task for the sake of the inheritance of his sister and his nephews. He refused at first, making the difficulties an objection: it was a hazardous journey through a mass of enemies on both sides of the sea; it would be dangerous for his sister, whom others could hardly protect while he was away, men who had practically abandoned her when he himself was captured, without confidence in their own cause. Deferring at length to the unanimous wish of all, he demanded hostages from each of those who were reckoned of highest rank, to be taken to Normandy with him and serve as sureties both to the count of Anjou and the empress, that all would stand together and guard her from wrong while he himself was away, remaining at Oxford in his stead.[281] His speech was applauded, and the hostages given to be taken to Normandy.

74. So Robert, bidding farewell to his sister and taking the hostages with him,[282] made his way with knights ready for action by safe places of sojourn to Wareham, the township and castle of which he had long since entrusted to his eldest son William.[283] There, some time after the feast of St John [24 June], he committed himself by God's grace to the deep, and set sail with the ships he then had. When they had almost reached the middle of the Channel a storm arose, and all the ships but two were carried in different directions; some turned back, some were driven beyond their destination. Two only, in one of which was the earl with his most faithful retainers, kept straight on their course, and put in at a suitable anchorage. So he came to Caen, and summoned the count of Anjou by messengers. The count came without reluctance, but on hearing the proposal he pleaded his own difficulties in objection, and they were many, one being that he was kept from coming to England because a number of castles

pp. 84–5; HH, pp. 712–13; OV vi. 518–19); the entrusting of the castle to William must be later than this. On Wareham castle, see *County of Dorset*, ii; *South East*, 2 vols. (Royal Commission on Historical Monuments, 1970), ii. 323–5; *Castellarium Anglicanum*, i. 128. On the distinction between the *vicus* and the *castella*, see Crouch, 'Robert, earl of Gloucester', p. 235.

detineretur quo minus in Angliam ueniret. Ea res moras redeundi comiti Gloecestriae ultra placitum innexuit. Nam ut Andegauensem omni occasione nudaret, cum eo decem castella *a* in Normannia expugnauit.*a* [284] Sed propemodum nichil quantum ad legationem hac promouit industria. Andegauensis enim*b* comes et alias occasiones,[285] prioribus solutis, substituit, quibus in Angliam aduentum excusaret suum. Magni sane loco benefitii filium suum ex imperatrice primogenitum auunculo concessit in Angliam deducendum, cuius intuitu proceres iusti heredis partes propugnare animarentur.[286] Henricus uocatur puer, nomen aui referens, utinam felicitatem et potentiam quandoque relaturus.

520   **75.**[c] Interea rex in Anglia, comitis absentiam aucupatus, subito ad Warham ueniens, et uacuum*d* propugnatoribus offendens, *e*succenso et depredato uico,*e* statim etiam castello potitus est. Nec eo contentus, qui fortunam sibi aspirare uideret, tribus diebus ante festum sancti Michahelis inopinato casu Oxeneford ciuitatem concremauit, et castellum, in quo cum domesticis militibus imperatrix erat, obsedit, ita scilicet offirmato animo, ut nullius spe commodi, nullius timore detrimenti, discedendum pronuntiaret, nisi castello reddito et imperatrice in ditionem suam redacta. Mox optimates*f* omnes imperatricis, confusi quia a domina sua preter statutum abfuerant, confertis cuneis ad Walingeford conuenerunt, eo proposito ut regem bello impeterent si ipse in aperto campo martem experiri uoluisset.*g* Sed eum*h* intra ciuitatem aggredi consilium non fuit, quam ita comes

---

a–a expugnauit in Normannia *Ce adding* Quorum hec sunt uocabula: Tenerchebrai, Seithilaret, Brichesart, Alnai, Bastonborg, Triueres, Castel de Vira, Plaiseiz, Vilers, Moretoin.   *b* om. A   *c* Rubric Quomodo rex ceperat Waram, absente comite *Ce*   *d* non bene munitum *Ce*   *e–e* succensa et depredata uilla *Ce*   *f* Igitur optimates quidem *Ce*   *g* uellet *Ce*   *h* om. A

[284] According to the annals of Saint-Aubin, Geoffrey took Mortain and 'castella plurima' (*Chroniques des églises d'Anjou*, ed. P. Marchegay and E. Mabille, pp. 35, 145); John of Marmoutier mentions Mortain and Saint-Hilaire-du-Harcouët (*Chroniques des comtes d'Anjou*, ed. Halphen and Poupardin, pp. 226–7); while Robert of Torigni mentions Mortain, together with Tinchebrai, Aunay, Cérences, and Le Teilleul, 'castella propria comitis Moritoliensis' (RT i. 226). These passages make it clear that the capture of the county of Mortain, which was under Stephen's own lordship, was the focus of the campaign in which Robert of Gloucester and his men took part. Bastebourg and Trévières

were in revolt against him in Normandy. This involved the earl of
Gloucester in longer delay than he wished before he could return.
For to deprive the Angevin of every pretext, he joined with him
capturing ten castles in Normandy [**Ce** *names them as* Tinchebrai,
St Hilaire, Briquessart, Aunay, Bastebourg, Trévières, Vire,
Plessis, Villers, and Mortain].[284] But by this service he accomplished almost nothing towards the object of his mission. For the
count of Anjou invented fresh pretexts,[285] when the first were
removed, as excuses for not coming to England. He did indeed, as
a great favour, allow the boy's uncle to take to England his eldest
son by the empress, so that on seeing him the nobles might be
inspired to fight for the cause of the lawful heir.[286] The boy is
called Henry, recalling his grandfather's name, and would he may
some day recall his prosperity and his power.

75. Meanwhile in England the king, seizing the opportunity
offered by the earl's absence, came suddenly to Wareham, and
finding it undefended [**Ce** not well fortified] he set fire to the
township and plundered it, and also gained immediate possession
of the castle. Not satisfied with this, as he saw fortune was
favouring him, three days before Michaelmas [26 Sept.] he
burnt the city of Oxford by an unexpected chance and besieged
the castle, where the empress was with the knights of her household, with such determination that he stated that the hope of no
advantage, the fear of no loss should make him go away, unless the
castle had been surrendered and the empress brought into his
power. Then straightaway the nobles of the empress's party,
ashamed at having left their lady contrary to the agreement,
mustered their forces at Wallingford with the intention of
attacking the king if he would risk a fight in the open field. But
it was not their plan to assail him within the city, which the earl of

are close to Caen and Bayeux respectively; Briquessart (the Norman *caput* of the earls of
Chester), Villers, Plessis-Grimoult and Vire, lie between Bayeux and Mortain: K. Norgate,
England under the Angevin Kings, 2 vols. (London, 1887), i. 338–40; Haskins, pp. 128–9.
   [285] He said that he feared rebellion in Anjou: RT i. 226.
   [286] The dates of Henry's first visit to England are established in A. L. Poole, 'Henry
Plantagenet's early visits to England', *EHR* xlvii (1932), 447–52, as probably commencing
in Nov. 1142 and lasting about a year.

Gloecestriae fossatis munierat, ut inexpugnabilis preter incendium uideretur.

521 **76.**^a His rumoribus in Normannia^b disseminatis, comes^c Rotbertus reditum maturauit. Trecentos itaque milites et aliquanto plures, quorum tamen numerus ad quadringentos non peruenit, nauibus quinquaginta duabus imposuit. His duas,^d quas redeundo in pelago expugnauit, adiunxit. Itaque piae uoluntati Deus per ^esuam gratiam^e egregie fauit ut nulla e tanto numero nauium longius euagaretur, sed omnes, uel pariter iunctis lateribus uel leniter unae ante alias progressae,^f placida sulcarent maria. Nec uero uiolentia fluctuum nauigia impetebat, sed quodam famulatu prosequebatur; sicut aspectus maris solet esse gratissimus, cum placidis allisa lapsibus alludit unda littoribus. In portum ergo Warham delatae, comitem^g et omnes sotios desideriis suorum felices carinae restituere.[287]

522 **77.**^h Cogitauerat primo ad Hamtunam appellere, ut dispendio ciuiumⁱ simul et domini eorum iniurias suas ulcisceretur.[288] Sed flexerunt eius impetum precibus multis Vituli, qui artissimarum necessitudinum parentes, quos apud Hamtunam habebant, erumnis ceterorum inuolui timerent.[289] Genus hominum nauticorum est quos Vitulos uocant. Qui quia fide^j clientes comitis sunt,[290] preces eorum non negligendas arbitratus, cepto destitit. Simul et honoratius uisum, ut in locum de quo egressus fuerat reuerteretur, quod per uiolentiam amiserat ui recuperaturus. Statim ergo portu

---

^a *Rubric* De reditu comitis Gloecestre in Angliam *Ce*   ^b Anglia *Ce*
^c Gloecestre *add. Ce*   ^d duabus *AB*   ^{e–e} gratiam sui *Ce*   ^f gresse
B   ^g comites *AB*   ^h *Rubric* Quomodo comes Gloecestre reditu suo Waram
ceperit *Ce*   ⁱ burgensium *Ce*   ^j fidi *Ce*¹, fidei *Ce*²

---

[287] 'Robert and Henry must have crossed from Normandy to England at the beginning of November at the latest' (Poole, 'Early visits', p. 449), arguing that a month must have been taken before the muster at Cirencester (*HN* §78)).

[288] Southampton was a royal borough (C. Platt, *Medieval Southampton. The Port and Trading Community, A.D. 1000–1600* (London, 1973), pp. 12–16), but the peace settlement of 1153 provided that Henry of Winchester should surrender 'munitionem Hamtone' on Stephen's death (*Regesta*, iii, no. 272), and the likelihood that he is the lord referred to here is only strengthened by William's circumspection.

[289] On this prominent burgess and seafaring family, see Platt, *Medieval Southampton*,

Gloucester had so strongly fortified with earthworks, that it seemed impregnable unless it were set on fire.

76. When these reports were spread abroad in Normandy, Earl Robert hastened his return. So he put 300 knights and somewhat more, though the number did not reach 400, on 52 ships. To these he added two that he captured at sea on his way back. Then God of His grace showed signal favour to his dutiful intention, so that of such great a number of ships not one wavered from its course but all cleft calm seas either side by side or in orderly line ahead. Nor did the billows assail the ships with fury, but escorted them like an attentive retinue, the way in which the look of the sea is wont to be most pleasant, when the waves glide gently up and play against the shores. So the happy craft entered Wareham harbour, and restored the earl and all his companions to their longing friends.[287]

77. He had thought first of putting in at Southampton, to avenge his wrongs at the hands of the citizens [**Ce** burgesses] and their lord.[288] But his anger was assuaged by many entreaties from the Veals, who feared that very close relations of theirs, whom they had at Southampton, would become involved in the troubles of the others.[289] Those whom they call Veals are a seafaring family. As they are loyal dependants of the earl,[290] he thought that he should not disregard their entreaties, and so he abandoned the idea. At the same time it seemed a more glorious thing to return to the place from which he had set out, and recover by force what he had lost by force. So he at once made himself master of the harbour and the

pp. 7, 10 n. 6; but the co-identification there of *de Sigillo* (Seal) and *Vitulus* (Veal) is queried by E. O. Blake in *The Cartulary of the Priory of St Denys near Southampton*, 2 vols. (Southampton Rec. Ser. xxiv–xxv, 1981), i. 24–5. The *Vituli* appear as leaders of the men of Southampton, Hastings, and Bristol in the capture of Lisbon in 1146: *De Expugnatione Lyxbonensi: The Conquest of Lisbon*, ed. C. W. David (New York, 1936), pp. 100–4, 110–11; C. Tyerman, *England and the Crusades, 1095–1588* (Chicago, 1988), pp. 167–8, 181–2.

[290] It is clearly the Norman branch of the family that is making these representations to the earl, their link with him being provided by their base in Caen: *Recueil des Actes de Henri II concernant les provinces françaises et les affaires de France*, ed. L. Delisle and E. Berger, 3 vols. (Paris, 1909–27), i. 266.

et uico in potestatem subactis, castellum obsedit, quod lectissi-
morum[a] militum quos ibi rex locauerat munitione sua confirma-
bat[b] animositatem, ne dicam contumaciam. At enim paulo post
milites, machinis comitis labefactati et consternati, petierunt[c]
indutias ut, sicut moris est illorum hominum, efflagitarent a rege
suppetias; die dicta, si forte uenire negaret, castellum reddituri. Id,
spe regem ab obsidione sororis abducendi, acceptissimum comiti
fuit, quanuis impatienti desiderio castelli habendi teneretur. Qua
putamus animi confidentia, ut nullo ex Anglia fultus adhuc auxilio,
cum trecentis et paulo plus militibus regem intrepidus operiretur,
qui mille milites et eo amplius habere ferebatur. Multi enim non
tam imperatricis odio quam auiditate predae ad obsidendum
conuolauerant.

523   78.[d] Veruntamen, cum relatum esset quod obsessis apud Warham
a rege negaretur auxilium, ea scilicet obstinatione qua predixi
castellum recepit;[291] eodemque[e] impetu insulam Portland, quam
incastellauerant, subegit.[292] Nec minus et tertium, cuius nomen
Lulleworda, armis perdomuit.[f][293] Inde omnes fautores imperatricis ad Circecestram conuocauit, iam ingresso Domini[g]
Aduentu.[295] Ibi igitur ad dominae suae succurrendum omnibus[h]
uiribus conspirati, profectionem ad Oxeneford meditabantur,
infensis mentibus cum rege, nisi abscederet, [i]preliatum iri.[i]
Enimuero iam progressis plausibile nuntium allatum est, egressam
imperatricem ab obsesso castello Oxeneford, et[j] apud Walingeford
tuto manere.[296] Illuc[k] ergo diuertentes, eiusdem dominae[l] consilio,
quia et milites, qui ea exeunte remanserant, castello reddito

---

[a] electissimorum B   [b] confirmarat Ce   [c] petiuerunt Ce   [d] Rubric
Quomodo comes Gloecestre congregato exercitu tetendit ad liberandam imperatricem
Ce   [e] et eodem A   [f] quod Willelmi de Glastonia cuiusdam cubicularii fuerat,
qui nuper a fide imperatricis desciuerat add. Ce   [g] om. Ce   [h] suis add.
Ce   [i-i] preliaturum iri Ce, preliaturi Mynors   [j] om. Ce   [k] Illic
Ce   [l] sue add. Ce

---

[291] The capture of Wareham from the king's forces is noted in GS, pp. 144–5.
[292] The Isle of Portland had been granted to the monks of Winchester by Henry I
(Regesta, ii, no. 745), and so any fortification might be presumed to be the work of Henry
of Winchester; but no fortification has been identified from earlier than the fifteenth
century: County of Dorset, ii; South East, ii. 247–59; Castellarium Anglicanum, i. 127.
[293] This is the only mention of the castle: Castellarium Anglicanum, i. 129.
[294] William of Glastonbury inherited the chamberlainship of Walchelin his uncle:

township, and besieged the castle, which by its strength had encouraged the resolution, not to say the obstinacy, of the picked knights whom the king had stationed there. But soon afterwards these knights, shaken and terrified by the earl's siege-engines, asked for a truce so that, as is customary with those people, they might beg aid from the king; they would surrender the castle on a fixed day supposing he refused to come. This proposal was most agreeable to the earl, though he was filled with an impatient longing to possess the castle, because it afforded a hope of bringing the king away from besieging his sister. What must we think of his resolution, seeing that, as yet supported by no aid from England, he fearlessly awaited with only a few more than 300 knights the arrival of the king, who was said to have 1,000 knights and more? For many had flocked to the siege not so much from hatred of the empress as from greed for plunder.

78. However, when the reply came that the king refused to help those besieged at Wareham, the earl recovered the castle with the determination I mentioned before,[291] and with the same vigour subdued the Isle of Portland, which they had turned into a castle,[292] along with a third castle named Lulworth[293] [Ce *adds* belonging to William of Glastonbury,[294] a chamberlain, who had recently deserted the empress]. Then he summoned all the empress's adherents to Cirencester after the beginning of Advent [29 Nov.].[295] So there they united all their forces to rescue their lady, and they were preparing to march on Oxford, intending to fight a desperate battle with the king if he did not go away. But when they had already started, the welcome news was brought that the empress had left the besieged castle of Oxford, and was staying at Wallingford in safety.[296] So they directed their course thither, and then, on the advice of their lady, because the

Haskins, p. 89 and n. 19, and, making some qualifications, Green, *Henry I*, p. 256. He witnessed a charter of Stephen at Oxford 1139 × 1140: *Regesta*, iii, no. 293.

[295] Nothing more is heard of the muster at Wallingford (*HN* §75), and forces were now gathered at Cirencester, closer to the main Angevin bases in the west country.

[296] The dates of the siege are clearly established: it commenced on 26 Aug. (*HN* §75), lasted for three months (*GS*, pp. 142–3), and the empress escaped shortly before Christmas 1142 (HH, pp. 742–3).

indempnes abierant,²⁹⁷ et sancti dies quiescere uel parum admon-
ebant, bello abstinendum rati, ad sua quique ᵃsunt reuersi.ᵃ

524 79.ᵇ Modum sane liberationis imperatricis gratanter apponerem, si
pro certo compertum haberem. Est enim euidens Dei miraculum.
Illud satis constat, quod, metu aduenientisᶜ comitis, obsessoribus
plurimis apud Oxeneford, quo quisque poterat, dilapsis, reliqui
laxiores custodias et remissiores excubias fecere; magis, si ad
bellum ueniretur, saluti suae solliciti, quam aliorum exitio infesti.
ᵈQua re ab oppidanis animaduersa, imperatrix cum solis quattuor
militibus per posterulam egressa amnem transiuit. Mox, ut
nonnumquam et fere semper necessitas et remedium excogitat et
audaciam subministrat, pede Abbendoniam profecta, hinc ad
Walingeford equo subuecta est.²⁹⁸ Quae tamen latius persequi
fert animus si umquam, dante Deo, ab his qui interfuere ueritatem
accepero.ᵈ ᵉ

ᵃ⁻ᵃ reuersi sunt A   ᵇ Rubric Explicit Liber Tertius Nouelle Historie Ce¹
ᶜ aduentantis Ce   ᵈ⁻ᵈ om. Ce¹   ᵉ Sed hec in uolumine sequenti, Deo uolente,
latius expedientur add. Ce

²⁹⁷ GS, pp. 144–5, refers to the surrender of the castle.
²⁹⁸ GS, pp. 142–5, says that the empress went on foot 'about 6 miles' (the distance to
Abingdon), and reached Wallingford the following night. Other accounts of the escape are
in HH, pp. 742–3; John of Hexham, in SD ii. 317.

knights who had stopped behind when she went out had surrendered the castle and gone away unharmed,[297] and also because the holy season urged rest if only for a little while, they thought they should refrain from war, and went back each to his own home.

79. I should certainly be pleased to add the manner of the empress's escape if I had sure knowledge of it, for it is a manifest miracle of God. This is well established, that, from fear of the earl's arrival, very many of the besiegers at Oxford slipped away whither each man could, and the rest were slacker in their guard and more careless in their watch, more anxious for their own safety if it came to a fight than eager for the destruction of others. When this was noticed by the garrison of the castle, the empress went out by a little postern with only four knights and crossed the river. Then, since often, indeed almost always, necessity both invents the cure and supplies the boldness to effect it, she went on foot to Abingdon, and then on horseback to Wallingford.[298] I am, however, disposed to go into this more thoroughly if ever by the gift of God I learn the truth from those who were present.

INDEX OF QUOTATIONS AND ALLUSIONS

A. BIBLICAL ALLUSIONS

B. ALLUSIONS TO CLASSICAL AND PATRISTIC SOURCES

GENERAL INDEX

Cholsey (Berks.), abbey 30 n.
Christian, clerk of queen Matilda 94–6
Cirencester (Glos.) 130
Clermont Ferrand (Puy-de-Dôme, France)
    18 n.
Cluny (Saône-et-Loire, France), abbey
    18 n.; monks of 30 n., 99 n., *see also*
    Henry of Blois, Peter Moraunt
Cnut, kg of England 104
Conrad, cardinal bp of Sabina 12, 14
coinage, Kg Stephen debases 74; of the
    empress lviii
Cornwall, earl, *see* Reginald
Cricklade (Wilts.), castle xciii n.
Crusade, First lxv

David, kg of Scots xxvii, xli, xlii–xliii, 8,
    30, 98, 102, 112
Devizes (Wilts.), castle xxvii, xxviii n., l, lv,
    lxvi, lxxxi, 44, 48, 50 n., 54 n., 74, 76,
    106, 122
Devon, earl, *see* Baldwin de Redvers
Domfront (Orne, France), castle 26
Dover (Kent) 27 n.; castle 43 n.
Dunstable (Beds.) 39 n.
Dunstan, St, abp of Canterbury xx
Dunster (Somt.) 64
Durham, bps, *see* Ranulf Flambard,
    William of St Calais; Treaties of (1136,
    1139) xliii, 30 n.

Eadmer, monk of Canterbury xx n.,
    xxiv–xxv
Eadwulf, abbot of Malmesbury xxvii
earldoms, created by Kg Stephen 40
Ecgberht, kg of Wessex 6
eclipses xcix–c; (1133) 22; (1140) 74
Edmund Ironside, kg of England 8
Edward, abbot of Reading 88
Edward the Confessor, kg of England 6
Eleanor of Aquitaine 20
Ely (Cambs.), abbey, 67 n.; bp, *see* Nigel;
    bpric 67 n.
England 22, 30–2; suffers from civil war
    xxvi–xxvii, xlix, liv–lv, lxiv, xcvi, 40, 70–
    2, 110
Essex, earl, *see* Geoffrey de Mandeville
Étampes (Essonne, France) 18 n.
Eustace III, ct of Boulogne 98; wife of, *see*
    Mary
Eustace IV, ct of Boulogne, son of Kg
    Stephen lx–lxii, 98–100
Évreux (Eure, France) xlvii

exchequer lviii
Exeter (Devon) 33 n.
Eye (Suff.), honour of lx

Flanders, counts, *see* Robert, William Clito;
    mercenary troops from lv, 32, 38 n., 72,
    106 n.
France 18, 78
Fulk V, count of Anjou xxxvi, 4; daughters,
    see Matilda, Sibyl

Galbert of Bruges xliv–xlv
Geoffrey, abbot of Abbotsbury 70 n.
Geoffrey, abp of Rouen 8
Geoffrey V, count of Anjou xxxix–xlii, lxi,
    lxvi–lxvii, lxxx, xcvii, 8–10, 41 n., 122–6
Geoffrey de Mandeville, earl of Essex
    lxii–lxiii, lxvii, lxxx–lxxxii, 102
Geoffrey de Waterville xcvi
Gilbert Fitz Richard de Clare, earl of
    Hertford 43 n., 116
Gilbert Foliot, abbot of Gloucester lii n.,
    42 n., 88
Glastonbury (Somt.), abbey xx, xxv, lx;
    abbot, *see* Henry of Blois; library
    lxvii–lxviii, lxxiii
Gloucester liv, 39 n., 62, 84, 86, 88 n.,
    100 n.; abbots, *see* Gilbert Foliot, Serlo;
    castle 43 n., 62; district of 64; earls, *see*
    Robert, William; honour of 89 n.; Vale
    of xxiii
Godfrey VII, count of Louvain 6
Godfrey, prior of Winchester xxxvi
Godfrey of Bouillon, ruler of Jerusalem lxv
Godfrey of Jumièges, abbot of Malmesbury
    xx–xxi
Gregory, cardinal deacon of S. Angelo, *see*
    Innocent II
Guildford (Surrey) 100
Gude, Marquard lxx
Guy, cardinal bp of Tivoli 16

Haimeric, cardinal deacon of S. Maria
    Nuova and papal chancellor 12
Harptree (Somt.), castle lxxxiii, 43 n., 72
Hastings (Sussex), townsmen 129 n.
Heber, Richard lxxv
Henry V, empr xxxvi, xxxvii 4
Henry I, kg of England 6, 10, 12, 18, 22,
    64–6; wives of, *see* Adeliza of Louvain,
    Matilda; daughter, *see* Matilda, empress;
    sons, *see* Reginald, earl of Cornwall,
    Robert, earl of Gloucester, William;

Peter, cardinal bp of Porto 14; letter
concerning papal election (1130) 14–18
Peter Moraunt, abbot of Malmesbury
xxx–xxxi, 88
Peter Pierleoni, cardinal priest of S. Maria
in Trastevere, *see* Anacletus II
Peterborough (Northants), abbot, *see*
William de Waterville
Philip, son of Kg Louis VI of France 20
Philip, son of Robert of Gloucester xciii n.
Phillipps, Sir Thomas lxxv
Plessis-Grimoult (Calvados, France), castle
126
Polydore Vergil lxxiii–lxxiv; use of *HN* cv
Pont-Audemer (Eure, France) xlvii
Portland, Isle of (Dors.) 130
Portsmouth (Hants) 12 n.

Ralph of Diceto, chronicler, links with *HN*
xcvi–xcvii
Ranulf I (Meschin), earl of Chester 80 n.
Ranulf II (de Gernons), earl of Chester
xlviii, lxxxvii n., 80–2, 102, 111 n.
Ranulf Flambard, bp of Durham
xxxvi–xxxvii
Reading (Berks.) xlii, 70 n., 90 n.; abbey
30; abbots, *see* Edward, Hugh of Amiens
Reginald, abp of Rheims 20 n.
Reginald, earl of Cornwall lv, 74
Rheims 20; abp, *see* Reginald
Robert, bp of Bath 88; suggested author of
Gesta Stephani xciii n.
Robert, bp of Hereford 88
Robert, count of Flanders 110 n.
Robert (Curthose), duke of Normandy 64

ROBERT, EARL OF GLOUCESTER:
birth xxxix n.; father, *see* Henry I; wife,
see Mabel; sons, *see* Philip; William,
earl of Gloucester; daughter, *see*
Matilda, countess of Chester
career: swears oath to support empress
(1127) xxxviii–xxxix, 8; involved in
Angevin marriage 9 n., 10; at Henry
I's death-bed (1135) 24; declines to
claim throne xli; remains in
Normandy 26; accepts Kg Stephen
(1136) xliv–xlvi, 30–2; in Normandy
(1137) xlvii, 36–8; defies kg (1138)
xlviii, 40–2; accompanies empress to
England (1139) liii, 62; military and
diplomatic activity in her support
(1140–2) lv, lx, 72–4, 78, 86–8, 96–8,

100–2, 128–30; at battle of Lincoln
(1141) 82–6; captured at Stockbridge
104–6; negotiations for his release
lxiii–lxiv, 106–8, 116–20; goes to
Normandy (1142) lxvi, 122–8;
recapitulation of his career lv,
lxiv–lxv, 112–16
character 2, 24; religious foundation, *see*
Margam
connection with WM: *GR* dedicated to
him xxiii, xxxvi, xxxvii; commissions
HN 2; revised edition of *HN*
heightens his importance
lxxxii–lxxxiv, lxxxvii–lxxxviii,
xci–xciv; his possible involvement in
this revision xciv

Robert, earl of Leicester 46 n., 50 n., 111 n.
Robert Fitz Alured 124 n.
Robert Fitz Hamon 9 n.
Robert Fitz Hubert, mercenary lv,
lxxx–lxxxi, 62, 74–6
Robert Wyvill, bp of Salisbury lxxii
Rochester (Kent) 106, 114–16; bpric 76 n.;
castle lxiii, lxv
Roger, abbot of Tewkesbury 88
Roger, bp of Salisbury xxvii–xxviii, xxxix,
xlii, 10, 28; arrested at court (1139)
xlix–l, 44–8; his trial l–lii, 50–8; death
and obituary xlix, 64–8; his nephews, *see*
Alexander, Nigel; his son, *see* Roger
Roger, bp of Worcester xxvi, xci–xciv
Roger, son of Bp Roger of Salisbury 68
Roger de Clinton, bp of Chester lii n.
Roger Fitz Gerold 80 n.
Roger de Mortimer 54
Roger the Poitevin lx
Roger of Wendover, chronicler lxxiii; links
with *HN* xcviii
Rome 18, 20, 58; Lateran council (1139)
li–lii, lxxxiv n.
Romsey (Hants), nunnery lii
Rouen (Seine-Maritime, France) 18, 21 n.,
26; abp, *see* Hugh; convent of Notre-
Dame-du-Pré 26; Jews of 18
Ruald de Calva lxix
Rudborne, Thomas, chronicler ciii–civ

St Albans (Herts.) lix; historical writing at
lxxiii–lxxiv, xcviii–c
St Davids (Wales), bp, *see* Bernard
Saint-Hilaire-du-Harcouët (Manche,
France), castle 126
Salisbury (Old Sarum, Wilts.) 68, 70 n.,